The Gospel of Survival

Revealing the good news of Biblical Preparedness

Jason Hunt

Barefoot Prophet Media

The Gospel of Survival

©2021, Jason A. Hunt
All rights reserved. No part of this book may be reproduced, stored in a retrieval system, or transmitted in any form or by any means without the prior written permission of the author, except by a reviewer who may quote brief passages in a review to be printed in a newspaper, magazine or journal.

Cover Design by Nick Dunham

Printed in the United States of America

Library of Congress Control Number: 2021904149

Published by Barefoot Prophet Media
www.barefootprophetmedia.com
ISBN: 978-0-578-83790-1

To Robyn, my best friend, bride, and partner on the narrow path to eternity with Jesus; thank you for bringing joy, laughter, and balance to our home. You are the greatest blessing God has bestowed to me; your patience and grace with me over the last twenty-one years of marriage have given me the confidence and peace needed to continually press on against the grain.

To my children, Ethan, Sydnee, Lindsay, and Daniel, thank you for letting dad work all those long days and nights and for being the best kids a dad could dream of. Thank you for the laughs and for enduring *Dad's Survivalin' Adventures*. I love you all.

Finally, a shout out to all my Campcraft brothers and sisters, you are what makes my outdoor ministry awesome and challenging; thank you for joining me on this journey.

ACKNOWLEDGMENTS

I want to acknowledge the people that have graciously shared their knowledge with me over the years in chats, emails, books, and videos that have enabled me to reach thousands with the gospel of survival and preparedness for the coming of Jesus Christ.

Thank you to my late-grandfather Milton Kenney and my uncle Jerry Kenney who mentored me in ministry and offered me opportunities to share the gospel. Without their influence, the gift of evangelism would not have been fanned to the flame it is today. I want to thank my parents, Victor and Sheila Hunt, who took us camping, hunting, and fishing for our entire childhood. While we didn't always like it, we most certainly needed it, and I've put those many years of adventuring to fair use. Thank you to Lonnie Hunt, my grandfather, who inspired me at age 35 to figure things out before I turned 40 and has provided us the proving-grounds to test these outdoor ministry skills for so many years. It's funny how an off-the-cuff comment can turn into such a driving motivation.

Special thanks to my martial arts instructors, specifically Rorion Gracie that revolutionized my mindset when it came to curriculum design and development. Also, the late-Woodsmaster Ron Hood. His videos inspired me early on in my career and enabled me to lend all my previous martial arts knowledge to survival methodology. I'm grateful to Dave Canterbury, who took an unknown preacher and gave him a shot as an instructor, then coauthor, and also a product developer. Thank you for your friendship over the years; our business grew because of the platform you provided. I am indebted to Creek Stewart for being a positive influence and mentor to me in the outdoor industry; thank you so much for all you've done. Thank you James Gibson for your friendship and mentorship. Learning from you and working on the biblically-based survival projects we have has been a great joy. Thank you, Jim Cobb, for giving me so many writing opportunities over the years. Lastly, special thanks to Robert Onken, Greg Laughlin, Bryant Garibay, Jamie Burleigh, Jamie Boggs, and Aaron Branch; and others within our instructor cadre. Without all of your help, Campcraft Outdoors could not have grown to what it is today.

CONTENTS

DEDICATION v
ACKNOWLEDGMENTS vii

1 My Story 1
2 Leave me behind! 21
3 Exit and Return 28
4 The Smooth Stones 35
5 Renewing the Mind 38
6 Kit Mentality 45
7 Pentecost: The Wilderness Refuge 53
8 Tool Safety 60
9 The Ministry of Fire 70
10 Sukkot: Camping in Debris Huts 90
11 Emergency Survival Shelters 100
12 Water and the Spirit 117

CONTENTS

13 | Food to Endure 130

14 | Rescue Essentials 144

15 | Bracing for Winter 160

16 | Woodsman Skills 180

17 | Backwoods Hygiene 200

18 | Wilderness Self-Aid 217

19 | Enduring Trouble, Together 227

20 | Urban Awareness 241

21 | Urban Kit Development 262

22 | Prepping on a Budget 274

23 | Field Craft 283

24 | Urban Movement 304

25 | The Wheat and the Tare 322

26 | Experimental Archaeology Applied 336

27 | Tactical Ministry 346

References 349

Training Resources 351

CONTENTS

ABOUT THE AUTHOR **352**

1

My Story

Who am I to write a book such as this? Well, I'd like to share a bit about myself and, more specifically, how Jesus Christ has radically changed my life. I was born in Southern Indiana in 1978 and spent my first week of life in the hospital due to low blood platelets. My parents, who were young Catholics, prayed for God to heal me. My dad even dedicated me to the service of the Lord should I be healed. Little did he know at that time that God would call in this dedication twenty years later.

I enjoyed an average childhood in the 1980s. We played outside every day, rode our bicycles all over creation. We recreated episodes of the Dukes of Hazzard, Knight Rider, The Super Friends, He-Man, and Rambo on the weekends and drank water straight from the hose. In the summers, my dad would abandon his obligations to take us camping for weeks at a time. My siblings and I would swim in the river, fish, and learn about camp life's hardships in canvas tents. "Don't touch the roof!" my dad would say every time it rained. Of course, we always did, and we each experienced water torture for the rest of the night. My dad was a carpenter, trapper, and outdoorsman, and my mom was the quintessential 80's mom and could do anything. We were poor, but we kids never lacked anything. Being poor meant I had to sleep in the living room most of the time as we only had a two-bedroom trailer, and I had two sisters that shared a room. During the week and especially on the weekends, I was often stuck trying to sleep while my dad and his friends would drink, smoke, and sing the night away. I had woken up to hungover men puking in bowls and dishes more times than I care to recall. I spent many nights crying myself to sleep in that living room which is when the seeds of resentment for my dad took root.

> *"Fathers, do not provoke your children to anger but bring them up in the discipline and instruction of the Lord."*
> ~Ephesians 6:4

Since 85', I was eaten up with martial arts. Living at the height of the karate and ninja craze of the time was like adding jet fuel to my imagination. I trained myself constantly out in the woods, building forts, gadgets, weapons, traps, and more. I often subjected my sisters to my devices and the neighbor kids. By the time I was a tween and young teenager, I was pretty proficient in karate and had grown tired of camping and developed quite a distaste toward it. My dream was to be in BlackBelt magazine, and camping wasn't going to get me there, and doing anything my dad told me probably wasn't either. The wind of change came through when I was a teenager as my uncle Jerry had come to know Jesus and was called to the ministry. Growing up Catholic, we pretty much went to church twice a year, that being Easter and Christmas.

Jerry would preach at us about Jesus, and we would pray with him every visit. I think I was saved and baptized at least eight times between the ages of 13 and 16. None of it ever took. We moved to the house my dad grew up in when I was 15 and, I now had my own space, his old room when he was a kid. This place gave me the escape I so craved. Now I was no longer confined to the same room my dad and his friends would be. My dad would take time nearly every night when he got home to talk to me, drunk or not. When he was drunk, he was overly philosophical and extremely condescending and would often vent his frustrations so that I would not have to endure what he had taken. Even though I resented him for many things, I always took his advice to heart. I also acted upon it.

> *"Train up a child in the way he should go; even when he is old he will not depart from it."*
> ~*Proverbs 22:6*

Between 15 and 17, I fell into a dark pit emotionally. I was a ball of rage. I took out as much frustration in my martial arts practice as I could, and whatever was leftover was doled out on anyone that looked at me funny. I started a gang; we primarily vandalized things and would steal. I taught them how to fight, and we would often stir up trouble. I started talking to the devil; in my mind, I knew Jesus was real. But I would purposely talk to the other guy out of spite. I was very into black-magic, demonology, and anything dark. My bedroom was all decked out in skulls of all types and looked like a satanist temple because it was! I looked like every other person, though; I played football, wrestled my senior year, did martial arts, I didn't look goth, I never drank nor did drugs. I despised the boredom and monotony of high school and ended up graduating in the bottom 25% of my class. I pretty much tried to avoid my family and worked as often as I could.

On my last day of high school, a girl asked me as we walked out to graduate what I would do next. I told her I'd get rich and do what it took. After a month off of high school, I went right into college at Indiana University Southeast. My grandparents were helping to make sure I had everything I needed to get me through college. In my first class on my first day, the professor set the tone for my college career. He said he and none of the other professors cared if we showed up or not. It was our responsibility as adults to learn and do the work required to complete the classes. That positively hit me for some reason. It was a challenge I accepted. My first two semesters were all A's and only a couple B's. College was different, and I liked it.

I worked part-time at the local mall at a nutrition store. I was enrolled in college as Pre-Med with a minor in Recreational Leadership. I was also teaching martial arts on the side as often as possible and even did a bit of bodybuilding and modeling for catalogs. By my third semester of college, I met Robyn, who would later become my wife. She worked with my sister, and upon seeing me for the first time, she said to her coworkers as I walked in, "Here comes my husband in the door."

I had just come from my first and last modeling shoot. It was creepy, and when the guy wanted to oil us up, I was out. I was looking pretty good when I walked in that day. Robyn and I were introduced, and I honestly thought no more about it until my sister came home that night. My sister lamented about how she would be fired if I didn't go out with her supervisor (Robyn). She even got my parents lecturing me about it! They all badgered me the next couple of days until I finally broke and called her to make a date.

We finally went out, and we hit it off. It would be five years before I spent a full day apart from her. Due to our meeting, my grades started to suffer in my third semester. Taking that 7 am Anatomy class wasn't the best of ideas. I ended up dropping half my class load so that I didn't fail. I used that extra time to obtain my Personal Trainer Certification. Robyn's family attended the same church that had trained my uncle Jerry, now an established pastor. She wanted me to go to church with them and, to be the good boyfriend I did. After all, I believed everything in the Bible; I just chose to do the opposite.

After six months of dating, Robyn and I moved out together, both aged 18. We worked long hours to save up money from our jobs and stole money right from the till to grease the wheels a little extra. All the while attending church every week. Two weeks after moving out, my dad was in a catastrophic motorcycle accident that resulted in him avulsing his foot. The accident happened while he was in the middle of building a new house and starting a new job the following Monday. To add to all this, the place they were currently living in had just sold. Talk about bad timing. A few years before, my dad had broken his back while working (a genuine accident), and before that, he had shattered his heel bone during a party. These and other drunken escapades and accidents over the years added to the resentment and bitterness in my heart. My parents and siblings had it very tough, practically camping in a wooden box without plumbing for about a year. My mom was undoubtedly the glue the kept it all together; she's tough as nails.

Finally, after years of robbing Peter to pay Paul, I heard the voice of God for the first time. In the church we had been attending for well over a year now, the pastor preached a sermon on stealing. It affected me deeply. So much that I decided to leave the job I had that next morning, and I told Robyn to do the same. I told her if God was who he said He was, then she would have a new job that day. That Monday, she received a fair job offer, and I would start in a new direction. I started working in the church's gym as a trainer, and I decided to pursue my martial arts career and open a school of my own. I had only been doing private lessons around town until then. It was the summer of 1999, we had been married that June. My uncle allowed me to use a room in his church to offer classes, and I started a Christian martial arts organization that would grow over the next several years to become the second-largest in the United States.

By now, we were pretty active in church life. On December 21, 1999, we were invited to go with my uncle and grandparents to a church service. When we got there, it turned out to be a fundraising event. There was a single light bulb hanging in the center of the old, rundown building in downtown Louisville, KY. The service was like any other at the start. Some singing, an announcement, and message, then call to prayer.

I couldn't tell you what was preached that night because I started fighting against the holy spirit at some point during the message.

By the time the speaker gave the altar call, I had already been experiencing what I could only describe as a heart attack for the past thirty minutes. A small man looked over the crowd and said someone was wrestling with God and needed to come forward for prayer. I knew it was me, and I wasn't going. He came back after a few minutes and said that God would make it worse if whoever it was wrestling did not respond. At that moment, my breath left me, and I jumped to my feet and took a single step out to the aisle. I looked at the man, and he said, "Fire." I felt like I kissed a freight train; I flew back, bounced off the pews, and landed flat on the floor. God swept my legs! I was not someone to give in to this sort of thing, but there was absolutely nothing I could do about it.

I saw a flash of a clear image in my head. I was wearing a wide brim hat, had a shawl over my shoulders, Bible in the left hand, staff in the right hand walking across an emerald green field with a trail of people following me. I knew that God called me to preach the gospel. I opened my eyes and saw Robyn crying and my family in awe. I couldn't move at all; as hard as I tried, nothing. So, I just laid there, soaking wet in my sweat. It looked like I had played in a bathtub; I was completely soaked. After a few minutes, I was able to lift my head, and again, the preacher shouting this time, said, "Fire!" after a while, I was able to crawl over to a pew and hide. I hurried out to my grandpa's van as soon as I could. When my uncle jumped in, he asked, "What did you see?" and I told him. He confirmed my feeling that I was to preach the gospel. The next morning I enrolled in the first online bible college I could find and I spent the next 10 years struggling to find my way in ministry.

I used my martial arts as a bridge to ministry opportunities. I offered Christian Karate and Jujitsu outreach programs and, after a year of

Bible school, landed my first job as a Youth Pastor. The people of this church supported me in building a large Christian martial arts organization. We stayed at this church, even though we were not spiritually on the same page while teaching martial arts at various locations.

In 2001, Robyn became pregnant; I was inducted into the U.S. Martial Arts Hall of Fame, and my organization went national. I had martial arts instructional videos on the market and had done some appearances in small martial arts journals. I inherited ownership of the first American martial arts college at the time from a very large organization. I was chosen as its President due to my state's leniency on accreditation at the time and my ability to provide sound leadership. I was well on my way to Blackbelt magazine, but growing in my relationship with Jesus now too. Then, 9/11 happened. We were living in a house near Robyn's parents, my parents and siblings were doing okay, and we had our first child, Ethan, that October. I was asked to train outgoing troops at Ft. Knox. I felt compelled to make the martial arts college a full-fledged Bible College due to my own ministry training so I started the ship in that direction. 2001-2004 was very hectic, Robyn had our daughters in August 2003 and October 2004 and I was in bible college and trying to run my own bible college, teaching, and running a martial arts organization with over two thousand members and schools while still working for free at area churches. I was engaged in heavy spiritual warfare, experiencing breakthroughs in wisdom, knowledge, and spiritual gifts constantly. I graduated with my Bachelor's in Church Ministry in 2003 and scraped out my Masters of Ministry in December of 2004 and was Licensed for ministry finally to start my own churches. It all came to a head in late 2004 as I was in prayer one night. God asked me if I still wanted to be rich. I told him I would rather win a million souls than have a million dollars. Within a week or so after this time of prayer, a local church I was affiliated with offered to buy my Bible College. By this time I had achieved over a dozen approvals from various denominations and had trained hundreds of area and national ministers. The catch was, I could not teach what I had been teaching, which was some of what you will learn in this book. They wanted me to limit teaching to their program, which they also wanted me to write!

In the church service that week, a proven prophet shared a word that there were several people in the congregation that would be millionaires. He even pointed some out and they were in fact on the precipice of becoming so. After service, he came to Robyn and me and said he also had seen my name, but he could not say it aloud as it was up to me to make the decision. The decision had already been made and within the following days, doors began slamming in my face. We spent the latter part of 2004 and all of 2005 living off all our belongings as we sold them off. We went bankrupt, lost our house, and eventually our car. I sold off what remained of my martial arts organization and my martial arts video rights for pennies on the dollar. All the years of robbing Peter to pay Paul had caught up. I decided to end my professional martial arts endeavors there. On the way to the car lot to return the car I could no longer pay for, God asked me what car I wanted. I frantically looked around and pointed at the most oversized, luxurious passenger van I saw at the time. On the ride back home from the car lot, my cell phone rang (a $10 Tracfone), and someone said they felt like they needed to buy me a new car that day. I had that van, which ended up being a used one that very day. I knew God was still listening, but good grief was it hard losing all we had. I asked God that night as I went to pray to teach me how to do it properly. I felt I had no idea how to do pray right because we were losing all we had.

"You have to cast your idols if you want to be in the army of the Lord. The greatest idol is you and me, we best get on the threshing floor."
~Jason Upton

I knelt with my elbows resting in my chair as I always did to pray, and a few minutes later, Robyn knocked at my office door, asking if I wanted lunch. I'm pretty explosive, so I run out all wild and am like, "What are you talking about!", well, it was, in fact, lunchtime the next day. I felt amazing. I knew I didn't fall asleep, so I ate lunch and went to church to ask my pastor what this was. My pastor just laughed at me and called me a radical. My friend Brian, my ministry sidekick, understood it, though, and encouraged me to press in deeper.

That following night I went in to pray, and before I could even begin, I was ambushed by the Holy Spirit with a flood of emotion and information. I was praising God throughout the night, studying things I had not learned before, and emerged each day with revelatory knowledge of those in my church. I had words of knowledge about people and their hidden sins, thoughts, deeds, and more. I became feared because I would openly correct anyone, at any moment, anywhere! I was not sleeping either but was continually refreshed by the Spirit of God.

I spent two months praying like this. I'd work at church all day, do my family duties and go to pray. When released from prayer, I would sleep if and when I was able. During this time, God began speaking to me about traditional holiday practices, my ambitions, my pent-up resentment, and more. An old martial arts and ministry mentor of mine, 'Dr. Neal' reached out during this time and said that the Lord would move us to a new house. He said, "son write this down and save it because it will make sense one day." He then described a house and property down to the gates' color and the brand of locks used on the doors. This move was great news to us as the bank had begun foreclosure proceedings on us, and we knew we needed a new place. I was excited when I went to pray that night. I thanked God for the new home and started pleading as to what my ministry role was to be. Undoubtedly, I would be an apostle to the nations I thought because of all this intimate prayer time.

That night, the room became filled with a sweet scent and moisture that was palpable. There was a heaviness in the air. Suddenly, as I was praising Jesus, I felt what I could only describe as a wet blanket drop over my shoulders and warm oil pour over my head. I felt hands placed on my shoulders; I felt the literal weight. In absolute terror, I went dead silent, not even breathing. Then a gentle voice, the likes of which I felt across my right ear, "You are my Reformer." I fell to the ground, knowing who had just manifested himself to me and who forever removed any doubts about His existence. I had just spent over sixty consecutive nights learning from and hanging out with him.

"Jesus has set me ablaze, and the people come to watch me burn."
~ Jonathan Wesley

The bank that foreclosed on us actually did a short sale after 13 months of letting us live there rent-free and thanked us for taking care of the place, so that was a silver lining financially. I would love to say life was terrific afterward. But, things became more difficult for another season. Robyn and our three kids ended up moving in with my parents in that house they had built years before. They had also taken in my great-grandmother, and my brother and younger sister still lived at home. Full-house was an understatement. There was a lot of latent hostility. Understandably so. My parents didn't want us there any more than we wanted to be there. I had gotten over a lot of my past resentment by now, and my dad didn't understand why I did the things I did; he thought I was pretty worthless. The family didn't even believe I had graduated from Bible College or was an actual minister. Keep in mind; I never invited them to anything I did. I couldn't afford to go through graduation ceremonies, so I always had diplomas mailed to me. I realize I robbed them of a lot of those accomplishments parents yearn to see, and because of the resentment I held, it turned back against me making some matters worse.

Well, distraught over living with family, I prayed with my friend Brian every Friday night, all night long. My main petition was getting our own house. God told me that I preached my way in, so I could preach my way out. So, I started spending days during the week preaching at my dad's friends as they came over and drank around the dinner table after work. I even baptized some in his bathtub. We had some excellent meetings, and little by little, things changed. After 90 days, my grandfather called for me (another person we had a bad relationship with). None of my phone numbers worked anymore, and he needed to speak with me. As he and I talked on the phone, he explained that he had a farm and that the farmhand had attacked him and he needed someone he could trust to live on the farm and help him raise his cattle. My grandpa invited Robyn and me to look at the farm's house, which we would get as partial payment for working on the farm. In February 2006, we rolled up to the farmhouse. Disappointing is an understatement. The previous tenant had trashed the place and used the upstairs as a dog kennel. There were twelve inches of dog poop in each upstairs room, and the downstairs was just as bad in other ways. My grandpa pretty much tossed us the keys and told us to decide, then he left. With tears in our eyes, we decided to take the plunge. This place was an hour away from anything we knew and thirty miles from a decent grocery store. We came back the next day and started tearing out the house and cleaning. It took Robyn and me two weeks to get it clean enough to want to bring the kids. In the process of cleaning, however, Dr. Neal's note popped into mind from years before. We were able to take the message and, like a checklist, check every box on the note.

We were where God wanted us. Moving to the country was hard. We were used to grabbing groceries daily or as needed due to them being a couple of miles away. Now, driving a gas-guzzling van and being thirty miles away from town meant learning how to juggle wants and needs in a new way. We ran out of gas a couple of times making the trip; thankfully, country neighbors were always helpful. Once we settled in, we started a church on our farm, right in the living room. We called it the Kentucky Cowboy Church, and this made us fast local celebrities. It seemed everyone in town suddenly knew us. The newspaper came out and did a front-page spread. No sooner than we began to hit our stride after about six months, change again came. My grandpa said he didn't want our church to operate on his farm because we didn't believe the same way his church did. Nevermind the fact I had more education on the subject than anyone in the family. He said what we do in the house is our business, so long as we don't have signs or any other feature that we're doing anything religious.

> "No one who puts his hand to the plow and looks back is fit for the kingdom of God."
> ~Luke 9:62

That decision made us find a new building, and right after, God told me that we were going to start traveling for ministry. Worried about how to tell our congregation, I waited. I told Robyn I felt that Leon, the first to attend our little church, was supposed to take it over for us but didn't know if I should put that responsibility on him. Within 24hr Leon called, saying he needed to leave to start his own church because he had been running from the call for 35 years. When I dropped all the work on him, we were both excited. He grew the church quickly and kept it going until he retired years later. All things work for the good of those who love God and are called (Rom. 8:28).

We set out on the road preaching from Texas to Pennsylvania and everywhere in between for the next three years. I interviewed for pastorates and sometimes just filled in or was a guest. We were going somewhere every other weekend. I was making just enough money on the farm to keep us going and building a relationship with my grandpa (my Father's dad), who I didn't honestly know. I spent dozens of hours in a delivery truck with him on the weeks between preaching engagements;

he got into doing freezer beef deliveries. So, we had a great chance to talk in-depth about everything. It seemed when we had finally said all we could say after three years together; he retired from the beef business. But, he and I got to know each other well in that time and healed a relationship we never really had. He's been a great blessing to us. I continued to manage the farm for the next three years with various tenant farmers until I was able to lease it for myself and have since taken it over for the family.

Our travel adventures were something to behold. We burnt through a few vans, and churches would invite me to speak, and sometimes instead of paying me, would kick us out. In particular, we went to a church in Tennessee, and the meeting ran over their usual time. It was a good meeting, someone got healed of a back issue, and I think I prayed for most people in the church. When we got back to our host's home to pick up our luggage, he handed me a single Dr. Pepper (which I loathe) and told me to never come back to his town. We put 100% of our money in the gas tank to get there and did not have enough money to get back home.

Well, we started home. Robyn began to cry in worry, and I started praying. Just before empty near the Kentucky/ Tennessee border, that voice I was so familiar with told me to pull over and be ready to fill my gas tank. So, I pulled into a gas station and sat there for about 15 minutes. A car whipped in fast, and a guy got out looking frantic. So I hopped out and smiled, and he said, "You're the one that needs gas?". He handed me $50, which filled the tank enough to get home. This example is just one of a few such stories. God will always have your back, even when you think he's stopped listening.

My uncle and I decided to join together to grow his church in Southern Indiana. By now, I had been in ministry full-time for several years, and one church had helped with schooling, so I now had a doctorate in theology and had been fully ordained. I became his associate pastor, again without pay, but I could glean from the food pantry and pick up side work as needed with him painting and cleaning houses. We were like the power team; people were getting saved, healed, and delivered all the time. It was like things had finally started to come together in the ministry work I was striving to remain a part of despite never making over $1000 in any single month the previous several years. We made enough to survive. If I didn't hunt or have a garden, we went without at times.

The kids were all school-age by now, and Daniel, the 4th child, was a few years old. We had started prepping and had been doing survival skills to celebrate the Biblical holidays for the past handful of years at this point. I had a dream in late 2008 that my uncle and I would go to a town and bless every person there. We would feed them and clothe them in abundance, somewhere in the mountains. I told my uncle the following day, and he said, "Cool, where are we going?" I, of course, had no idea.

Several weeks later, my uncle called and asked if I was telling people about our mission trip. Another church had dropped off a revival tent, and he had a 50 ft box truck ready with food and clothing. Well, I decided to pray again. I got a call from a stranger out of the blue a couple of days later from Arkansas. He interviewed me to make sure I was the right person for his message; then he told me I was going to Manchester and hung up. Okay, where's that?

That weekend, my uncle and I had been invited to visit a prominent pastor from Texas who was in town. We took our wives and had dinner. A small-framed woman with a long skirt and long hair sat in the corner during the pastor's dinner meeting. She looked out of place compared to the others in attendance, and I probably stared a hole through her. I grabbed Robyn, and we went to visit with her since she looked lonely.

She was, of course, super friendly with a thick but lovely country accent. She asked us to come to her town to preach at the bible school. When I asked her town name, she said "O'Neida"; me having no idea where that was, she said, "You know, by Manchester." Well, we found the place.

When we arrived in Manchester, it was everything we had expected. Only one helper came with my uncle and me, but the woman who invited us had some helpers to distribute food and clothing. We gave pickup truckloads of food, new clothing of all types, and even toys to every resident living in Oneida and even those outside the town. We had a fantastic day of ministry and blessing, which was a Thursday. On Friday morning, we finished off the truck's remaining items and served hot meals (we still don't know where that came from because we loaded the truck!). Then we started trying to erect the revival tent that was 60 feet x 100 feet in size. We three guys had no idea how to set up a tent of that size. We ended the day exhausted with only the edges spiked out.

Saturday at 7 am, we were back at it. Slowly the men of the town came and started to watch us. Most of them just drinking beer and laughing at us. After five hours and no progress, they began to help out. We had twenty men helping us all to no avail. The 25-foot tall center poles were just too cumbersome to get in place. This event is the only time in my life that I can say I gave 100% of my physical effort to do anything; I strained every bone and muscle in my body trying to move the poles. One man hooked his tow truck to a pole to drag it in place, and it didn't budge. We had a big sag in the tent you had to crawl under to enter. The local sawmill owner brought a load of slabs down, and we created bracing to lift the sag out. After completing the Stonehenge-like bracing, it started to rain. We were able to have our ministry meeting that night, we had only a handful attend due to the rain, but it was still a fruitful meeting.

"... Not by might nor by power, but by my Spirit,' says the LORD.."

~Zechariah 4:6

Sunday morning, we arrived, and the tent was again on the ground. It was full of water. We had about three hours until the morning service, so we got to work. We cleared the water in time for the wind to kick up. The wind was so strong it was lifting the entire tent into the air. It had pulled stakes a few times, and one guy went around hammering them in sequence. At his wit's end, my uncle started preaching against the weather and commanding the wind to stop. I stood at the edge of the tent, lamenting. The tent started breathing; it would rise to its full height, then slowly drop, only to do it again. I watched this happen a few times before hearing the voice of the Lord say, "Stop your uncle." I grabbed Jerry, and instinctively we grabbed the poles, undid the bolt, extended them to full length, reinserted and tightened the bolts, and set them in place. The tent rested perfectly upon them, and the sun came out immediately. We rejoiced, and the people stood in awe.

We expected the meeting to be off the chain! Yet again, meager attendance. We had a smattering of people compared to all those we had fed and clothed, but we had nonetheless accomplished our mission. After the meeting, a couple introduced themselves to us. They turned out to live near my uncle, and they wanted us to come to their home for dinner that same week. A couple of days later, we arrived, and the husband ended up being a Congressman, and his wife was from that town. They had been visiting her family and kept up with our meetings. They offered to fund our continued work in that area as long as we wanted to pursue it.

Robyn and I all this time had continued praying to move to raise a new church work, and we felt this was finally the place. Keep in mind; this was a 4hr drive one way for us every weekend. My uncle, Robyn, and the kids would all climb in the van Friday mornings, and we'd go to the mountains all weekend. The first several months, everything went beautifully. We established a wonderful congregation, lives were being changed, and disciples being made. Then, the stranger from Arkansas called me again, this time with bad news. He described that I would be attacked, having my throat cut in my next service. The person he described perfectly matched the lady that had essentially become an elder in our church. As I got up to speak that week, the woman asked to share something. Being in the moment, I said, "sure," as I had forgotten what the guy had told me. Well, she proceeded as he described, so I reared back as if to hit someone, only to play it off as she went to the pulpit. Relieved, I sat down as she began her announcement. It started as any other church announcement, but that's all I can say because I shook out of a stupor an hour later to see her still talking. I looked around and noticed everyone, over sixty other people with a glazed-over look, numb to anything. Then I heard my friend Jesus' voice as loudly as I have ever heard him speak to me. He said, "Dust your feet!"

> *"Whoever does not welcome you, nor listen to your message, as you leave that house or city, shake the dust [of it] off your feet [in contempt, breaking all ties]."*
> ~Matthew 10:4 AMP

I scrambled out the door, bewildered. It was December 21, 2009, my birthday, and ten years to the day since God called me to ministry. Five minutes later, Robyn came out with the kids, and she was upset. I go into fight mode, and she just said, "I think the Lord told me to dust my feet." At hearing that, I flip out. "Get in the Car!" I'm expecting something drastic. Well, another ten minutes pass before my uncle comes out saying the same thing. Fifteen more minutes pass, and everyone comes out. He, being more pastoral, still accepted their invitation to the house for coffee. I refused and warned him I would leave him in five minutes. Of course, I had to go in after him, and when I did, he showed me keys to a new building that a congregant had built for a new church but never used. I wasn't interested! But, he talked me into looking it over that night and convinced me that dusting our feet just meant the current building. I knew better but still went along with it.

We went back on December 24th to prepare for a New Year's Eve kick-off service. We cleaned the church up, but oddly, no one came around to help. December 31st arrived, and no one showed up to the service. So, we started going door to door to all the member's homes, as many as we could recall anyway; again, none were home. We ended up sitting in the house of our worship leader all day waiting. When they arrived to find us, they all but fell to their knees. The woman who gave the announcement came to each of them when we left the last time and threatened them. She even went to the church building owner and somehow convinced them that she was a prophet of God and would remove the blessing from their family if they didn't sign the building over to her. They did, but she instructed them all to allow us to continue using her facility. Upon hearing this, I stormed into the woman's house like a SWAT Team member, removing the door from the hinges. She met me with a sly grin and demonic look I was also familiar with, as I had it when I was a teen. All I could do was say, "you won this fight, devil," and we left.

> "For we are not fighting against flesh-and-blood enemies, but against evil rulers and authorities of the unseen world, against mighty powers in this dark world, and against evil spirits in the heavenly places."
> ~Ephesians 6:12

On the four-hour ride home, I decided I was finished fighting to remain in church ministry and that I was done with organized religious activity. I told those with me that as soon as I got home, I would start a new business teaching people how to prepare, how to fight, and survive. I did just that as the clock struck midnight that New Year's Eve, I had filed the incorporation papers online for Hunt Survival, which would become the catalyst for our current outdoor ministry and Campcraft

Outdoors. It was a full twenty years later, in 2019, that I realized that the emerald green field I had seen when God called me to ministry was the one on our farm. It struck me like lightning as I was wearing my wide-brimmed hat, wearing a shemagh across my shoulders with a Bible in my haversack and staff in my hand, leading students during a class. I had finally arrived at the place he showed me so long ago.

This story is only the abridged highlight reel version. I could write another book on ministry experiences alone. While I never tried to get into Blackbelt Magazine, I have had over 200 articles published in national and even a couple of international magazines. I became a firefighter, EMT, and wilderness emergency care instructor. I've co-authored a best-selling Bushcraft book and have taught with the top instructors in the United States and have even done some television work. I was even asked by a Bible Seminary to design their ministry leadership program which they ran for several years, they awarded me my second doctorate in outdoor ministry leadership. I share my story to let you know that I'm no one special. I grew up playing in the woods, was poor, had family problems, fought personal demons, went bankrupt, have been on food stamps, have been a thief, bully, liar, lusted over pornography, and lost all my worldly possessions. I struggled in life too. The difference is that I met Jesus Christ along the path and spent time with Him personally. I used to have a "why me" attitude until Jesus showed me it was because of me that He had overcome death, hell, and the grave on my behalf. He knew everything I would ever do- but he still chose me and loved me unconditionally. I continually choose the hard path because, in my weakness, He shows His strength. The more I boast about my weakness, the more of Jesus you will get to see.

"My grace is sufficient for you, for my power is made perfect in weakness." "Therefore I will boast all the more gladly about my weaknesses, so that Christ's power may rest on me."
~ 2 Corinthians 12:9-11

And what about the resentment, anger, and bitterness I held in my heart. Thankfully Jesus took that too. My dad spoke wisdom into my life when he was unable to use it for himself due to the burdens of life; whether he was too drunk to remember what he said at the time or not, it happened. He had his own struggles to overcome as we all do, and I certainly didn't make resolving any of them easier growing up. Being fully transparent here, I honestly believe that the ministry I fulfill today was actually meant for my Dad. He has so much skill and woodsy knowledge it's amazing, but for whatever reason, the world has quenched that. It was nothing I was remotely interested in until... it just was. We buried the hatchet years ago and made peace and he's an amazing grandpa and yes, my mom is still the Rockstar keeping all the knuckleheads in check. I'm grateful for all those experiences growing up, good and bad, because they armed me with hundreds of life-lessons for my children. In raising my kids, I've had the opportunity to course-correct what past generations could not.

So, who am I? Just a guy that's hung out with Jesus in the woods. I am the man that you will see tell the mountain to move and fully expect it to tuck tail and run before I dig in, and I am the one that will confidently say if you come with me, I promise you will meet my friend Jesus along the way. The following pages of this book are things that Jesus and I have discussed over the past twenty years. I've had help, good and bad, along the way, all of which taught me valuable lessons, some of which you will read about in their best light.

2

Leave me behind!

When a Christian thinks of the words *left behind*, it often conjures up thoughts of people being unworthy to meet the Lord in the air at his second coming. This concept is known as the *rapture*. The majority of those professing to be Christians believe that the word rapture is a theological term used to describe the church's catching away at the second coming of Jesus Christ. The word rapture, however, was not used widely within Christian theology until the twentieth century. The word rapture is not a theological term, although many dictionaries now include a theological definition due to its everyday use within modern religious circles. The word rapture comes from the Middle French word of the same spelling *rapture*, which means *seizure, rape, and kidnapping*, which comes from the root Latin word *raptus* or *carrying off to be molested*, originally of women and cognate with rape.[1]

Most Christians would be surprised to learn that *rapture* has a sexual meaning. However, the rapture is entirely befitting the theory that has raped the modern church of its Biblical mandate to prepare for and equip others to be watchful of the second coming of Jesus Christ. "Leave me behind!" It should be our hope, which is the polar opposite of what the rapture theory teaches.

Matthew 24:15-22 *The day is coming when you will see what Daniel the prophet spoke about—the sacrilegious object that causes desolation standing in the Holy Place. (Reader, pay attention!) "Then those in Judea must flee to the hills. A person out on the deck of a roof must not go down into the house to pack. A person out in the field must not return even to get a coat. How terrible it will be for pregnant women and nursing mothers in those days. And pray that your flight will not be in winter or on the Sabbath. There will be more remarkable anguish than at any time since the world began. And it will never be so great again. Unless that time of calamity is shortened, not a single person will survive. But it will be shortened for the sake of God's chosen ones.*

We must first realize that Jesus is speaking here to believers. That's right, his disciples! He is admonishing them to pray that their flight (as in escape) is not at a time they would be unprepared to take it on, such as on a Sabbath when they rest or in the winter when it would be difficult. This series of passages should alert you to the need to have your EDC (Everyday Carry) with you and have your Bug-Out-Bag always ready. Jesus is telling those in Israel living near Jerusalem (the Holy Place) to run to the hills because the stuff has just hit the fan; the urgency in his words equates to saying- Get out while you can because it's going to be so bad that nothing and no one will survive. But this period of destruction upon the earth will be shortened for our sake, not because we're undeserving of punishment but because the world would be utterly destroyed.

Matthew 24: 23-28 *Then if anyone tells you, 'Look, here is the Messiah,' or 'There he is,' don't believe it. For false messiahs and false prophets will arise and perform great signs and wonders to deceive, if possible, even God's chosen ones. See, I have warned you about this ahead of time. "So if someone tells you, 'Look, the Messiah is out in the desert,' don't bother to go and look. Or, 'Look, he is hiding here,' don't believe it! For as the lightning flashes in the east and shines to the west, so it will be when the Son of Man comes. Just as the vultures gathering shows there is a carcass nearby, these signs indicate that the end is near.*

Jesus warns those living in the hills not to leave their places of refuge in the wilderness because many will claim to have exceptional knowledge of the Messiah's location or arrival on the earth. In contrast, others will claim to be the Messiah- don't believe any of them because He will come without notice as quickly as lightning flashes across the sky.

Matthew 24:29-31 *Immediately after the anguish of those days, the sun will be darkened, the moon will give no light, the stars will fall from the sky, and the powers in the heavens will be shaken. And then, at last, the sign that the Son of Man is coming will appear in the sky, and there will be deep mourning among all the people of the earth. And they will see the Son of Man coming on the clouds of heaven with power and great glory. And he will send out his angels with the mighty blast of a trumpet, and they will gather his chosen ones from all over the world—from the farthest ends of the earth and heaven.*

Again, we're warned about the sun, moon, and stars not giving their light, as John revealed in the book of Revelation (Rev. 8:12). It's in the midst of this darkness that the sign of Jesus' coming will be known to all remaining upon the earth, and it's at that moment that they'll realize their folly, and with the blast of the trumpet, God's chosen will be gathered together. The phrase *'gathered together'* is interesting because the Greek word for gather, episynago, is rooted in the word episynagogue, which does not mean to gather into one specific place, nor does it mean an escape. It does, however, point to be assembled as a synagogue[2] or *be called to worship*. Interestingly, this specific Greek word episynago is linked to the word echthros, which means enemies[3]. When reading the Greek text, the picture painted for us is that God will assemble us to await His coming, hidden from our enemies!

Matthew 24:32-36 *Now learn a lesson from the fig tree. When its branches bud and its leaves begin to sprout, you know that summer is near. Similarly, you can understand his return is very near, right at the door, when you see all these things. I tell you the truth; this generation will not pass from the scene until all these things occur. Heaven and earth will disappear, but my words will never fade. However, no one knows the day or hour when these things will happen, not even the angels in heaven or the Son himself. Only the Father knows.*

The generation living during these events will see the coming of the Messiah, and we are again reminded for the third time in this discourse of Jesus to be ready and prepared because we will not know the day or hour when He will come.

Matthew 24: 37-41 *When the Son of Man returns, it will be like it was in Noah's day. In those days before the flood, the people enjoyed banquets and parties and weddings right up to Noah entering his boat. People didn't realize what was going to happen until the flood came and swept them all away. That is the way it will be when the Son of Man comes. Two men will be working together in the field; one will be taken, the other left. Two women will be grinding flour at the mill; one will be taken, the other left.*

These series of statements are probably some of the most misunderstood about the end-times. The world will be as it was in the days of Noah. We need an understanding of what life was like at that time. Genesis 6 gives us some insight, as verse 5 states The Lord observed the extent of human wickedness on the earth and saw that everything they thought or imagined was consistently and totally evil. The word translated as evil in this passage is ra', which essentially means anything contrary to God's desires[4]. We're fast approaching the time in which complete wickedness and evil will rule the earth for a time. Now imagine what happened to Noah and his family as they spent all that time building a boat. The ridicule they must have endured! Constant persecution, people running off with their supplies, etc.; then when God told them to enter the ship, people were still out and about partying and doing their thing. As the floodwaters rose, imagine the screams of those begging to be let into the ark to escape the flood, the anguish Noah and his family must have felt as they heard the cries of men, women, and children they have known for years perishing only a few feet away outside. However, God hid them in the ark to escape his wrath as He will hide us at His coming.

Now the challenging part, "one will be taken, the other left." According to Strong's entry for 'taken,' the Greek word here is #3880 paralambano, which means to be taken upon oneself like you would carry something away and accept one to be as he professes. Instantly, this would lead one to believe that this is the rapture, but let's not yet get ahead of ourselves. The Greek word for 'left' in this same series of passages (Matt. 24: 40-41) is aphiemi, which appears 47 times in the King James Bible as forgiven and has Strong's definition #863 of being 'left alone' or 'to leave so that what is left may remain.' Both of these Greek words can have good and bad meanings depending on the context. It appears that within this context, it says that those professing to be non-Christian by word or deed will be those taken away, just as the chaff is removed from the good wheat (Matt. 3:12). In contrast, those who are left are forgiven and the same that will inherit the earth (Matt. 24:13). The context of the following verses reiterates this sentiment.

Matthew 24:42-51 *So you, too, must keep watch! For you don't know what day your Lord is coming. Understand this: If a homeowner knew exactly when a burglar was coming, he would keep watch and not permit his house to be broken into. You also must be ready all the time, for the Son of Man will come when least expected. A faithful, sensible servant is one to whom the master can manage his other household servants and feed them. If the master returns and finds that the servant has done an excellent job, there will be a reward. I tell you the truth; the master will put that servant in charge of all he owns. But what if the servant is evil and thinks, 'My master won't be back for a while,' and he begins beating the other servants, partying, and getting drunk? The master will return unannounced and unexpected, and he will cut the servant to pieces and assign him a place with the hypocrites. In that place, there will be weeping and gnashing of teeth.*

Again, we are warned to keep watch, be prepared, and know that we must be ready at all times for His return. We shall not be snatched away to live in the sky, but we shall do the job of managing all that our Master owns, just as humanity was created to do in the very beginning (Gen 2:15). The earth is the Lord's and the fullness thereof (1 Cor. 10:26). Those that survive to the end shall be saved, and those that die beforehand shall be resurrected, and we will all meet together at His coming- so whether we live or die, we know that we're in Christ and where he is, we will also be. So, this isn't a time to worry or be fearful, but a time of excitement and purpose. Any gospel that includes an escape clause is not the gospel of the Kingdom of God.

Not everyone who calls out to me, 'Lord! Lord!' will enter the Kingdom of Heaven. Only those who do the will of my Father in heaven will enter. Many will say to me on that day, 'Lord, Lord, did we not prophesy in your name and in your name drive out demons and in your name perform many miracles? But I will reply, 'I never knew you. Get away from me, you who break God's laws.' Matthew 7:21-23

Jesus gave us the good news of the coming kingdom and what to expect: *Then you will be handed over to be persecuted and put to death, and you will be hated by all nations because of me. At that time, many will turn away from the faith and betray and hate each other, and many false prophets will appear and deceive many people. Because of the increase of wickedness, the love of most will grow cold, but the one who survives to the end will be saved. And this gospel of the kingdom will be preached in the whole world as a testimony to all nations, and then the end will come.* Matthew 24:9-14.

We are now living in a time when the gospel of the kingdom is occurring. We see people turning from the faith daily, hatred among churches that believe differently, false prophets are everywhere. We see true believers worldwide being persecuted for their faith, being killed and jailed in socialist nations. In the United States, we see Christianity quickly becoming the faith of the minority. The love of pastors, parents, and children for one another, for others, grows colder by the moment. We are consistently reminded by the news media the next disaster is just around the corner. These things result from the transition from the kingdom of Satan to the Kingdom of God. Trials, tribulation, and hardship are indeed good news to those awaiting their savior and the establishment of his throne on the earth as they prove his soon coming.

Please understand that tribulation is not wrath. While the church shall not receive the fury of God's anger (1 Thess. 5:9), the church has a promise that it will endure many a tribulation (John 16:33, Acts 14:22, Romans 5:3, 2 Thess. 1:4, Rev. 2:10). So, let us endure difficulties together. Let's stop robbing our brethren of the mandate to prepare for the coming of the Lord with a story of escape from hardship.

Make sure that the light you think you have is not actually darkness. Luke 11:35

3

Exit and Return

Archaeology is ultimately the process of solving riddles. It borrows its tradecraft from various academic disciplines ranging from history, anthropology and biology, to geography, linguistics, and geology, to name only a handful. Archeologists use what's necessary from such disciplines in their quest to answer historical questions so we may better understand life in the ancient and not so ancient past. Biblical Archaeology uses these same investigation systems to provide ample and ongoing evidence of the absolute proof that God exists. Experimental archaeology is one of many forms of specialization. By doing the things described in discoveries, we learn how and why they were and remain essential in many cases. We seek to understand why God gave specific skills in certain situations and how the annual training cycles, also known as the Feasts of the Lord, apply to God's chosen people past, present, and future and ultimately how these things fit within His plan for the believer today. It is through the practice of experimental biblical archaeology that I not only fully realized the depth of my calling after a decade of church ministry, but God's desire to have a prepared church.

Upon their banishment from the Garden of Eden, Adam and Eve found themselves at odds with the surrounding world that had fallen into a cursed state. Thorns, briars, and pestilence had fallen upon the face of the planet. Adam and Eve had not been prepared for such hardships during their time in the Garden. They would now have to exert constant effort to live from the land, and they, now having the knowledge that they were nude, first needed clothing beyond the leaves they used to cover themselves. So, God taught them how to make clothing from animal skins (Gen. 3). The word for 'make' in that sentence may seem simple enough to comprehend- but in the Hebrew language, it is the word *asah*, which adds more depth to the meaning as it fully translates as to toil with and transmit an idea. When God made them clothing, the idea was fully conveyed to Adam and Eve, no doubt by way of example. We know they left the Garden in the garb of skins, and they could not return.

Thus, the processes of animal identification, harvest, butchery, cooking, hide tanning, sewing, stone, and bone tool-making were all fully transmitted as these things were all necessary to make clothing and use the entirety of the animal. So, we gather that the first thing God did after expelling humanity from paradise was teaching them how to survive apart from his presence. He taught them self-reliance. Throughout the Bible, the themes of survival, such as trapping, hunting, water filters, debris shelters, and warfare tactics, are all taught.

Exitus et Reditus or exit and return is a gothic theological concept that was written by Thomas Aquinas. In a nutshell, how things depart from God is how they shall return to God. Humanity left the presence of God by first learning skills of self-reliance. It only makes sense that as his return draws closer, the feelings of the need to be prepared and be more self-reliant that are shared worldwide have been affecting believers in more dynamic ways over the past few decades. God is preparing us for our return to Him. In his infinite wisdom and eternal love, God did not just show Adam and Eve how to survive; he poured out his grace continually on his people by giving them annual holidays that trained them in the cycles of survival. These holidays pointed to Jesus in the Old Testament, reveal the power of Jesus in the New Testament, and give us a blueprint for training and preparedness in modern times. These festivals represent our Survival Triangle- Passover, Pentecost, Sukkot.

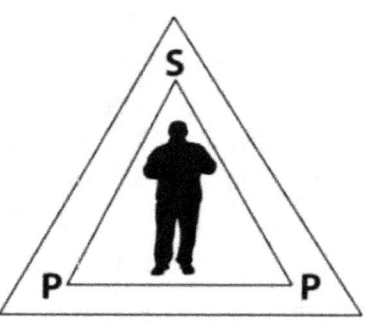

PPS Survival Triangle (Eph: 215)

Only three holidays in the Bible are obligatory (Ex.13: 14-19). These festivals are also known as the Feasts of the Lord; the word festival/feast in this context is the Hebrew word *Moed* which means *appointed time, rehearse, or practice*.5 These three annual rehearsals are times of great importance spiritually and prophetically in the yearly biblical calendar. Passover is a Spring festival inaugurated at Moses's time as a dramatic, week-long Bug-Out. After enduring weeks of harsh judgment from God, Pharaoh finally conceded. In the middle of the night, after the final plague of death had killed all of Egypt's firstborn children that did not have the blood of a lamb on their doorposts, Pharaoh demanded that Moses take all of his people, the Hebrew slaves, and leave Egypt. So, beginning just after midnight, Moses gathered his people, their belongings, including their unleavened bread loaves, and with their livestock, made their way out of Egypt. About 600,000 men were on foot, and their families and livestock and an unnumbered quantity of foreigners among them. Their first stop was Sukkoth (which means temporary camp) [Ex. 12:37] and was quite a distance away from Goshen (the land ruled by Pharaoh) at about 25 miles. Hiking this distance was a colossal undertaking by so many people and spoke of the event's urgency. It took them seven days of travel to reach the Red Sea, where they would cross into Arabia. They took the southern route as they had more people to pick up for the trip at the copper & turquoise mines south of the Suez. It was longer than the necessary journey but essential in collecting the other slaves who had yet been unaware of their recent freedom.

Meanwhile, Pharaoh, having a change of heart after realizing his slaves would never return, rallied his armies and took the wilderness road across the desert, catching up to the Hebrew people. Their lives were again in danger, and this is when God parted the sea to allow the people to escape—at the same time, destroying Pharaoh and his army within the sea as the water tunnel walls thundered down atop them. They then traveled six more weeks to Mt. Sinai's foot for a total of 50 days, learning to depend upon God for their survival. The skills remembered within this festival revolve around the need to be prepared for danger, flee at a moment's notice, always be watchful, and carry our belongings with family and animals in tow. Other skills include items to always have at the ready, cook over a fire, leave a minimal trace, and rely upon those called to lead us out of immediate danger. Passover is a festival for all believers that is mostly foreign to the modern church. These skills are timely when applied to a modern context as a spring festival in that they prepare us for the unknowns that lie within the storm season. According to the Insurance Information Institute, spring flooding and tornadoes account for over 55% of insured losses. Power outages and late-season cold snaps and ice are also potential issues to contend with, making the need to evacuate our home or primary area of operation a grim reality. Spring is also the time we begin sowing our garden crops in preparation for the months ahead. By practicing the emergency survival skills conveyed through the Passover story, we'll be better prepared to endure these events, especially with our families and pets.

Highlighted Passover Skills

- *Get meat for the family, maybe friends: Ex. 12:3-6*
- *Apply the blood of Lamb (Jesus): Ex. 12-7*
- *Start a Fire: Ex. 12:8*

- *Cook over a fire: Ex. 12:8*
- *Cook bannock over a fire: Ex. 12:8*
- *Leave no trace of meal: Ex. 12:10*
- *Eat quick, EDC in hand: Ex. 12:11*
- *Prepare for Calamity: Ex. 12:12*
- *If you know God, you're safe: Ex. 12:13*

In the New Testament, this rehearsal's spiritual elements are fulfilled by the advent of Jesus Christ. He died on the cross as the Lamb of God for the sin of the world (John 1:29). Prophetically, however, Jesus himself warned in Matthew 24 that the sign of his return would look much like it was during the time of Noah and that we should get to the wilderness into our places of refuge for protection. Noah had the Ark, and ancient Israel had the desert. We shall have the woods.

Pentecost is a Summer festival that took place 50 days after Passover. In Hebrew, it is called Shavuot or the Feast of Weeks and marks the counting of seven weeks of seven days. On this 50th day, a new grain offering (Wheat) was made. In the Old Testament, God gave the 10 Commandments as the ancient people encamped around Mt. Sinai (Barley). In the New Testament, the Holy Spirit came to those waiting in the upper room in Acts chapter 2 (Wheat) after the resurrection of Jesus. In both of these festival events (Passover and Pentecost), the people were waiting to learn from and understand the Creator God's will, mind, and heart. Without getting into the deep spiritual matters at work, I'll suffice to say that it is so fitting that this festival falls in the early summer months. All the wild edible and medicinal plants and trees are blooming, and the animals are moving around often. It's the ideal time to make things off the landscape, to take advantage of the foliage for fair weather shelters, and to begin thinking about the garden harvest soon to come.

This season is one of dependence upon God for our needs. They began to rely upon the landscape and the things of the natural environment created by God designed to enable their survival. Things such as the heavenly manna, trapped quail, and water from the nearby desert. Again, this festival is an annual rehearsal wherein we learn to identify natural resources and use them in survival situations. By applying this mindset, we will meet God in the wilderness to learn from and rely upon him. Technically speaking, due to the disobedience of the ancient Israelites to enter into their promised land the first time they arrived (Deut. 1: 7-35), they lived in the wilderness for another forty years. The results of this time permitted the people to fully come into their skills as they mastered the crafts needed to build, defend, feed, and clothe their families and govern themselves. They became fully self-reliant apart from the world's systems around them, which gave them great might in the face of their enemies.

Highlighted Pentecost Skills

- *Camp outside: Ex. 15*
- *Make Water Filters: Ex. 15:22*
- *Survival is hard; train your mind: Ex. 16:2-3*
- *Make bird traps: 16:13*
- *Learn where to find water: Ex. 17:5*
- *Learn self-defense: Ex.17:8*
- *Appoint camp helpers: Ex.18:20*
- *Practice good hygiene: Ex.19:10*
- *Make use of the landscape: Ex. 21:24*

Sukkot (Sue - Koat), also known as the Feast of Shelters, Ingathering, or Tabernacles, took place in the Fall. It was the most extraordinary celebration of the annual festivals as it was the harvest season and last holiday before the rainy season of winter. During this eight-day festival, God's provision of food, water, shelter, clothing, guidance, light, and heat are celebrated. To practice this festival, God required the family's men to gather materials off the landscape to create a shelter made of trees and leafy boughs (a debris style shelter) wherein they were to live for a week.

They were to partake of the seasonal harvest and fellowship together daily, and God promised to meet with them during this time. The book of Revelation notes that this festival continues after the return of Jesus to the earth. It's a season of rest- where we are to come into our knowledge and inheritance of the world around us- we inherit the Kingdom. We're ready to rest from our labor as we know how-to live-in relation to the land; thus, the holiday represents our restored fellowship with our Creator. The eighth day of the festival is called Simchat Torah or Joy of the Torah and marks the end of the yearly cycle of readings from the Torah (first five books of the Old Testament), and the scroll is rolled back to the beginning in the synagogue. This act of rolling the scroll represents our proverbial going back to the beginning of humanity when we dwelt with God in the garden.

Highlighted Sukkot Skills

- *Build a debris shelter: Lev. 23:42*
- *Camp out for a week: Lev. 23:43*
- *Collect Seasonal Harvest: Duet. 16:13-14*
- *Rejoice! Duet. 16:14*

These three annual training cycles have a much greater spiritual, prophetic, and practical meaning than has been given here. God has laid out a survival training plan that includes skills training, and through the practice of the skills that you are already interested in, you can come into closer fellowship with Him through His only begotten Jesus Christ.

4

The Smooth Stones

Now that we have a Biblical foundation for skills training as revealed in the three annual rehearsals, let us move into survival training, beginning with wilderness skills as they are the most sought after, then work our way back toward town with urban survival skills.

Campcraft Instructors and other students training with Shepherd's Sling at ESEE

Our survival priorities derive from the story of David and Goliath. David, a shepherd and survivalist who had fought and killed bears and lions while tending, his sheep entered into another survival situation when he volunteered to fight the Philistine champion, Goliath. David stopped by the creek on the way to fight the champion to choose five smooth stones, which he dropped into his haversack. He selected one stone to throw from his sling, and the rest, as we know, is history.

The five stones were smooth so that when thrown from the staff sling, they would fly straight, hitting their intended target. Creek stones smooth out through the constant ebb and flow of water movement they're in, rubbing against other rocks in the rainy season and the droughts. Our priorities consist of skill areas that must be equally abraded and practiced in good and bad times. When the need arises, we can use the skill to overcome our survival situation with confidence.

- Safety: Unless we demonstrate good safety skills ranging from pre-planning our trips to tool use and rescue, we have no business engaging in regular outdoor endeavors. Practicing safety is a daily skill.
- Fire: We must understand several methods of creating and sustaining fire to manage our body's core temperature, cook effectively, make medicines, and signal for rescue.
- Water: We must understand how to purify raw water to make it safe to drink. Including understanding how chemicals affect the body short and long term.
- Shelter: We must understand how to shelter from extreme elements to manage our core temperature and engage with wild environments long term.
- Food: We must understand how to take food resources from the landscape and in a way that makes the most sense. Hunting, Trapping, Fishing, and handiwork such as simply flipping rocks.

These five skill areas or 5 Smooth Stones are life-long skills, each with its season of training and regional variance. By tapping into the three annual festival cycles, this significance becomes more defined and realized over time. These stones are the pillars of daily survival and shall require constant maintenance. The good news is that so long as we focus on each of these five areas every day, we should be able to endure tough times, in theory. In later chapters, we will cover skills-based training for the woodlands, wintertime, first aid, and urban environment. You will see how these five areas adapt to seasonal/regional variance.

5

Renewing the Mind

And be not conformed to this world: but be ye transformed by the renewing of your mind, that ye may prove what is that good, and acceptable, and perfect, will of God. ~ Romans 12:2

Renewing our minds to align with God's plan for our lives related to home, family, and wilderness preparedness and safety is vital. Without the guidance of the Holy Spirit in all we do, we're only planning to fail and will ultimately veer off the path that leads us to Jesus. Just as a compass always points magnetic north, there is only one true north. By aligning all the skills and guidelines I provide throughout this text with your map (The Bible), your compass (The Holy Spirit) will always take you where you're supposed to be. Before we ever seek to bug out away from our homes, we should always strive to first take shelter at home where the majority of our belongings are, and our family members will assemble in times of crisis. Your group should discuss alternative meeting locations or rendezvous locations as well. These contingency meeting locations are vital to a good home survival plan.

Storm & Disaster Preparedness

- Know the risks for your area. While some weather-related disasters are seasonal, others are not. Fires, Floods, Earthquakes, and power outages are all risks that face everyone.

- Have a Plan. Understand how to shut off utilities to your home, where to meet if the house is no longer safe, have alternate routes to get to or leave your home, and have a back-up method of communicating with loved ones.
- Refrigerated foods begin to spoil in as little as four hours. Have a plan in place to circumvent this obstacle. FEMA recommends a 2-week shelf-stable food supply for each family member at a minimum!
- If you have pets, make sure that you include them in your plan as a family member.
- Remember to have back-ups of any necessary prescriptions and, if possible, back-ups of your important documents and prescription eyeglasses.

Essential Supplies (Per Person)

- Small Tool Kit (that includes lighters, wrenches for utilities, and a can opener)
- Weather Radio
- Lanterns & Flashlights
- Phone Chargers with Emergency Phone if possible
- Extra Batteries
- Duct Tape
- Roll of 3mil Plastic Sheeting or a Tarp
- Rescue Whistle
- Wool Blanket
- First Aid Kit
- Toilet Paper
- Map of Area
- Change of Clothing
- Three days of back-up Food
- Three days of Water (3 gal.)

Food Storage Recommendations
Do not put all your eggs in one basket. Food diversity is a necessity. If you do not already eat it regularly, do not store it!

Vitamins, Minerals, and Dry kinds of milk and Protein options are vital to good health

Consider adding fiber supplements to your stored foods

2-week minimum food supply per person in your family

Survival for the Wilderness

The mind is the most incredible tool for survival; the more you know and experience before a crisis event, the less you will need so far as tools and equipment and the better prepared you will be when such an event takes place. Training such as a Modern Survival course will help prepare you mentally and physically for such a crisis event, but all skills are perishable if they are not maintained. Do not permit weeks or months to go by without refreshing the muscle memories we seek to develop in this course.

General Safety

Maintaining a basic level of personal fitness is a vital component of survival. Suppose you are unable to hike extended miles across potentially rugged terrain with even a basic survival kit. In that case, it is doubtful you would survive a potentially life-threatening situation with less gear, more than likely in worse conditions. Get yourself accustomed to moving your body in functionally related tasks such as chopping wood, lifting a heavy backpack (up to 50lb), and hiking over rough terrain with time limitations. These simple fitness goals will better prepare you for the rigors of survival and hiking in general. Begin by walking at least 20 minutes daily purely for exercise and increase the time and mileage as you are able. When ready, add a backpack and increase the pack's weight load as you get in better shape (Rucking). Perform pushing and pulling exercises as well as squatting and crawling activities with a backpack. Overhead presses, lying/ bench style presses, triceps extensions, curls, air squats, calf raises, bear crawls, push-ups, burpees, and more are all types of exercises to be done while wearing a backpack. Begin with as little as ten pounds of weight and work your way up over time.

Controlling your body's core temperature (*CTC = Core Temperature Control*) is the most critical item on your survival "to-do list." Your body can typically only endure 3 hours of extreme exposure before it begins exhibiting symptoms of hypo or hyperthermia, assuming that the weather is not in perfect conditions. When you become wet due to perspiration or water drenching, you lose body heat 25 times faster than dry. Therefore, in damp or cold conditions, FIRE becomes your most needed resource.

Fire will enable you to:
Dry wet clothing
Dry and warm yourself
Prevent hypothermia

Use the acronym *HOT* as a CTC checklist:

- Hydrate Regularly
- Overheating, Avoid it
- Take time out

Conversely, if you are in hot and humid conditions, SHELTER becomes your most needed resource.

Shelter will enable you to:
Prevent overexposure to harsh sunlight, which prevents burning
Give you shade, which will result in a more relaxed area to rest
Aid in preventing hyperthermia

In cooler months, use *COLDER* as a CTC checklist

- Clean Clothing
- Overheating, Avoid it
- Loose and Layered
- Dry
- Evaluate gear often
- Repair clothing and footwear

The will to Survive

Without the will to survive, tools and training will only go so far. The mind has the unique ability to overcome stress and hardship even when there appears to be little chance of surviving. It is here when the will of survival comes into play. That mental attitude can bridge the gap between realizing the severity of the situation and resolving to endure it without quitting, no matter the costs. We read the historical accounts of men such as Daniel Boone, who ran 160 miles barefoot through the frontier from Chillicothe, OH to Ft. Boonesboro, KY in only five days to warn of an impending Indian attack and Hugh Glass. Despite being attacked by a grizzly bear and left for dead by his exploration party, he crawled more than 200 miles back to the nearest fort to recuperate before again setting out to the frontier. More recently, we consider the stories of Aron Ralston and Bill Jeracki. Aaron amputated his arm after being pinned in a slot canyon by an 800-1000lb boulder for 187 hours. Bill, a 38-year-old Colorado fisherman, cut off his leg at the knee after two boulders fell on his leg while angling in a remote canyon stream.

What explains the actions of these men? Their will, their sheer determination to live despite seemingly insurmountable odds. If not kept in check by your skills, faith, and training, fear and panic will make you a victim. Maintain a positive attitude and an optimistic outlook on your circumstances. Take dominion (absolute authority) over nature; it is our God-given birthright as the people of God to do so.

And God blessed them, and God said unto them, be fruitful, multiply, and replenish the earth, and subdue it: and have dominion over the fish of the sea, and over the fowl of the air, and over every living thing that moveth upon the earth. ~ Genesis 1:28

The Rules of 3 & 5's

- It takes 300-500 repetitions to begin to develop neural pathways when learning a new skill such as striking a Ferro rod.
- It takes 3000-5000 repetitions of that skill before muscle memory starts to develop.
- You cannot live more than 3-5 minutes without oxygen and adequate blood flow
- You cannot live more than 3-5 hours without maintaining your core body temperature
- You cannot live more than 3 days without hydrating your body properly and within 5 you may not recover
- You cannot function normally within 3 weeks of not eating any food and after 5 weeks of undernourishment you can die
- You will suffer emotional and psychological breakdowns after 3 months without companionship and usually, by 5 months you will suffer permanent psychological impairments.

With an understanding of these guiding principles, you may now begin to develop a Plan of Action, the first stage of which is summed up in the acronym STOP

S.T.O.P.

- S: Sit down, gather your thoughts

- T: Think about your gear and options
- O: Observe your surroundings and weather
- P: Plan and act

Preparedness

When it comes to avoiding a survival situation, proper preparedness is key, especially when you venture outdoors. Follow these guidelines as a measure of best practice:

- Plan trips, evacuation routes, and emergencies ahead of time with a good idea of the area and terrain you plan to visit
- Pack a proper survival kit
- Have a plan in place for your family to follow should you "be late" returning home
- Take with you in your kit extra emergency items to aid you in the event of injury, illness, or if you get lost
- When possible carry a cellular or satellite phone or HAM Radio

6

Kit Mentality

The acronym E.D.C. stands for Everyday Carry and typically represents a survival kit that you don't leave the house without, something you carry with you daily. God has also provided foundational guidelines for making what I would describe as an urban E.D.C. kit. Once again, this should further solidify in your mind how important it is to our Heavenly Father that we plan to live and survive as the early, first-century church did- as one enduring tribulation and persecution.

In Luke 22:35-37, we find Jesus instructing his disciples, saying, *"When I sent you out to preach the gospel without any money, a haversack or extra clothing did you find that you needed anything? "No," they replied. But now, Jesus said, take your money and a haversack and if you don't have a knife, sell your shirt to buy one! For the time has come for this prophecy about me to be fulfilled: "He was counted among the rebels." (Isa. 53:12) - Yes, everything written about me by the prophets will come true."*

Here we see that our basic kit should consist of some money or trade goods, a haversack or bag, and a knife. The followers of Jesus are identified as rebels from this point in the scripture. In this context, those that are without the law, according to their accusers. However, if you study church history, you will find that the Jews and Gentiles treated the early Christians as rebels and persecuted them vehemently.[6] Because we are rebels in the eyes of the world, God wants us prepared. In addition to our knife, pocket money, and haversack, we're instructed in other places to carry:

- A staff. Repeatedly throughout the Old Testament, we find that Moses, Joshua, and others are told to take up their staff as they went out to do as God led them. The description used most often is that of a shepherd's staff. Still, in Hebrew, we get a better understanding through the word *matteh*, which means *staff, rod, or club used for walking, discipline, guidance, and a symbol of identity within a tribe with the extension of royalty.*[7]
- A shelter. In Numbers, the Lord commanded Moses to instruct the people of Israel to set up their tents by divisions, each man in his camp under his standard (Num. 1:52). This camp occurred during their wilderness travels. As they reached the Promised Land, we find that they traded their tents for houses- but continued to carry tents with them daily because God commanded them to wear a particular fringe on the corners of their garment known as tzit-tzit. The tzit-tzit are tightly bound cordage with a blue thread interwoven to remind the wearer of God's omnipresence and his eternal commandments. The tzit-tzit is attached to a talith, also known as a prayer shawl. TAL means tent, while ITH means little. Thus, we have a small tent carried about a person throughout Biblical times and today amongst observant Jews and Christians. This little-tent or Talith (also spelled Tallit) is also called a cloak, robe, and prayer closet in the New Testament. When we read about the woman with the issue of blood grabbing the hem of Jesus' robe, it was the tzit-tzit on his talith she was grabbing hold of, the fringes of his prayer tent (Matt. 9:20-22). There are numerous examples of this throughout the entirety of scriptures: Ruth 3:9, Ezek. 16:8, Psalm 91, II Kings 2, Luke 8:43, Mark 5:41, to name only a few, not to mention the Apostle Paul's vocation as a tent-maker (Acts

18:3). He was not making goats' hair tents, which were common at the time. Paul was making prayer tents to support his ministry and because he understood the importance of having a place to commune with God daily. The talith also protected the wearer from the elements as needed, as it was based on the ancient Israelites and Bedouins' blankets that traversed the desert.[8] The shemagh is the modern equivalent to the ancient tallit for the common man.

These items are the only items that God said to carry daily, and thus far, our daily kit would consist of a knife, haversack, money bag, staff, and tallit. If we go by the Bible standard in modern times, we're going to look like someone from Lord of the Rings. Today, these items will all fit into most modern haversacks. You will have room remaining for the additional gear you may wish to carry.

These five items have many more substitutions that can and should be suited based upon your personal needs. The tools of the modern day's E.D.C. will, of course, vary by region and environment, especially considering we're no longer in an agrarian or farm-based society.

Essential Equipment: Emergent C's

Emergent means becoming of greater importance. These 12 C's represent categories of items that will serve as the basis for all kit layers.

The first five Tier 1 or E.D.C. items are essential to safe survival in nearly any environment:

- Knife
- Fire Kit: Lighter, Ferro rod, fire starters
- Jacket and Shemagh
- Water Filter or Bottle with a Steel Nesting Cup
- 100ft of #36 Tarred Bankline

JASON HUNT

The Author's Biblically inspired EDC for Day Hikes

These five items are essential because they are the most difficult to replicate in the field, especially when thrown into an actual survival situation. Therefore, it's recommended these 5, in some form or variation, serve as everyday carry items. These items are also something that can, for the most part, carried in your pockets without drawing any unwanted attention to yourself.

Equipped to Survive: The Complete 12 C's Survival Kit

The 12 C's represent categories of items that are essential to survival. The first five items we discussed are considered E.D.C. items, with the following seven regarded as items that make survival more convenient. This kit would be a Tier 2 kit or one attached to your body by way of a bag such as a haversack or small backpack. As more items are added to each category, a Tier 3 kit, one you carry by conveyance such as a cart, horse, or vehicle, could be created. Tier 3 or 4 would be more conducive for longer-term wilderness activities, building, and living.

1. Cutting Tools
2. Combustion Devices
3. Cover Elements
4. Containers
5. Cordage
6. Cargo Tape
7. Compass
8. Candle Devices
9. Combination Tools
10. Cotton Material & Repair Needle
11. Cerate
12. Circumvention

Cutting Tools: Choose a knife capable of cutting your way out of a house if necessary, yet elegant enough to defend yourself and perform all survival-oriented tasks. A small pruning saw may also be of great use.

Cover Element: Clothing is the primary cover you will use, so choose clothing that you can keep in your bag to change into should you work in an office environment. Beyond clothing, a sturdy tarp or emergency bivvy with a lightweight blanket will be all that required to rest for short periods.

Combustion: While building fire could give away your position, when prudent, making one can provide needed warmth during a chilly night and permit you to process water for the next day's travels. Have at least four ways to make a fire in your fire kits, such as a Lighter, Fire Starters, Ferro Rod, and Magnification Glass with Char Cloth.

Containers: A 2-3 liter water bladder inside your pack can be helpful in addition to a stainless steel container and nesting cup. With the bladder and bottle full, you'll have plenty of water for a day's travels, and with the addition of a Grayl or Sawyer brand squeeze filter and Sillcock key, you will be well supplied when it comes time to procure additional water, whether in town or the field.

Cordages: #36 Tarred Bankline is a favorite for camp-related chores, but paracord is also very handy for specific applications such as replacing a broken shoestring. A climbing rope or mule tape section will permit you to raise or lower yourself over potential obstacles.

Cotton Material & Repair Needle: You should carry a 3' x 3' section of 100% Cotton fabric. A shemagh fulfills this purpose very well. It can be made into an improvised dust mask or used as a bath towel when needed. The repair needle will be capable of mending your heavy-duty backpack or even your boots. Just make sure you get a #14 Sail Needle, and you're now set to complete in-field sewing repairs when you break down your paracord or bankline.

Cargo: In addition to the bag you choose to carry your gear, a roll of 1" wide Gorilla Tape is a must-have cargo tool. It will permit you to mend your bag and serve for first aid purposes (band-aids) and fire-starting purposes because the tape will burn when lit with a lighter or Ferro rod.

Combination Tool: A Leatherman multi-tool or Swiss Army Knife (SAK) will be extremely helpful during the transition between urban and rural environments. Tools will enable you to dismantle or create other devices and make potential repairs to your gear.

Candling Device: The headlamp is essential for hands-free movement; you cannot afford to tie your hands up by carrying a flashlight when it matters. Make sure your headlamp offers low light and red-light settings and bring at least two sets of additional batteries.

Compass: Carry a compass that has a sighting mirror along with pace beads attached. Also, add with it a notebook and pencil to make navigational notes. All of these items are also multipurpose.

Cerate: At the basic level, a cerate is simply a medicated ointment or salve. Chapstick is a type of cerate. By extension, cerate may include other medical or first aid category items. In the modern world, you should always expect the potential for gunshot wounds. You can efficiently address minor traumatic injuries with other entities within your kit (as we'll show later in the book). However, the threat of GSW is real, and a proper Blow-Out Kit (First Aid for Gun Shot Wounds) is a necessity.

1. Tourniquet
2. 2 Chest Seals
3. Nitrile Gloves
4. Quick Clot
5. Steri-Strips/ Duct Tape
6. Dermabond/ Vet-Bond
7. 12ft Gauze/ Wound Packing

High-calorie food items and hydration mixes are also part of your Cerate kit; meal replacement bars and the like provide nutritious and lasting meals when on the move.

Circumvention: An N95 Respirator Mask/ Dust Mask along with dust goggles and tactical or leather gloves will be of great benefit should you find yourself crossing a city during a period of unrest. Additional items in this category would be firearms and other defensive weapons. Lock picks and handcuffs keys, all of which can bypass restraints, aid in an escape, or in avoiding capture. Communication devices such as radios and cell phones may also permit ways of gaining local intelligence to go around potential choke points and ambush sites.

7

Pentecost: The Wilderness Refuge

I will bring you into the wilderness of the people, and there will I plead with you face to face. ~ Ezekiel 20: 35

Pentecost takes place forty-nine days (seven weeks) after Passover's day for a total of 50 days. Called Shavuot in Hebrew, the festival was a thanksgiving feast for Israel when the farmers gathered the first harvest of wheat. It takes place in early summer. It was on Pentecost that God gave his commandments to the covenant people of Israel from Mt. Sinai. Fire fell upon the mountain out in the desert, and God's people came under his divine protection through the covenant at Sinai. They would forever be able to dwell in this place of refuge should they be obedient to his instructions and continue to keep the covenant.

With the advent of Jesus Christ and the new covenant's inauguration, God once again demonstrated His love for His covenant people. After his resurrection, Jesus remained on the earth for an additional forty days (Mark 16:12-19, Luke 24:35-49, John 21, Acts 1:1-11), at which time he continued to eat, fellowship, and teach his disciples. He commanded them before his ascension to heaven to wait in Jerusalem for the coming gift of the Holy Spirit. The disciples returned to the room they had just used for the Passover dinner. Altogether, there ended up being about 120 in the room before Peter finally started to talk about replacing Judas. They remained in that room for ten days, praying, waiting, and fellowshipping with one another. Suffice to say, the Feast of Pentecost is a great day of celebration as not only did we receive God's Commandments at Sinai, but the gift of the Holy Spirit who gives us all revelation and truth (1 Cor. 2:10-11).

On this holiday in the summer-time, God gave us the ability to discern his will apart from the religious services of the temple and priests. As followers of Christ, no more would we be bound to a temple, to an earthly intercessor (priest), or make a sacrifice for our sins. Anywhere we go, we can hear from and speak forth the oracle of God.

"For where two or three gather in my name, there am I with them."
~Matthew 18:20

By abiding in God's word, by being obedient to His instructions, we're wrapping ourselves in a protective bubble of sorts. This protection hinders the fiery darts of the enemy and the troubles of this world.

Deuteronomy 33:27: *"The eternal God is your refuge, and his everlasting arms are under you. He thrusts out the enemy before you; it is he who cries, 'Destroy them!'"*

Nahum 1:7: *"The LORD is good. When trouble comes, he is a strong refuge. And he knows everyone who trusts in him."*

Psalm 119:114: *"You are my refuge and my shield; I have put my hope in your word."*

Isaiah 25:4: *"You have been a refuge for the poor, a refuge for the needy in their distress, a shelter from the storm and a shade from the heat. For the breath of the ruthless is like a storm driving against a wall"*

Isaiah 57:13: *When you cry, let those who you have gathered deliver you; but the wind shall take them, a breath shall carry them all away: but he who takes refuge in me shall possess the land, and shall inherit my holy mountain."*

This verse in Isaiah 57 mimics the language of Thessalonians. When read in Hebrew it is incredibly powerful and specific as well. The Holman Christian Standard Bible gives a more accurate word for word translation:

Isaiah 57:13: "When you cry out, let your collection of idols deliver you! The wind will carry all of them off, a breath will take them away. But whoever takes refuge in Me will inherit the land and possess My holy mountain."

Again, those that are serving idols shall be carried away by the wind (chaff) while the wheat, those taking refuge in the Lord, shall be left behind (Matt. 24:40). Additionally, Shavuot (Pentecost) is the annual wheat harvest in Israel. Remember the First-fruits festival, which is the first Sunday after Passover, was for the former harvest, the first of the barley grains to harvest. In comparison, the wheat farmers collected the last or latter of the grains at Shavuot[9]. Again, this is another important lesson as it defines the context of the former and latter rain (Joel 2, Hosea 6) and the grain harvest process. Followers of Jesus are referred to as wheat (Matt. 13:24, Luke 22:31), and in the Parable of the wheat and tare, we learn that the enemy will come into a good field of wheat and sew tares that will grow up right alongside the wheat. The plowman cannot remove them because they'll uproot the excellent wheat beside them, so the harvester must remove them at the time of harvest (Matt. 14:24-30). John the Baptist said about Jesus, *"His winnowing fork is in His hand, and He will thoroughly clear His threshing floor; and He will gather His wheat into the barn, but He will burn up the chaff with unquenchable fire"* (Matt. 3:12).

Enter the Tribulum

A tribulum was a tool used at the time of Jesus and beforehand to crush the hardened outer shell of wheat and tare alike[10]. It was a wooden platform that had stone or metal teeth on one side. The thresher would stand on the flat side and rock back and forth over the wheat to separate the good wheat from the chaff. He would then take his winnowing fork and toss the harvest into the air, at which time the lighter chaff would be blown away and separated from the heavier wheat. The chaff would then be swept up and thrown into the fire. The bible uses this picture to describe the end-times harvest. There will be a significant crushing- a tribulation that will separate the good from the bad. And at the coming of the Messiah (the thresher), the thresher will burn up the chaff while we who are his will remain with him forever.

Those that have received the commandments of God and have the testimony of Jesus Christ shall find their place of refuge in him during times of hardship and suffering. Pentecost is not only a celebration of the receiving of the gifts of the commandments of God and blessing of the Holy Spirit; but a reminder that one day we shall all be sifted as wheat. We are called to be fully prepared for it, and we must have a stable relationship with and understanding (Revelation & Truth) of Jesus Christ. Passover is a symbol of our spiritual deliverance and subsequent escape from the sinful world. Pentecost is symbolic of our reliance upon God for all our provision and continual dependence upon Him for all our needs apart from the world. Learning to live like this in modern times will be very challenging.

THE GOSPEL OF SURVIVAL

The Tribulum of Aleppo
Public Domain

Just as Passover is a Bug-Out Rehearsal for us to practice annually, Pentecost is an annual rehearsal for us to learn to rely on God for guidance. So that the Lord can direct us to our literal place of refuge in the end-times; this literal place of gathering wherein we will commune with others to await his coming. In the end times, Jesus Himself said we must not waste time running back into the house to get what we need- we must run to the wilderness (Matt. 24).

Ezekiel 20:33-38: *"As I live, saith the Lord God, indeed with a mighty hand, and with a stretched out arm, and with fury poured out, will I rule over you: And I will bring you out from the people and will gather you out of the countries wherein ye are scattered, with a mighty hand, and with a stretched out arm, and with fury poured out. And I will bring you into the wilderness of the people, and there will I plead with you face to face. Like as I pleaded with your fathers in the wilderness of the land of Egypt, so will I plead with you, saith the Lord God. And I will cause you to pass under the rod. I will bring you into the bond of the covenant: And I will purge out from among you the rebels, and them that transgress against me: I will bring them forth out of the country where they sojourn, and they shall not enter into the land of Israel: and ye shall know that I am the Lord."*

The Apostle John confirms this as well in *Revelation 12:6: "Then the woman [the Church] fled into the wilderness, where she has a place prepared by God, that they should feed her there one thousand two hundred and sixty days."*

When the time to flee comes, God has a place of refuge prepared for those that are His! We take away these points from Pentecost:

- Pentecost is the day we received the 10 Commandments and the entirety of the Torah at Sinai. It was also the day the Holy Spirit birthed the Church.

- The day on which he (Jesus) began his ministry as a mediator and high priest in heaven, which is confirmed by the believers in the upper room receiving the Urim and Thummim (cloven tongues as of fire), also known as revelation and truth.
- It is a Festival of Thanksgiving, thanking God for giving us a covenant relationship and the ability to understand his desires without the need of an earthly mediator.
- It is a reminder that we will one day be sifted as wheat through a time of tribulation, which is required for us to be separated from the tares (False Believer) and prepared for harvest (Glory).
- It is a day that reminds us of the protection God provides for us should we cleave unto Him by remaining obedient to His teachings as revealed in His word.
- It's an annual cycle of training that will encourage us to listen to the leading of the Holy Spirit closely.

Now you are better equipped as to what you should take into the wilderness and the Biblical reasons to do so. Now let's examine some essential tool safety protocols before delving further into skills development.

8

Tool Safety

The Triangle of Death

The arteries of the thigh, the groin area, and the lower abdomen comprise the triangle of death. A deep knife wound in these areas when carving or cutting improperly could result in massive blood loss and death. Therefore, always cut and carve away from your body and away from these areas.

The Blood Bubble

The Blood Bubble is the area around you in which bystanders could be cut should you swing your knife around or, again, carve improperly. Make sure bystanders are outside of your circle when using your knife. You should look on both sides of your body and when in a class setting, look behind you to be certain you are not in someone else's blood bubble. If you find you are struggling to carve, do not try to carve off such large pieces (we call it hogging off). Slow is smooth, and smooth is fast when it comes to carving. When you hit a knot, work around it first, then through it, which will help mitigate skipping off the wood and into a bystander.

Knife Handling

When handing a knife to another, flip the blade back toward you so the handle is exposed enough for the other person to grasp the knife handle safely. Make sure the blade is facing up and away from your hand. Require the person taking the knife to acknowledge that they have it by saying "Got it."

Carving with a Knife

Create a Try-Stick to try out carving common camp notches on a single stick. According to Mors Kochanski, the purpose behind the try stick is to practice and demonstrate the skillful use of the knife as a wood carving tool and learn some of the practical operations that may be used in wilderness living. Any straight-grained, knot-free wood will do for the stick, with one of the better woods being a straight piece of willow. We shall only demonstrate the trimmed end, cabin notch, pothook notch, and round notch for this course.

THE GOSPEL OF SURVIVAL

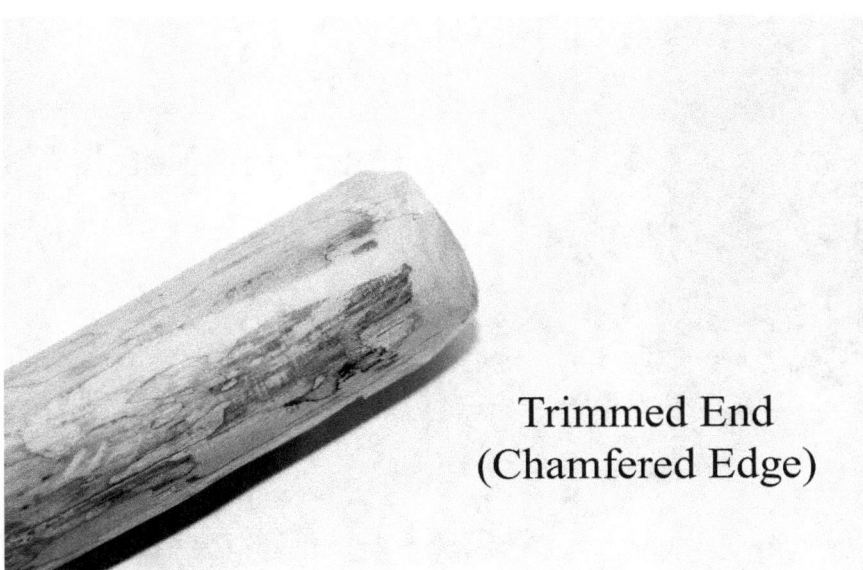
Trimmed End
(Chamfered Edge)

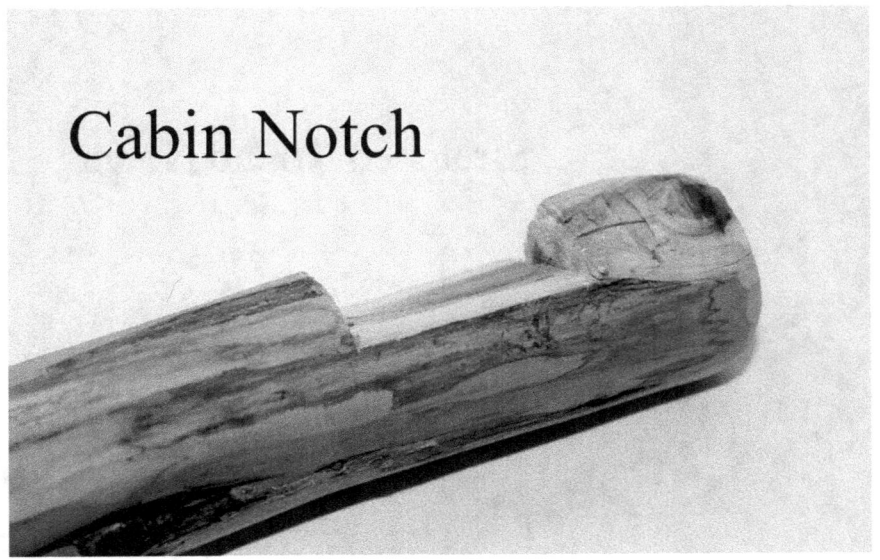
Cabin Notch

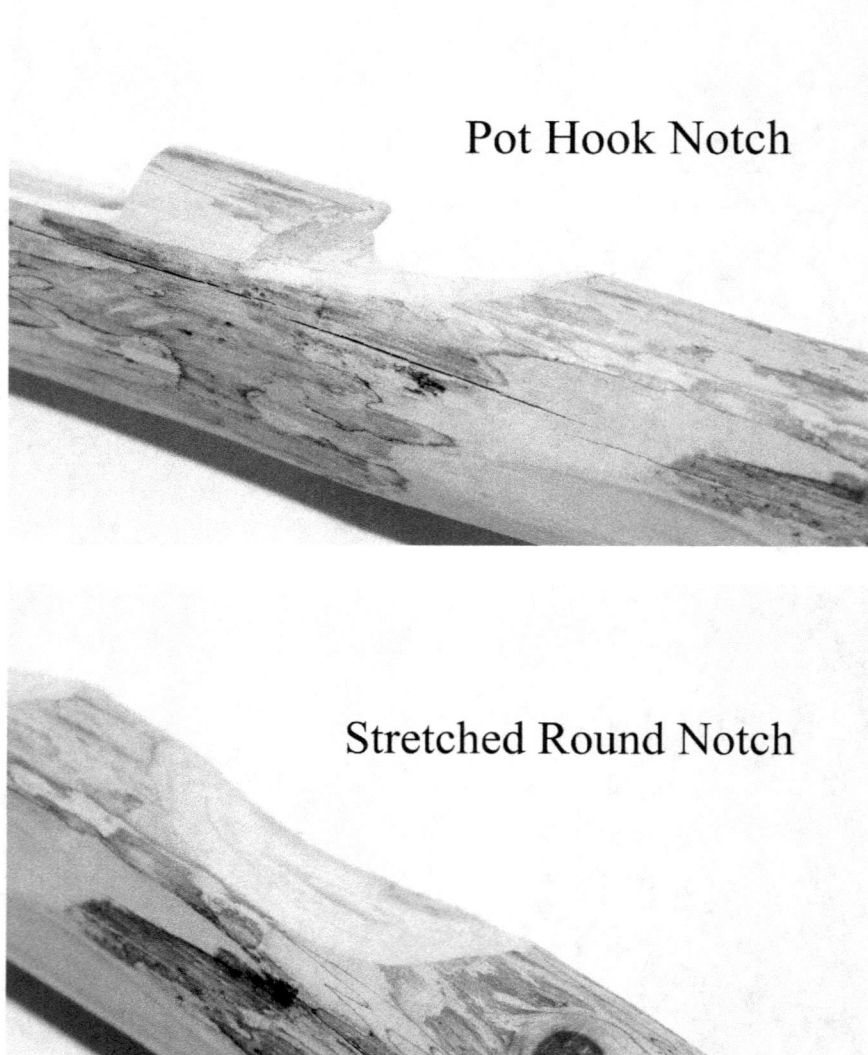

Pot Hook Notch

Stretched Round Notch

THE GOSPEL OF SURVIVAL

How to Scrape a Ferro Rod

There are three primary methods we utilize to scrape a Ferro rod with the spine of a knife or any other hard object such as a rock, file, or the back of a saw blade. We prefer using the 1/2-inch diameter by 5-inch long Ferro rods with a handle on them because they are easier for beginners to use and permit macro motor skills in extremely cold weather. The smaller the Ferro rod, the more fine the motor skills become to use it, and in cold weather, that can mean the difference between life and death.

1: *Rod Pull*: Holding the knife stationary at the end of your knee or even anchored to your foot, you pull the rod from the knife. This works best for dry materials.

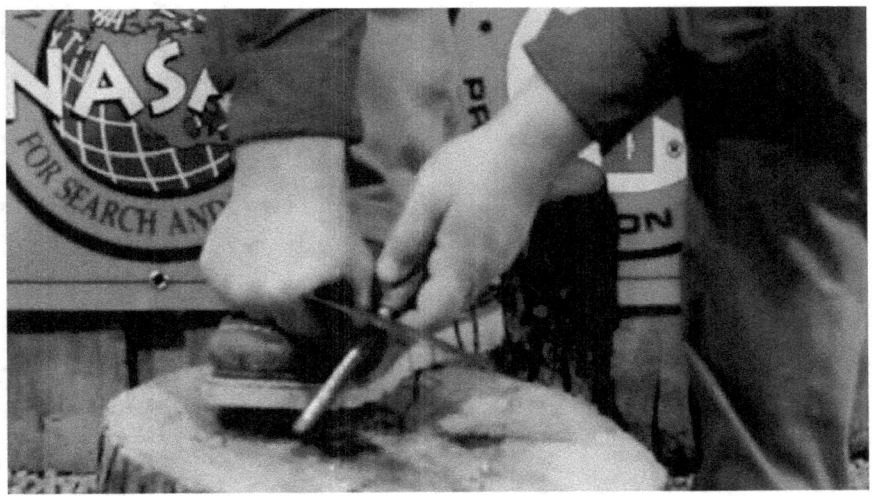

Press up against the scraper you use as hard as you can. Use the edge of the scraping device and pull hard to produce a shower of sparks. The stationary scraper will shield you and direct the majority of sparks into your fire lay.

2: *Pump*: Holding the rod stationary, pinning material to the fire making surface; you scrape the knife spine downward repeatedly to produce a shower of sparks. This works best on damp or poorly selected material.

Repeatedly using this technique can chew through a Ferro rod quickly if uneven pressure is applied. You may see a dish effect on the rod surface, which shows that you apply more pressure in the center of the stroke than at the top or bottom of the stroke. Firm and even pressure is the key to consistent success.

THE GOSPEL OF SURVIVAL

3: *Hard Scrape*: Press the knife spine as hard as you can against the rod and slowly scrape ribbons of material from the rod to create a small pile of shavings that can be ignited. This works best for duct tape and other difficult materials.

The hard scrape technique is also an effective way to clean up speed bumps along your Ferro rod. Speed bumps develop from not applying even pressure during strikes off the rod. Rotate your rod with each strike for even wear and the most longevity.

Cutting with a Pruning Saw
Use the Plumbers vice method to cut a long stick of wood. Step over the wood with your dominant leg and secure wood in the bend of the knee. Across the opposite thigh, hold wood tight, and then saw on the outside of the body for a safe, efficient cut. Consider pocket saws for smaller work for traps and finer woodcraft techniques.

This sawing technique is the safest to use for manageable pieces of wood for projects and camp shores. Large wood pieces for structures and the like would be sawn in place or on the ground. Once the saw is halfway through such pieces, roll the log to cut from another angle to avoid pinching the blade. In some cases, a wood wedge may be required to keep the saw kerf from closing on the blade.

Use of Baton and Anvil
Use a baton to gain leverage on your knife to cut through wood up to 5" in diameter. The baton should be living wood (green-wood) of about one-inch diameter and the length of your arm from the tip of your fingers to your elbow. The baton is not meant to be a woodworking miracle tool like a woodcraft maul. A baton is a multi-use tool for smaller tasks such as fire-prep, digging, throwing at animals, and defense.

The anvil is another piece of wood upon which you will process materials. This piece protects your cutting tools from being driven into the ground, thereby saving the edge. An anvil can be created from anything that will permit a steady platform. So, a log that's been flattened on one side, an old tree stump, or a 2-inch thick piece you cut from another log will all serve the same purpose.

9

The Ministry of Fire

Their work will be shown for what it is because the Day will bring it to light. It will be revealed with fire, and the fire will test the quality of each person's work. ~ 1 Corinthians 3:13

Fire Science 101

With fire skills reigning as one of the most critical survival skills to know and certainly one of the most popular to practice, it makes sense to invest time learning to understand it. What precisely is this elusive element, and what is it made of? We should understand these things before learning to wield fire as a tool.

So, what is fire?

Fire is a chemical process of combustion involving the oxidation of a fuel source at a high temperature. It releases energy and produces heat and light. Flames are made following the chemical reaction between oxygen and another gas and intensify by increasing combustion rate. Four elements, also known as the fire tetrahedron, must be present for a fire to exist. These fire tetrahedron elements include:

- Oxygen
- Heat
- Fuel
- Chemical reaction

When you remove any one of the four elements, you can then extinguish a fire.

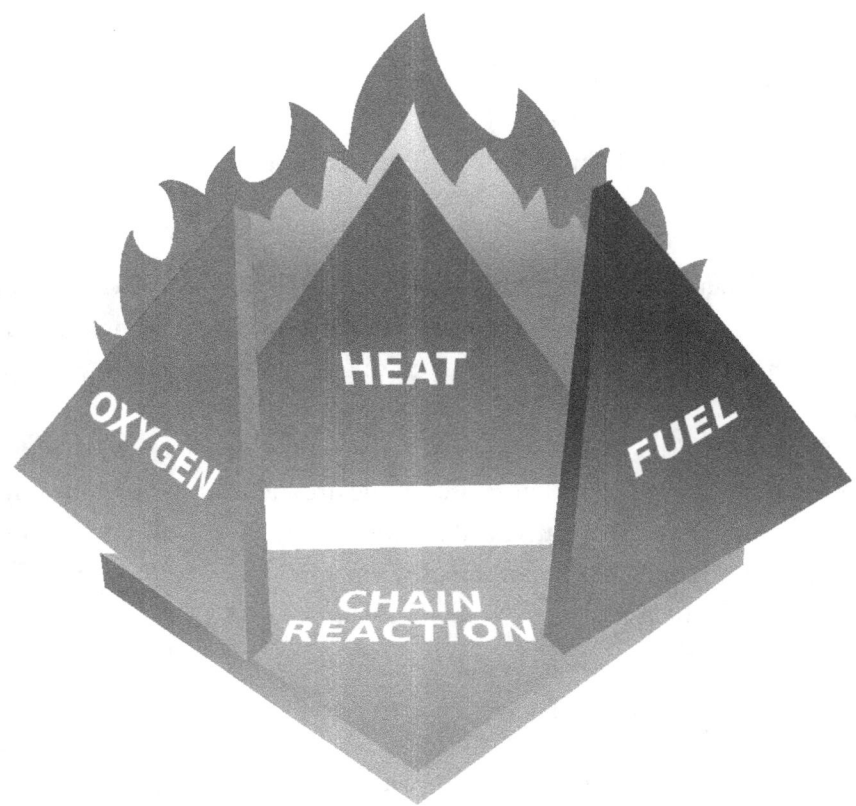

Fire Tetrahedron, Image in Public Domain

The 5 Stages of Fire

There are five stages of fire, including:

Ignition: At this stage, a fire extinguisher can control the fire, such as wind, rain, or snow.

Growth: Additional fuel ignites, causing the size of the fire to increase. At this stage, the fire's kindling begins to burn fuel sized sticks of at least thumb thickness.

Fully developed: This is when temperatures reach their peak, and the fire is sustainable and potentially self-feeding. Full-size logs are now burning, and there is a well-established coal bed.

Burnout: The fire gets less intense.

Extinguished: The fire is out with no hot spots.

The 5 Fire Definitions

In Modern Survival, we have specific fire-related words or phrases that require definition as people use different terms depending on their location or training. For the sake of getting everyone on the same page:

Venturi Effect: This is a jet effect that occurs when a fire lay is appropriately constructed. The center of the fire sucks air in from the bottom and projects the heat and flame up. That is especially important when boiling water and when creating emergency fires and signals. *The Venturi effect is named after Giovanni Battista Venturi (1746–1822), an Italian physicist.*

Sustainable Fire: A fire burning fuel at least the thickness of your thumb or one inch in diameter. Once a fire is burning fuel, it is sustainable enough to walk away from collecting more fuel for the fire.

QuickFire: A fire starter such as a cotton pad soaked in lamp oil, wrung out, then dipped in wax, or a commercially made fire starter designed to work in poor weather conditions.

Fatwood: Also known as *"fat lighter," "lighter wood," "rich lighter," "pine knot," "lighter knot," or "heart pine,"* is derived from the heartwood of pine trees. The resin acts as an accelerant even in wet conditions.

Scavenger Mentality: When scavengers see an opportunity to get something, they take it. We must practice the scavenger mentality when it comes to fire building resources. We must think of the current fire and the next fire we have to make, so we should always collect resources materials because WE NEVER KNOW WHEN WE WILL NEED THEM. So, when you see an excellent fire resource, grab it!

Tinder, Kindling, and Fuel

Tinder is the hair-like, fine fibers that provide a large overall surface area to take a spark. Finely processed inner and outer barks, grasses, and fibrous plant materials work well as natural tinder sources.

Kindling is small diameter wood pieces ranging in size from the sharp end of a pencil to your fingers' length, but not your thumb. Kindling is what enables the fire to become hot, fast. Feeding continually during the growth stage with kindling will establish a coal bed faster for later cooking.

Fuel is anything the diameter of your thumb or larger. Fuel sized sticks will not only enable you to reach fire stability but permit you to fully develop the fire for cooking, heating shelters, and other survival-related projects.

The 5 Natural Tinder Sources

Mnemonic Device: "As big as your head or your Fire is dead" Students will typically choose smaller amounts of tinder to make nests the size of songbirds. We want an Eagles nest to make a fire for survival; this is do or die!

"But they that wait upon the Lord shall renew their strength; they shall mount up with wings as eagles; they shall run, and not be weary; and they shall walk, and not faint."

~ Isaiah 40:31

1. Inner Bark

The stringy inner bark of a fallen Black Locust tree

The dry inner bark from dead trees and plants can be stripped and processed into excellent tinder material. Look for the dead inner bark from trunks and branches of tulip poplar, cedar, black locust, ash, basswood, and cottonwood, to name some of the more common to the Eastern Woodlands. Plants used for cordage material, such as milkweed, dogbane, and stinging nettle, can also provide inner bark tinder. Inner barks are processed by pounding, tearing, twisting, scraping, or buffing. Pounding is usually the best way to fluff up barks. When processing in the ways listed, catch the delicate fibers in some containers and use them as the finished bundle's core. These fine fibers have a large surface area and will ignite more readily.

2. Outer Bark

The outer bark of the Eastern Red Cedar

The outer barks of trees such as birch, cedar, and juniper can all be processed much like an inner bark. Cedar and juniper smolder more than anything, but they hold heat well and aid in increasing the tinder bundle's internal temperatures to achieve ignition. Birch barks are preferred by many as they will ignite readily from an open flame, and with some processing, they can accept spark ignitions from Ferro rods. The more the bark is processed, the more readily it will ignite due to the decrease in overall surface to be burned, so tearing into thin strips or roughing the texture goes a long way in achieving a fast ignition.

3. Fibrous Plant Material

A bundle of teasel hung at camp to dry

The dead tops from many plants work well as a tinder source. Some tops, such as goldenrod, have several grades of tinder in them. Goldenrod has a fine down that is surrounded by papery chaff, which is on slender twigs. These tinder mixed grades can burn furiously and serve as an example of how different tinder qualities burn well when combined. Seed down from cattail, thistle, or milkweed pods can also be used as flash tinder. These almost explosive materials combust quickly but do not burn but for a moment. Weed tops and grasses usually do not require processing. Some weeds have a white, Styrofoam like core called a medulla, commonly called a pith. Plants with a pith such as teasel, thistle, milkweed, and dogbane make excellent resources for charred material. By charring the pith, you create another fire-making resource that will readily accept a spark to become an ember. The ember that can be blown upon to ignite a fire.

4. *Fungus*

Cracked Cap Polypore on the side of a Black Locust tree

The fire-making properties of various types of fungi have been known for thousands of years. Ötzi, the Iceman, had fungus pieces (Fomes Fomentaris) among his belongings and likely used them for his fire-making and medicinal properties. Several types of fungi will carry a viable ember, the most common of which in North America are:

- Cracked Cap Polypore (Phellinus robiniae)
- Horse's Hoof Fungus (Fomes fomentarius)
- Chaga (Inonotus obliquus)

Each is used similarly so far as fire-making is concerned. You saw into or crush the woody fungi to increase its surface area to accept a spark that will grow into an ember. This ember is then transferred into a bird's nest tinder bundle to be blown into a flame.

5. Tree Accelerants

Resinous sap from a pine tree

Tree accelerants such as Pine resin, which is infused in fatwood, are fantastic resources for fire kits and permit survivalists' means of extending the life of their resources by creating new ones. By cutting slivers of wood and covering one end in pine resin, you can make a type of match that will accept an open flame. You can smear this same resin into flash tinders such as cattail, thereby extending their burn time and volatility and adding to any natural materials to create fire starters. Whenever you see pine sap globules hanging from a tree, take them and store them for later use.

THE GOSPEL OF SURVIVAL

The 5 Ignition Methods

Fire Kit photo by Anthony Awaken Photography

1. Lighter

I recommend the Bic brand lighter because they are guaranteed from the factory to ignite 3000 times per lighter and because the plastic body, when scraped into shavings, makes a viable option as a tinder source.

The lighter should always be your first go-to item when making a fire in an emergency. Users should understand how to rescue them once being submerged, rewarm them when cold, and make use of them when damaged or even broken.

2. Ferrocerium Rod

The Ferro rod is an excellent emergency fire starting device. It's been proven for decades by the military, and now that survival and bushcraft skills are main-stream, the improvements in available models are nothing short of staggering. We recommend a 1/2" diameter x 5"- 6" long rod for general kit use. This will permit the user to have many years of fire-making ahead of them while maximizing their ability to ignite marginal fire materials.

3. Solar Magnification

Solar magnification is the most economical method of making a fire because the sun is free and renewable. A magnification lens or card (Fresnel Lens) that is at least five power provides plenty of strength to capture the sun's rays and turn them into a mini laser beam. Sandwich bags filled with water, water bottles (glass or plastic), steel spoons, and even condoms can also be used as a means of achieving enough magnification to elicit a solar ember ignition.

4. Flint & Steel

Flint is not one specific type of rock but a collection of stones above a 7.5-8 on the Mohs scale of hardness. Cherts, Quartz, and Obsidian are all types of flints. For the flint to be useful, it must first be *dressed*, which means to have an edge put on it by breaking away some of the stone to create a sharpened edge. This sharpened edge is then struck against a high carbon steel striker or piece of metal. Upon striking the metal's surface, the flint cuts off particles of the steel, and upon contact with oxygen in the air, the bodies of the particles spontaneously ignite and give off heat as they oxidize (rust). Because the metal particles' surface area is so large compared to their volume, the particles quickly heat up and glow red hot. They become sparks. You must collect these sparks into a material that will accept a spark of relatively low temperatures yet will still ignite at said lower temperatures. Previously burned materials, known as charred materials, are capable of receiving such a spark. You can easily ignite charred cotton cloth, plant pith, fungus, and even wood with flint and steel sparks.

5. Friction

Friction fire is a skill you most certainly do not want to rely upon in an actual survival situation. Not because it's inconsistent to do, but because it requires a more advanced skill set due to its multiple moving parts and technical issues that need constant troubleshooting on the fly. Should you be injured, disoriented, dehydrated, hungry, or be suffering from a core temperature control (CTC) issue, performing this skill becomes exponentially more difficult.

The 5 Fire Lays

The way we lay down sticks to make a fire is an integral part of the fire-starting process. If we lay our sticks in one direction, packing them too tightly together, or conversely, too far apart, we would have too much or too little air and contact between burning surfaces. This improper stacking will not only prevent the fire from heating up properly but will starve it of fuel, thereby stunting its ability to sustain itself.

1. Emergency Fire (Chaotic Tipi)

The simplicity of the Tipi is hard to beat. Take a handful of sticks in each hand and place one over the top of the other to create an inverted V shape. In the center of the V, place your tinder bundle. Ignite the tinder, then grasp the top of the V and stand it up over your fire. This cone of sticks has an excellent fuel-to-air ratio, which equals a great burning fire lay that is quick lighting and dependable, even with damp materials. It looks like a tipi (tee-pee) that's a mess. That's okay; fire thrives in chaos, and the sticks going in different directions will help feed the fire faster.

THE GOSPEL OF SURVIVAL

2. Long Fire (Winter Warming)

This fire will provide a wider swath of radiant heat, which will last you through the cold winter nights. The idea is that you make the fire as long as your body or at least the length of the shelter's opening. This fire is commonly used with super shelter systems and does a beautiful job of maintaining heat within a half-faced or lean-to style shelter.

Dragging long trees and logs into camp and laying them in the fire is often the easiest method of maintenance, just make sure you leave space between the logs so air can circulate, otherwise, you'll smother this fire. You can also share this fire with another shelter set up across from you. With two people managing the fire you can each take turns on fire watch and get a more restful night's sleep.

3. Water Boil Fire Lay

While you can boil water in any fire lay, this specific fire-lay does so as quickly as possible. We begin by placing our steel bottle on the ground and then surrounding it with our tinder material. We then place kindling around the bottle in a log cabin style fashion, then tipi an armload of sticks over the top the whole thing before attempting ignition. Once ignited, we ensure that the fire is surrounding the bottle and burning well, then we add an armload of kindling to the top. Water will boil often in under five-minutes time, but most certainly in less than ten so long as there isn't a downpour of rain.

4. Cooking Fire (Hunters/Trappers Fire)

The Hunter's Fire Lay, also called the trapper's fire, is a widespread technique during the mountain men and fur trappers' age. It's essentially a long fire used for cooking. Align two 6" diameter logs, one on each side of your coal bed, from the previous night's long fire spaced apart as wide as your skillet or flat-bottomed cook pot. Ideally, the prevailing winds will travel into the fire between the logs, thereby keeping it nice and hot for cooking. You set your skillet or cook pot on top of the logs. You can cook several dishes this way and have space to manage or feed the fire as necessary.

5. Siberian Fire Lay

The Siberian fire is one specifically suited to protect your fire from rain or snow. The roof provided over top your main fire shields it from the elements while still permitting the roof logs to burn overnight. It offers suitable warmth and leaves a relatively small footprint when compared to the long fire. The great thing about this fire lay is that it's meant to be scaled up. It's called Siberian for a reason! Harsh winters and frigid temperatures are endured by the Evenk people of Siberia annually, and this fire lay helps them trap and camp all winter long. Scale this up to 4", 6", or 8" logs to increase all the heat, burn time and sleep time you can get while afield.

How to hear from God

God will often use the elements to speak to His people. He spoke to Moses, Isaiah, and Elijah from the midst of the fire. He led his people across the desert in a pillar of fire by night and smoke by day, and Jesus revealed himself in his set ablaze, glorified form to his followers (Mk.

9:2-50). Our God is a consuming fire (Heb. 12:29). For those willing to still themselves around the fire in times of personal crisis, distress, or even when in need of counsel- God will reveal himself to those that seek him (Psalm 14:2 Acts 17:27-28).

Here's how to train your Fire Skills

The following fire skills are listed in their progression as I teach them in my Modern Survival course. A brief explanation of the technique and testing elements is included to get the most from your training and be better prepared.

1. *Rescue a Wet Lighter:* Once a lighter has been submerged in water, remove excess water with a few flicks of the wrist. Then, remove the child safety covering from the flint wheel, make sure you bend the barbs that hold it in place back down on the shroud. Now, dry the flint wheel by either wiping it off as you rotate it or by running it back and forth over your pants across your thigh briskly. Once you see sparks and a hint of flames, it's ready to light.

2. *Lighter Tinder Fire:* Using the spine of your knife, scrape off the body of your lighter to create a pile of shavings roughly the size of a quarter (25 cents). Ignite the pile using your Ferro rod, then ignite a tinder bundle with it as a way to prove viability. Ensure scrapes from all sides of the lighter and not just one side, which may inadvertently cause a leak or explosion of lighter fuel.

3. *Create Char Cloth & Material:* Place 100% cotton or plant pith material inside a metal tin. If the container is tight and without hinges, poke a small hole in the top or edge of the rim (through the top and bottom pieces) and cook it on the fire for at least 7 minutes (you can't overcook it). You'll see a small gas exhaust jet often ignite from the hole; this is normal. Once the flame goes out from the exhaust jet, it's typically completed charring. You may now remove the tin from the fire, but do not open it

until it's completely cooled, as the reintroduction of air will cause the material inside to combust. Once cooled to the touch, open the tin and examine your char material. It should be completely black; if not, cook some more. Try making some charred material from cloth and plants. Note the items you used to make char and which worked best for you.

4. *Fire with Flint & Steel:* Now use your charred material with your flint & steel set to create a fire. You may rain sparks down into your char tin or elect to place the charred material on the flint, then strike that way. Whatever your chosen technique, make a note of which method you favor and which charred materials you found worked best for you.

5. *Fungus Fire with Mag Lens:* Locate a piece of fungus from a local tree if at all possible. Process the material using your saw and ignite it with your Ferro rod. Transfer that ember into a bird's nest once it reaches about the size of a dime. Then blow it into a flame. Once you have successfully used your Ferro rod, try using your magnifying lens to do the same thing. Finally, try charring the fungus and using flint and steel. Note your findings- Did one method prove more consistent? Did you prefer one method over another? What types of fungus did you use?

6. *Carry fire across distance:* This skill will enable you to take your fires with you should you decide to move camp. There are three methods to try for this skill, one is to ignite an ember into a piece of fungus, two is to ignite an ember into a bit of charcoal, and the third is to braid some natural cordage and get an ember glowing on one end of it. Try all three techniques, cover some ground with each one, and walk at least a mile. Note about how long each piece lasted you and how far you were able to travel. This information will give you a better idea of how large or small the material should be based on the distance traveled.

7. *Duct Tape Tinder Fire with Ferro-rod:* Duct tape, Gorilla brand specifically, works well as tinder resources even in the rain.

Process a tinder bundle from tape and ignite it using the pump technique with your Ferro rod. Note how long it took you to ignite it the first time, then perform the procedure a few more times to become more proficient. Not all duct tapes are created equal, so if you use other brands, jot down those that worked the best for you.

8. *Fire with Ferro-rod and Natural Material:* Create a tinder bundle the size of your head from the surrounding landscape's material. Your objective is to ignite the material using only your Ferro rod to create a sustainable fire in less than 5 minutes.

9. *Fatwood Fire with Ferro-rod:* Go afield and locate some pine trees and try to harvest your fatwood. If that is out of the question, then use store-bought fatwood. Process some down to create a pile of tinder and then split or feather the remaining pieces into your tipi fire lay. Ignite using your Ferro rod to create another sustainable fire in 5 minutes or less.

10. *3 Minute Fire with Quick Fire:* Use a pre-made fire starter for this sustainable fire effort. The firestarter can be a store-bought item or one you have made yourself. The tipi fire lay will again be used, but only give yourself 3 minutes to achieve sustainability! This skill will test your ability to select the best of dry materials and your fire lay skills.

11. *10-minute Water Boil Fire:* The ability to boil water quickly will enable you to stave off hypothermia by creating a fire and getting warm liquids in your body. This skill is also useful when you have to treat a patient while afield or if you're on the move and have little time to waste. Make sure to get a good tinder bundle surrounding your bottle and choose good kindling too. Log cabin stack it around three sides of the bottle leaving room to start the fire in the front. Pile on kindling to about knee-high, then let the fire do its job.

10

Sukkot: Camping in Debris Huts

It's incredible to learn that God gave us an everlasting command in the Bible to go out and camp by making a natural debris shelter. More than that, he even tells us to live in it for an entire week every year! Talk about survival skills; it's all part of the annual cycles of God. The Feast of Tabernacles, also known as Shelters or Sukkot (Booths), celebrates the reality that Israel's children lived in natural tents (sukkah) as they crossed the desert wilderness on their way to the Promised Land of Israel.

Leviticus 23:42-43 *"For seven days you must live outside in little shelters. All native-born Israelites must live in shelters. This will remind each new generation of Israelites that I made their ancestors live in shelters when I rescued them from the land of Egypt. I am the LORD your God."*

Sukkot is the memorial celebration of Israel's wilderness wandering. But like all of the Feasts of God, Sukkot is multidimensional in its applications. Leviticus 23 describes the Feasts of God as being a 'moed' or 'appointed time' and, as stated earlier in this book, a 'miqra' or 'rehearsal.' Therefore, when we celebrate the feasts, we are keeping an appointed time of rehearsal. An annual practice will train us well in something we will one day have to do, if you will. By maintaining God's rehearsals in each generation, we keep the memory of historical and potential prophetic (future) events into our present collective consciousness. God

THE GOSPEL OF SURVIVAL

did not merely command us to mentally remember the wilderness wandering events, but act them out.

"But wait!" you may say; "Leviticus only required the native-born Israelites to celebrate this feast. It has no application on Christians because it's under the law." Native-born Israelites indeed had to observe it under the Old Testament law; it also requires that all that call themselves Christian observe it because they are grafted into Israel as one native-born. Please read: *Romans 11:13, 17, 18, Eph. 2:15, Ezekiel 47:22- 23, Genesis 49:10, Micah 5:2, Matthew 2:1, Luke 3:23-34, Matthew 1:1-16, John 15:1-8, 1 Corinthians 3:27-28, 12:12- 13.*

Furthermore, while the "law and its requirements" were nailed to the cross, God's commands and desires for humanity remain intact. (I John 5:3, John 14:21, John 15:10, 1 John 2:3-6) The "law and its requirements" refer to the penalties for breaking the Law of Moses, not the Law of God (10 Commandments), this is evidenced in the fact that if we commit adultery, we still sin and can go to hell, but we are not stoned in the streets. God's Commandments define sin and are eternal, while the cross has obliterated those given to Moses (Ceremonial and Sacrificial rules). However, the Feast Days have always been how non-Jews were grafted into Israel and covered by God's grace.

Exodus 12:48: *"If there are foreigners living among you who want to celebrate the LORD's Passover, let all their males be circumcised. Only then may they celebrate the Passover with you like any native-born Israelite. But no uncircumcised male may ever eat the Passover meal."*

All of the appointed rehearsals contain physical aspects such as circumcision, which translate to matters of the heart and mind that we are to embody in our lives fully. In the Appointed Rehearsal of Sukkot, all of Israel's men go up to Jerusalem and camp in booths made of branches, palm fronds, and leaves. As each generation endeavors to build their temporary living quarters, they remember and relive wilderness wandering events by scouring around to find material suitable for a temporary shelter and making the shelter with simple hand tools. Each generation may then experience the same type of experience from Egypt to the land of promise. By keeping the festival of Sukkot, each generation may lay claim to this rich heritage and remember that it is God who sustains them through the wilderness and not their works of self-reliance.

By keeping the three main Biblical holidays of Passover, Pentecost, and Sukkot, we fully realize our identity as the covenant people of God. Failing to recover this identity leaves us lost in religious Christianity, one with a form of godliness but denies the power to set us free (2 Tim. 3:5). So, by recalling and reclaiming the past, we find our place and calling in the present as Christians skilled in outdoor living, survival, and preparedness. Remember that the Biblical holidays prepare us for something yet to come, a specific appointed time. Beyond reliving the past, the celebration of Sukkot is a rehearsal for a prophetic time in history. While the children of Israel were capable of reading and writing, books were rare and very expensive. Unlike today, every believer did not have his own Bible to study. For this reason, the Torah (Old Testament) was read publicly every seven years at Sukkot.

Deuteronomy 31:10-11 *"And Moses commanded them, saying "At the end of every seven years, in the solemnity of the year of release, in the feast of tabernacles, when all Israel is come to appear before the Lord your God in the place which he shall choose, thou shalt read this Torah before all Israel in their hearing."*

The Bible also teaches that parents are responsible for teaching their children the Commandments, statutes, and ordinances of God.

Deuteronomy 4:9-10 *"Only take heed to thyself, and keep thy soul diligently, lest thou forget the things which thine eyes have seen, and lest they depart from thy heart all the days of thy life: but teach them thy sons, and thy sons' sons; Specially the day that thou stoodest before the Lord your God in Horeb, when God said unto me, Gather me the people together, and I will make them hear my words that they may learn to fear me all the days that they shall live upon the earth, and that they may teach their children."*

Deuteronomy 6:6-7 *"And these words, which I command thee this day, shall be in thine heart: and thou shalt teach them diligently unto thy children and shalt talk of them when thou sittest in thine house, and when thou walkest by the way, and when thou liest down, and when thou risest up."*

Deuteronomy 11:19 *"And ye shall teach them your children, speaking of them when thou sittest in thine house, and when thou walkest by the way, and when thou liest down, and when thou risest up."*

In each of these quoted passages, when read in their larger context, there is a direct connection to verbally teaching the Bible and diligently doing what the Bible says, which is what we're doing by celebrating this feast and building our shelters the way God desires (James 1:22). It is something we're to do daily in practical and dynamic ways for the rest of our lives after coming to know Jesus Christ. Practically speaking, doctrine is what we do and not merely what we believe. Belief alone in or for something means nothing unless it's backed with conviction and action. Teaching in ancient times was done mostly by example. How did parents diligently teach their children the Torah? They taught their children by doing what the Bible said in their homes. Thus, by keeping the Biblical holidays, parents not only taught their children the past, allowed them to connect with their heritage in the present, but they also prepared them for all that was about to come.

So, how does this lead us into the preparation of the New Testament? Jesus and the Apostles repeatedly warned us of the consequence of not being prepared.

Matthew 24:42-43 *"Watch therefore: for ye know not what hour your Master doth come. But know this, that if the Goodman of the house had known in what watch the thief would come, he would have watched, and would not have suffered his house to be broken up."*

Luke 12:47 *"And that servant which knew his Master's will, and prepared not himself, neither did according to his will, shall be beaten with many stripes."*

Revelation 3:3 *"Remember therefore how thou hast received and heard, and hold fast, and repent. If therefore thou shalt not watch, I will come on thee as a thief, and thou shalt not know what hour I will come upon thee."*

1 Thessalonians 5:2 *"For yourselves know perfectly that the day of God so cometh as a thief in the night."* 2 Peter 3:10 *"But the day of the Lord will come as a thief in the night; in the which the heavens shall pass away with great noise and the elements shall melt with fervent heat, the earth also and the works that are therein shall be burned up."*

Because the Bible teaches that what happens to the fathers also happens to the children, we should look to the past to understand what will happen in the future. When Jacob and his children reunited with Joseph in the land of Egypt, the Bible tells us that the children of Israel were quite at home there.

THE GOSPEL OF SURVIVAL

Genesis 47:27 *"And Israel dwelt in the land of Egypt, in the country of Goshen; and they had possessions therein, and grew, and multiplied exceedingly."*

The Hebrew of this verse tells us a little different story. It is possible to read this verse in Hebrew as saying that the 'land possessed Israel's children.' We might remember that Israel's children left the land of promise because of a severe seven-year famine. When they came to Egypt, Joseph placed them in the plushest land in the kingdom. There was plenty of food, land, and water for their families, herds, and crops. Their hearts were satisfied and content. But this was not to be the land of their heritage. Thus, we witness Jacob causing his children to swear an oath that they would not bury him in the land of Egypt but would return him to the land of promise.

Genesis 47:29-30 *"And the time drew nigh that Israel must die: and he called his son Joseph, and said unto him, If now I have found grace in thy sight, but I pray thee, thy hand under my thigh, and deal kindly and truly with me; bury me not, I pray thee in Egypt: But I will lie with my fathers, and thou shalt carry me out of Egypt, and bury me in their burying place."* Genesis 49:29-30 *"And he charged them, and said unto them, I am to be gathered unto my people: bury me with my father's in the cave that is in the field of Ephron the Hittite, in the cave that is in the field of Machpelah, which is before Mamre, in the land of Canaan, which Abraham bought with the field of Ephron the Hittite for a possession of a burying place."*

By this oath, Jacob assured that his sons, beginning with Joseph, who had been in Egypt the longest and had most to leave behind, would leave Egypt and return to the promised land. Unfortunately, once they completed their promised task of burying Jacob, they all returned to their possessions in the land of exile and turned their back on the ground of their heritage. Here we may remember the contrast between Abraham and Lot. When God called Abram to leave his country, kinfolk, and father's house, Abraham departed as God had spoken to him. On the other hand, an angel commanded Abraham's nephew Lot to leave the city of Sodom, for God was about to destroy the city.

The report of Lot's response to the commandment of God to leave this land:

Genesis 19:14-16, 26 *"And Lot went out, and spake unto his sons in law, which married his daughters and said, Up, get you out of this place, for God will destroy this city. But he seemed as one that mocked unto his sons in law. And when the morning arose, then the angels hastened Lot, saying Arise take thy wife and thy two daughters which are here; lest thou be consumed in the iniquity of the city. And while he lingered, the men laid hold upon his hand and upon his wife, and upon the hand of his two daughters; and God being merciful unto him: and they brought him forth and set him without the city....but his wife looked back from behind him, and she became a pillar of salt."*

Lot and his family were so comfortable where they were that they hesitated to leave, even when God enumerated the danger and destruction they were facing. Jesus tells us that where our treasure is, there our heart will also be. Israel's children found their treasure in Egypt, though their calling was to be a Holy Land people. Therefore, when the time was right, God turned Egypt against the children of Israel. What once was a life of pleasure and leisure slowly becoming a life of bitter hardship and oppression. Eventually, Israel's children would cry out to be delivered from Egypt's land and live in the land promised to their fathers. Eventually, God would drive Israel from the land of Egypt into the wilderness. For those of us that have made our homes, raised our families, and put down roots in the land of exile, we need to be mindful that an *appointed time* is coming when God will gather those scattered to the ends of the earth.

Deuteronomy 30:3-4 *"That then the Lord your God will turn thy captivity, and have compassion upon thee, and will return and gather thee from all the nations whither thy Lord hath scattered thee. If any of thine be driven out unto the outmost parts of heaven, from thence will the Lord your God gather thee, and from thence will he fetch thee."*

Isaiah 11:12, *"And he shall set up an ensign for the nations, and shall assemble the outcasts of Israel, and gather together the dispersed of Judah from the four corners of the earth."*

Jeremiah 32:37 *"The Lord which gathered the outcasts of Israel saith, yet will I gather others to him, beside those that are gathered unto him."*
Isaiah 56:8 *"Behold, I will gather them out of all countries whither I have driven them in mine anger."*

Ezekiel 37:21 *"Thus saith The Lord, Behold, I will take the children of Israel from among the heathen, whether they be gone, and will gather them on every side and bring them into their own land."*

Unfortunately, it may take bitterness and adversity to drive us from the comfort of our countries, kindred, and homes and ultimately into a survival mode when preparing in advance by rehearsing God's festivals would have made the transition somewhat easier; at least from the point of it being expected. Most likely, it will be at this time that many of the true believers in Jesus will be persecuted, driven from their land, family, and homes. The appointed rehearsal of Sukkot is a means of preparing us for the day when we are again called to leave the world's comfort in exchange for exile as we return to our Saviors arms.

Daniel Hunt reading his Bible in a Sukkot shelter

Once again, we may be wandering through the wilderness and living in natural shelters of leaves and branches, trusting that God will deliver us and provide for us as we endure the purging fires of the outdoors. So, by keeping God's appointed times, we prepare our families for the day of His return for His Bride, the church. We teach them the way Jesus desired for his actual birthday to be celebrated, and we learn to perfect our outdoor skills by building shelters in the wilderness, how to give and share our resources, how to set up a camp, and how to orient ourselves to the land. By this, we shall be preparing each generation for what yet lays ahead of them.

Therefore, we take away from this chapter the following details:

1. Like all of the Biblical Festivals, Sukkot is a rehearsal for something to come and remembrance of past events.

2. Families are to build a natural shelter and camp out in it for a week in the fall of the year; while this was primarily the men's duty, women are certainly welcome to join and the children.
3. It is the actual time of the birth of Jesus on the earth*.
4. As an appointed time on God's calendar, He promises to visit with us!
5. It is an event that requires us to hone our survival skills of building shelters with natural material, yet more evidence of Christians' need to be trained in survival and preparedness skills.

*In my book Origins of the Christian Holidays, I outline in great detail ample evidence for the birth of Jesus (Yeshua) during the festival of Sukkot based upon the priestly concourse of the Temple, birthing requirements according to the Law of Moses, and the historical record of Rome at the time. This book is available on Amazon.

11

Emergency Survival Shelters

5 W's of Shelter Site Selection

Where we place our shelter, even if only for one night, could make or break us in an actual emergency. The 5 W's will help keep things in perspective- safety is priority number one, then we can look at the ease of use, comforts, etc.

Widow Makers refers to those treetops and large branches, dead tree parts, or other natural phenomena that break off during high winds and storms, often getting caught up in the woodland canopy. Look above you, look closely, to ensure there are no dead branches or broken tree parts hanging anywhere above your proposed campsite. Also, look around you to be sure that there are no dead or damaged trees leaning against another in a precarious fashion that would permit a single high wind to blow them over into your camp. Finally, before you anchor any tarps or hammocks to trees in your camp, look down at the roots to be sure that once weight or force is put on the tree, that it won't fall over on top of you.

Wind is a continual concern as it changes directions from time to time. Check for the prevailing winds, the most consistent direction the wind blows, and make sure that the opening of your shelter doesn't face into the wind. By facing into the wind, you'd have all the smoke and ash from the fire blown into your shelter, which is a fire hazard. Not to mention, it would keep you too cool throughout the night. Instead, set your shelter to take advantage of the prevailing wind direction for the area. Shelters should be set to allow wind to pass between your shelter and campfire.

***Wood**, look* for a shelter site with access to plenty of fires and survival-related projects. Collect three times the amount of firewood you think you'll need. Scavenging for wood in the middle of a cold night is another hazard we want to avoid. Remember that living trees offer shade and can serve as a natural windbreak, but you should always avoid dead standing trees.

Water should be no more than 200 yards away and no fewer than 100 yards. Flash flooding can occur unexpectedly in certain areas, and camping away from the water mitigates this potential issue. Creek and river bottoms tend to stay soggy, retain the cold and are insect magnets, avoid camping there whenever possible.

Wigglers are those things that creep, crawl, and slither under the leaf litter. Check your shelter site for potential hazards such as snakes, hornets' nests, ground hornets, fire ants, etc., so you don't have to make a sudden camp evacuation in the middle of the night.

The 5 Mechanisms of Heat Loss

Conduction occurs when you come into direct contact with a surface that's colder than your body. Instead of transferring heat to the environment, you move it into the cooler object. If you're camping, you can lose heat to any surface on which you're sitting or lying. If you don't insulate yourself, you'll get cold when you're lying on the ground. You'll be uncomfortable even when you're sitting on a log or rock. Conduction happens even faster when you're in the water as the cool water sucks heat away from you at about 30 times faster than the ambient air, which is why 70-degree water feels so much colder than 70-degree air. When it comes to insulating against conduction, use a hand depth of compressed debris such as leaf litter, moss, or boughs in the late spring and through the summer months. By autumn, we should use elbow depth of compressed material and in winter a full arms depth. This depth will create a nice thick cushion on which to rest through the night.

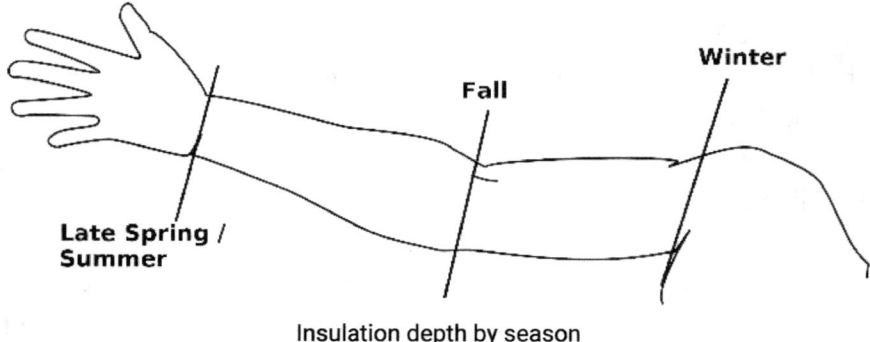

Insulation depth by season

Convection involves losing heat to the environment. However, it requires some air movement to occur. Convection explains why you can cool yourself off while sitting in front of a fan. The circulating air touches your skin. As it does so, it takes away some of your heat. As more cool airbrushes by your body, you lose additional heat, which explains why it's essential to shield yourself from windy conditions.

Radiation is the transmission of electromagnetic waves through space. We naturally heat our bodies to an average temperature of 98.60 F. We lose an average of 65% of our body heat through radiation as our body tries to equalize the climate around us; we give off heat, which displaces it to the cooler area around us. Therefore, the more surface area that is exposed to cooler air, the more heat we lose. The fires we make also radiate heat to the surrounding environment, such as the trees, ground, and us. For every meter we move away from the center of a fire, we lose about ¼ of the heat from the fire. This rule is known as the Rule of Inverse Squares. So, we should seek shelter in the sweet spot between too much and too little heat to best manage our core temperature.

Respiration is merely breathing. When you inhale air, your lungs absorb oxygen, exhale, and breathe out air that your body has warmed up. Your core temperature experiences a slight dip when this happens. Compared with the amount of heat that you lose through the other mechanisms, it's minor. However, it can be a significant factor when you're spending time in cold weather, especially while sleeping, as this warmed air creates condensation (moisture). This moisture is why you should never cover your head while sleeping; this moisture will accumulate on your blanket or sleeping bag, making you wet and potentially colder. Maintain an air hole for adequate air exchange and to better manage condensation issues.

Perspiration is, of course, sweat. When you increase your core temperature, you sweat to keep your body cool. This sweating is a built-in mechanism that prevents you from overheating. As the moisture evaporates, it cools the surface on which it's sitting. If your skin is wet, it can be challenging to maintain your core body temperature. Although sweating can be dangerous when you're camping in cooler weather, so can moisture of any kind on your skin. If you're exposed to rain, snow, or mist, you could be in danger of losing body heat in the same manner.

The 5 Shelter Knots

Siberian Hitch (Evenk Hitch)

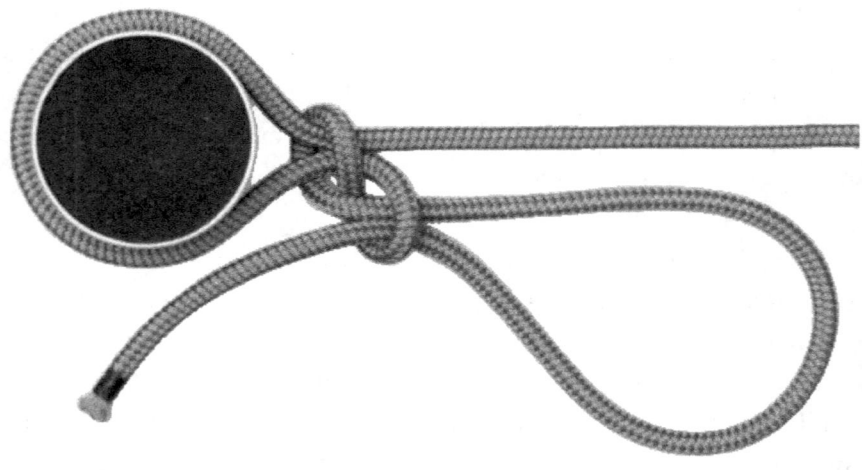

Image Capture courtesy of Animated Knots.com

The Siberian Hitch, also known as the Evenk Hitch, was used initially for tying reindeer to a tree while in mittens by the Nenets people of northern Russia. It was made famous among bushcrafters and survivalists by Ray Mears, who used it regularly in his television series. What makes this hitch great is that it holds a load well and releases easily with a simple pull. This knot is the first knot we tie when setting up our tarp ridge-lines.

Truckers Hitch

Image Capture courtesy of Animated Knots.com

The trucker's hitch got its name because it's a knot commonly used for securing loads on trucks and trailers. This general arrangement, using loops and turns in the rope itself to form a crude block and tackle, has long been used to tension lines and is known by multiple names.

Knot author Geoffrey Budworth claims he can trace the knot back to the days when coachmen and merchants used horse-drawn conveyances to move their wares from place to place. This knot is the second we generally tie when setting up our tarp ridge-line.

Double Fisherman's Bend

Image Capture courtesy of Animated Knots.com

The double fisherman's knot, also called a necklace knot or grapevine knot is a bend or knot that joins two pieces together. This knot and the triple fisherman's knot are the variations used most often in climbing, arboriculture, and search and rescue.

The knot is formed by tying a double overhand knot, in its strangle knot form, with each end around the opposite line's standing part. We utilize this knot to create the four loops used to secure our tarp to the ridge-line.

Prusik Knot

Image Capture courtesy of Animated Knots.com

The term Prusik is a name for both the loops of the cord and the hitch. A Prusik is a friction hitch used to attach a loop of cord around a rope, applied in climbing and rope rescue. The Prusik hitch is named after its inventor, Austrian mountaineer Karl Prusik.

We utilize this knot to create a point at which we can attach our tarps to our ridge-lines with a tent stake or stick. By sliding the Prusik away from the trucker's hitch, tension is placed across our tarp, thereby making it taught.

Larks Head

Image Courtesy SurferToday.com

Correctly called a cow hitch, it has been known since the first century when Greek physician Heraklas described a monograph on surgical knots and slings. The common alternate name "lark's head" is attributed to Tom Bowling in the 1866 work *The Book of Knots*, which is presumed to have been adopted from a French manuscript. Lark's Head is a literal translation of the French name for the knot, tête d'alouette. We utilize this knot for securing loops to grommets on our tarp. Once connected, we are then able to stake the loose end of our tarp to the ground.

THE GOSPEL OF SURVIVAL

The 5 Shelter Configurations

All 5 of our shelter configurations can be erected using the same ridge-line system and knots. So, once you master the knots associated with the ridge-line, you'll not need to deviate to other systems.

The Lean-To tarp shelter is one of the most common shelters we utilize as it is an "on the go" shelter because it's easy to carry, easy to set up, and you can quickly take it down. It provides excellent wind deflection, and it will keep you safe from rain or sun heat. The downside is that this shelter doesn't have sides to offer protection against other elements.

You can add side deflectors by filling drum liners with debris or piling up some green or leafy branches. This practice will make you feel more secure and help prevent too much wind from coming through your shelter.

| 109 |

The Plow Point is another one of the more common setups we use, especially when we need to protect ourselves from high winds and driving rains. The pointed side should face the wind. While there's not much room for your gear, the benefits of better protecting yourself from the elements and more efficiently heat the shelter due to its smaller interior area far offset the drawbacks.

By wrapping some plastic across the front of this shelter, you can create a super shelter. The low profile and added plastic will greatly increase the heat retention capabilities of this shelter style. It's an excellent option to consider when the weather is cold or wet.

The A-Frame shelter is a great option when you need to minimize your profile, block wind, snow, rain, or treat an injured patient. When using a 10' x 10' tarp, a 30-degree angle of the tarp's roof will create a ten-foot-long area 8.6 feet wide and 2.5 feet tall. Great for multiple people or when you need more space. When using this style with an emergency tarp, it's best suited for a single user at times when core temperature control is most needed. The smaller space inside will be more comfortable to warm while still providing adequate coverage from the elements.

THE GOSPEL OF SURVIVAL

The Fly is the preferred set up for hammock camping or for creating a large covered work-space. It provides a good sunshade and ample headroom; it keeps the rain at bay. This shelter is a good set up in hot climates because it allows for good ventilation and adequate sun coverage.

The Author's A-frame Fly for Hammock Camping

The Super Shelter, invented by Mors Kochanski, a Canadian wilderness expert, and prolific author, is based on the concepts of what a shelter should provide to a person in the cold environment of the boreal forest. He inserted plastic in front of a shelter to serve as a conductor of point radiation from a fire. This light would refract, thereby trapping and heating the air within the shelter, enabling the user to stay warm and dry their clothes. The super shelter is fire-dependent. Without a continual fire, the shelter will not hold heat. There are several ways to build this shelter, the easiest of which is accomplished by draping plastic over our standard emergency space blankets. With proper ground insulation and plastic coverage over a lean-to or plow point tarp shelter, one can easily reach interior shelter temperatures of 80° F or more, so long as the fire is maintained.

Greg Laughlin with a super shelter built during a class

Rest and Sleep while Afield

"The quality of a survival kit is determined by how much it can help you when you need to sleep. If you can sleep well at night, you have it made."

~ Mors Kochanski

Gear

The right gear certainly makes a difference. We've already mentioned insulation layers, and these are important in all sleep situations, including hammocks. The only time you would want to omit that would be at the hottest time of the year. The clothing you wear is essential and will always serve as your first cover element for survival. Loose and layered to trap or release heat is still important. The blanket vs. sleeping bag dilemma usually comes next. The fact is that a queen-size high-quality wool blanket, like a 6-point Hudson's Bay Blanket, will permit you to sleep comfortably down to about 40 degrees. After that, you need more ground insulation, more significant fires, or coal beds to make them work. But they can and do work below freezing. Sleeping bags are the way to go otherwise. Whatever your predicament in a survival scenario, think outside the box. Use trash to insulate your body to mimic the effects of quality gear.

Sleep Cycles

A quality night's rest in the woods takes time. It would not be uncommon to go as long as 36 hours of little or no sleep in a real emergency. Regardless of why you are afield, you'll often find the first night is usually the one you find yourself the most restless. This restlessness is because you're still set on your home sleep pattern, assuming you're not completely exhausted. By your second night, you settle in better and begin moving back toward a normal biphasic sleep cycle. This cycle may be new to you, but historically people slept in two phases through the night. One lasted about 4 hours when they would wake for 1-3 hours and do things like reading, snack, have sex, or even chop wood! Then, they would sleep again 3-4 more hours until dawn. It was called first sleep and second sleep in pre-industrialized Europe. There's a book on the subject called "At Day's Close: Night in Times Past" by Roger Ekirch if you're interested in the history of nighttime escapades. Nessmuk also references biphasic sleeping in his book Woodcraft in Chapter 3 on the Indian Camp.

"Ten o'clock comes. The time has not passed tediously. You are warm, dry, and well-fed. Your old friends, the owls, come near the fire-light and salute you with their strange wild notes; a distant fox sets up for himself with his odd, barking cry, and you turn in. Not ready to sleep just yet. But you drop off, and it is two bells in the morning watch when you waken with a sense of chill and darkness. The fire has burned low, and snow is falling. The owls have left, and a deep silence broods over the cold, still forest. You rouse the fire and, as the bright light shines to the furthest recesses of your forest den, get out the little pipe and reduce a bit of navy plug to its lowest denomination. The smoke curls lazily upward; the fire makes you warm and drowsy, and again you lie down—to again awaken with a sense of chilliness—to find the fire burned low and daylight breaking. You have slept better than you would in your own room at home. You have slept in an "Indian camp."

It's normal to wake in the night in the woods (usually to pee). Speaking of which, never fight off the urge in the night to get up and pee, as doing so makes you colder as the blood in your body pumps around the bladder in an attempt to keep the water warm. This cold feeling means your extremities get a lighter blood flow, which makes you cold. So, get up and go. Stoke the fire. Eat a snack. Go back to bed. Generally, the first thing you hear around the morning campfire is the question- "How did you sleep?" An answer other than good in the old days was often a sign of poor woodsmanship. Proper insulation, sound gear, and an understanding that it's okay to wake up at 2-3 am for a while- is all you need to know to start getting a better night's rest in the wilds.

Fear of the Unknown

I will make a covenant of peace with my people and drive away the dangerous animals from the land. Then they will be able to camp safely in the wildest places and sleep in the woods without fear. ~ Ezekiel 34:25

If you've never slept under a tarp shelter before, especially down on the ground and outside of a hammock, it's understandable to be a bit jumpy at anything that makes a sound in the dark. The animals are almost always more afraid of you than you are of them. They may be curious and sniff about, but you often have nothing to worry about unless you are in wolf, bear, or cougar country. Make sure you keep food outside of and away from your main camp if you are in predator country and keep a fire going overnight, and that will keep the beasts at bay.

In my forty years of camping experiences, the most prolonged period, I stayed in an unimproved tarp shelter was two weeks. While I certainly seen some wildlife and weathered some storms, I'll share my only animal experience with you here. It was mid-November, and we had been running a trap line. I was with a group, and my camp was nestled away from the others as I was sleeping under a tarp with no fire. I had an excellent sleeping bag, so I was plenty comfortable. In the middle of the night, I had an odd dream about my oldest son. For some reason, he had passed away; the funeral parlor put him on a conveyor belt heading up into a cremation furnace. As I watched him roll along, I saw him twitch, which made me run to him and begin to squeeze him with hugs and shake him to wake him up. Suddenly a loud burst of air with a hiss came from under his arm, which startled me and woke me. As my eyes opened, I realized the hissing was still going on as I had been squeezing a possum under my arm in my sleeping bag! As I let go, it scurried off into the dark as I laughed myself back to sleep.

If you find yourself in a covenant relationship with God through Jesus Christ, you have a promise of peace and protection while camping in the woods. Rest in that knowledge, and you'll be able to overcome anything.

For God hath not given us the spirit of fear, but of power, and of love, and of a sound mind... ~ 2 Timothy 1:7

Train yourself
Train your shelter skills by practicing the 5 Knots and 5 Tarp Shelters until you can set up each shelter type in under 5 minutes per shelter.

12

Water and the Spirit

Water appears throughout the scriptures as a symbol for the Holy Spirit. For example, in John 4:13-14, Jesus is speaking to the woman at the well.

Jesus answered and said unto her, *Whosoever drinketh of this water shall thirst again: But whosoever drinketh of the water that I shall give him shall never thirst, but the water that I shall give him shall be in him a well of water springing up into everlasting life.*

Water is also used as a symbol for God's Word in the scriptures, for obedience to God's word brings cleansing.

"How can a man cleanse his way? By taking heed according to your word." Psalm 119:9

Obedience to the word brings cleansing to our soul, while the Holy Spirit brings refreshing to our spirit as we are obedient. In Romans 6, we learn that being immersed or baptized upon our confession of Christ as Savior breaks the power of sin in our lives. Collecting spiritual water is likened to remaining obedient to God's will and teachings as found in the Bible. As with water collection in the natural, contaminants can creep into our water supply if we stray from God's path. In James 4:17, we're told that those that know the truth but don't do it are in sin. Knowing the way to Christ but doing your own thing instead is a contaminant in your water supply, which will lead to sickness and eventually death if left unchecked.

We can take lessons from the natural process of collecting water and apply these principles to our spiritual lives for understanding how to gather effectively, clean, and purify drinking water is a skill that everyone must understand. The days of merely drinking from the local creek are pretty much gone. The chemicals and waste being pumped or dumped into our groundwater systems today poison our supplies, just as taking the word of every "man of God" can lead us into error. In the end-times, the Bible tells us that all the waters will become bitter and as blood (Rev. 16:3-7), praise God for the provision that comes from He who is the living water!

Dangers in Drinking Water
Cholera – Cholera is the friendliest bacteria found in water as it typically only leads to diarrhea. It is treated by continually replacing the lost fluids by drinking clean water. Continuing to drink cholera-infected water can lead to increased infection, including leg cramps, vomiting, dehydration, and shock, requiring fluids to be replaced intravenously. Without proper treatment at an advanced stage, death can occur.

Hepatitis A – Hep A is not as friendly as a liver disease caused by a viral infection. Symptoms include loss of appetite, nausea, vomiting, fever, dark urine, tiredness, abdominal pains, and jaundice (yellowing of the skin and eyes). While the disease is not life-threatening, it can take months to overcome its effects with medication. Typically, once overcome, your body will create antibodies that will help prevent a recurrence of the disease.

Giardiasis – Giardia is a single-celled parasite that lives in the intestines ingested by drinking water contaminated by sewage. This organism can survive outside the body for a long time and is one of the most common waterborne diseases. Symptoms include greasy stools that tend to float, diarrhea, cramps, and nausea. Advanced symptoms can lead to weight loss and dehydration, while others have no symptoms at all. The problem is resolved by flushing the parasite from the body over several weeks with clean fluids and medication if required.

Chemical Pollutants – The big issue with chemical pollution is that it won't boil out of your water. Most of the chemicals are heat resistant and must be filtered out through charcoal or another type of filter system. If you find water in the middle of a tobacco, soybean, or cornfield, you can bet that some kind of chemical has contaminated the water. Check for flora around the area and look at their condition; do they look healthy? Are they thriving in the area? Is there fish or frogs in the water? Frogs in the water are a good sign of a good ecosystem, but this again is no guarantee of a chemical-free environment. When in doubt, filter and boil it out.

Natural Sources of Water
Seasonal creeks and runoffs – These areas are typically only active during and shortly after a rain and should be treated like chemically polluted water as anything sitting atop the ground surface will be flushed into the stream, thereby polluting the available water. These water sources should be filtered and boiled, or chemically treated.

Rainwater – Your best source of clean water comes from heaven above; collecting it is simply a matter of taking advantage of the weather and utilizing whatever containers you have available. However, if you are in a heavily industrialized area, you can get some chemical taste and possible infection. You can also collect rainwater in the way of dew by tying a cloth around your ankles and trekking through some tall grass. The fabric will quickly become filled with water, which can be wrung out into a bowl or container to be filtered of turbidity (solids in water).

Rivers and Streams – Like Creeks and runoffs, rivers and streams should be filtered whenever possible and boiled. Millions of people still rely on water from rivers and streams around the world for daily water. However, drinking straight from these sources is not advised because bacteria and viruses can more easily reproduce in slow-moving water. When the water is up, these sources fill with runoff from the surrounding areas and serve as nature's toilet system flushing waste out of the area.

Plant Water - Here in the Eastern Woodlands and many jungles, you can harvest water from vines by cutting a section three feet long at an angle on both ends; water will drip from the vine's cut surface and provide some needed hydration. If the water you find is cloudy or bitter coming from a vine, it should be avoided as it's the wrong species. You can also tap trees such as the maple or birch, which provides sap that can be drunk or boiled down to a sweet liquid like syrup. In the desert, Aloe and Agave plants survive an extended period of drought and store liquids in their leaves, which can be harvested for juice.

Coconuts also provide an excellent source of fluids, which aids in the replacement of electrolytes. Lastly, you can tie plastic bags over leafy boughs on live trees and allow the sun to heat and condense the air in the bag, creating water after several hours.

The 5 Hydration Factors
Maintaining proper body hydration is always essential in day-to-day life and more so in the wilderness. Cold weather especially tricks the mind into thinking it is hydrated due to the present damp and cold conditions. Drinking at regular intervals throughout the day is the best way to remain hydrated. Examine your urine each time it's evacuated, as it will aid you in determining your hydration levels.

5 Urine Colors

- Clear: Well hydrated
- Faint Yellow: Good hydration
- Straw Yellow: Hydrated
- Yellow: Dehydrated
- Dark Yellow/Brown: Extremely Dehydrated
  - Dark Yellow/ Nearly Brown urine is typical for most morning evacuations and a sign for you to rehydrate your body each day.

The 5 Factors Affecting Hydration

- **Heat:** In extreme heat, we sweat and lose water more quickly.
- **Cold:** In cold/wet weather, our mind focuses on maintaining core temperature more so than hydration, so drink more often.
- **Tea/ Coffee:** Are diuretics that trigger a urinary response regardless of how well or poorly hydrated we are. Thus, you will require more frequent hydration.
- **Soda:** Provides carbs by way of sugar and not hydration. There is a lot of salt and sugar in soda, and they should not be considered at all for maintaining hydration.
- **Medications:** Medicine may affect your body by making you urinate more or less frequently and even in odd colors. Talk to your doctor to discuss potential issues.

The best source of hydrating your body is always water, coupled with minerals, salts, and sugars. You could eat regular snacks such as trail mix with water intake or elect to include electrolyte aids.

The 5 Water Purification Methods

Boiling (Water from an unknown source)
Boiling remains the best method of killing off the pathogens within the water. In heating water above 131°F, pasteurization occurs, destroy-

ing cysts, and by 149°F, most pathogens are destroyed. Water boils at 212°F at sea level and drops by 1oF for every 500ft above sea level. So, at an elevation of 5000ft, water will begin to boil at about 203°F. So, by bringing water to a rolling boil, you can rest assured that you are destroying all pathogens within the water. Boiling is a visual indicator that a sufficient temperature has been reached for the destruction of waterborne pathogens. I liken boiling water to receiving an impartation of the Fire of God; this is a radical call to holiness. It's a simple and the most direct way to eliminate toxins in your life, seek out the righteousness of God by the power of the Holy Spirit. Johnathan Wesley said it best "The spirit of God has set me ablaze, and the people come to watch me burn." Let that be the example we leave to those around us- let us boil over with the Spirit of God!

Filtering (Water from a known source)

Filtering through a modern filter such as a Sawyer, LifeStraw, or Berkey is excellent for removing turbidity and chemical agents from your water source but has only marginal success at eliminating bacteria and pathogens. This is why filtering is best when you know where the water comes from and suspect minimal bacterial contamination. While mild farm runoff or suburban chemicals won't adversely affect you in a short-term survival situation (days), you might expect adverse reactions over weeks of ingestion. When you know you have some chemically affected water, you can also make a primitive filter from charcoal, grasses, and sand. Filtering through these sediments within a container removes some chemicals that could adversely affect your body over time. If you rely on a modern, commercial filter, take time to read the instructions to know how to use it correctly and under what conditions the filter will work most effectively. Spiritually speaking, we must filter out what we hear from others. Not everyone who speaks with claimed authority, such as a well-known pastor or teacher, will give us accurate information. We must understand that all men are fallible, and despite the best of intentions, they can often lead us astray. But by filtering their message through the Word of God, we can get to the truth of a matter and decide whether or not to receive the water they have offered us.

Distillation (Salt Water)

If all you can find is saltwater, you will have to desalinate it (remove the salt). The salt in saltwater overworks the renal glands quickly, which leads to kidney failure, shock, and a host of other issues. Distill the water by hanging a can full of water over a fire and placing a clean cloth over the lid to collect all the steam. From time to time, wring out the moisture into a potable water container to drink once it cools. The salt that remains behind can be utilized to season game meats as you harvest them. Alternatively, should you have access to some plumbing pipe or tubing, a still can be created from any metal container. Bring water to a boil and allow the steam to collect in the tube and cool as it drops over into another container. Desalination is the spiritual sense happens when you feel like you are stuck in a rut, waiting on God to move. The process adds pressure until you come to a decision, you'll continue to stew, or you'll shed the impurities holding you back and burst forth by the power of the Spirit. These ruts can go on for as long as you allow them to. God is always waiting on us; it's never the other way around; all we have to do is shed the dead weight (sin, disobedience, unforgiveness) that will allow us to get back on the narrow path to eternity with Him.

Solar Pasteurization

It is the process of bringing water to a temperature of at least 145°F. By maintaining that temperature for 30 minutes (Low Temp, Long Time), pathogens are destroyed. By using keep water in a bottle and allowing the sun's rays to refract through it, heating occurs. If maintained over a long time, this heat and UV radiation are enough to neutralize pathogens often present within the water. Place water in full sun when possible use heath reflectors such as foil, aluminum, or black surfaces to heat the water. Allow containers to collect the sun as long as possible;

small bubbles around the top of the water are a good sign as this denotes water has been heated to a pasteurizing temperature.

Spiritually speaking, the longer we remain in the light, the less darkness we'll perceive in our lives. Jesus said in John 12:46, *"I have come as a light to shine in this dark world, so that all who put their trust in me will no longer remain in the dark."* We should seek to spiritually pasteurize ourselves through regular fellowship with like-minded people in the light of Christ.

Chemicals (Bleach, Iodine)

If you use bleach or purification tablets of any type, read the instructions. They often make the water taste like bleach or iodine, but it's very safe to drink. When using these agents, shake the water well to ensure the chemical tablet reaches all the water in your container. If you have an enclosed container, be sure to flip it over so the chemically cleaned water hits that cap to kill off any hidden bacteria lurking in the lid.

Liquid Clorox Bleach

One gallon of Clorox Bleach can purify about 3,800 gallons of drinking water. When the infrastructure collapses and the waters stop flowing, bleach will be a valuable bartering item and a real lifesaver. As history has shown, the most significant demand in a long-term disaster is for drinkable water. During most big natural disasters, you'll find relief crews hand out free Clorox Bleach packets with simple instructions. Although bleach will kill the bacteria in water, it will not filter out the particles. To use bleach, follow these steps and be sure to store these directions with your emergency bottle of bleach:

- Filter water to remove large particles
- Pour the clear water into a clean, uncontaminated container
- Add Regular bleach containing 4% to 6% sodium hypochlorite (8 drops per gallon of water)

- Mix and shake well
- Wait 30 min
- Water should have a slight bleach odor, and if it doesn't, repeat the dose

Keep an eyedropper handy in your survival kit or attached by a string to your bottle of Clorox Bleach. Never pour purified water into a contaminated container. Sanitize water jugs, containers, and dishes with a little Clorox Bleach. Keep in mind that you should only use Regular Clorox Bleach and not Fresh Scent or Lemon Fresh; bleach is bad enough as it is, so try not to make it worse. Bleach will eventually lose its strength, and you should follow the expiration date, so try to replace your bleach bottle about every three months.

To clean dishes, utensils, and containers, follow these steps:

- Mix 1 tablespoon of bleach with about one gallon of water.
- Wash and rinse items.
- Let each item soak in the bleach/water solution for about 2 minutes.
- Drain and air dry.

Iodine

You can either get iodine in a liquid form or a solid tablet form, and you can use both to purify water. To use liquid iodine:

- Add 2-3 drops of iodine to each liter of clear water (8-10 for cloudy water).
- Mix and shake well.
- Let the water stand for 30 minutes.

Iodine in tablet form is usually easier to find and can be found at most drug stores and sporting goods stores. The names will vary, but they're most commonly known as Halazone tablets. Each manufacture will make them differently, so follow the directions on the package. Generally, the recommended dose is one tablet per liter of water and two tablets if the water is cloudy.

A purification tablet in the spiritual sense is a Rhema word from God. It's the written word made active and in the now; information that brings immediate clarity to a situation you may be struggling with. These "tablets" may come from the Spirit speaking to your mind or from a brother or sister in Christ that feels "led" to share something with you.

Urban Water Sources

Procuring water in an urban environment, especially in modern cities with a lot of foot traffic, will require a *sillcock key*. A sillcock is an outdoor water spigot, hose bibb, faucet, or valve attached to the exterior of a residential, commercial, or industrial building. Residential sillcocks most commonly have a handle or lever to control the flow of water. But commercial and industrial sillcock valves typically require a key to operate them, primarily as a deterrent of vandalism.

THE GOSPEL OF SURVIVAL

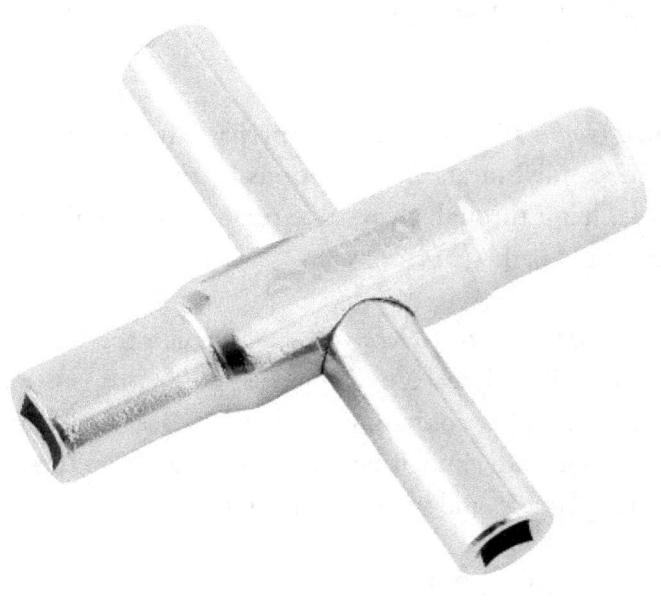

Standard 4-way sillcock key

Not having a handle readily available prevents would-be vandals from turning the water on and leaving it running, possibly flooding the area. Sure, you might be able to open some sillcock valves with pliers or a multi-tool, but most are engineered to protect against them. Water gained will be the same that comes from the tap.

Water heaters are another great resource to consider when procuring water in an urban survival scenario. Should the grid be down, many water heaters will be full of water. After a time, water can sour and begin to smell, but it is still safe to drink with filtering. For the most part, *water pipes* will also still be full of water, although not pressurized. If you can gain access to a multilevel home or at least get to the lowest level of a home, you can drain the water in the pipes by using gravity to your advantage. Cut the line and catch the water that drains out in a container. Open a faucet at a higher level to release any residual pressure that may have built up.

Canned Goods all have water in them that can be drunk. Fruits, vegetables, and canned meats are all options. If tuna flavored water isn't your thing, filter it through charcoal to remove some of that flavor. You can get meat and pathogen-free water.

Pools, Fountains, and Decorative Ponds can contain a variety of chemicals, including algaecide and chlorine. Even a properly maintained pool can contain other contaminants such as algae, fecal bacteria, and insects. To be safe, filter and, if possible, boil water from these resources to eliminate chemicals and pathogens from the water.

Boiling at Altitude Table
Based on standard sea-level atmospheric pressure (courtesy, NOAA):

Altitude, ft (m)	Boiling point of water, °F (°C)
0 (0 m)	212°F (100°C)
500 (150 m)	211.1°F (99.5°C)
1,000 (305 m)	210.2°F (99°C)
2,000 (610 m)	208.4°F (98°C)
5,000 (1524 m)	203°F (95°C)
6,000 (1829 m)	201.1°F (94°C)

8,000 (2438 m)	197.4°F (91.9°C)
10,000 (3048 m)	193.6°F (89.8°C)
12,000 (3658 m)	189.8°F (87.6°C)
14,000 (4267 m)	185.9°F (85.5°C)
15,000 (4572 m)	184.1°F (84.5°C)

How to make Boiled Water Taste Better

Many things can be dissolved in water, including air. When water boils, the dissolved air leaves the water, and the result is a flat taste. After boiling water, aerate the water by pouring it back and forth a few times between two containers. This process adds air back into the water, and it will taste better. You could also shake it violently in a closed container, open the cap to introduce more air, then shake again. Should the taste be off, introducing some charcoal chunks to the water, or filtering the water through powdered charcoal will significantly improve the flavor.

Train your purification skills

Train your water purification skills by boiling 32oz of water in around five minutes and by making regular use of a variety of filters. Also, train in using bleach and iodine-based chemicals so you know exactly how to do it before you ever need to rely upon it.

13

Food to Endure

"But he that survives to the end, the same shall be saved."
~ Jesus (Matt. 24:13)

Food Resources can be a complicated topic to cover when it comes to survival – it's one of the lower priorities for the Rules of 3's and 5's, as most humans can survive three weeks without food and still function. Most of us rely on the commercial availability of food and would be helpless if asked to fend for ourselves. So, we should first focus on simple food items that require the least number of calories and effort to obtain in a survival situation. As our skills, knowledge, and resources improve, perhaps through trial and error, we'll arrive at more extensive and more substantial food options for longer-term self-reliance. Survival begins at the water's edge.

The 5 Lower Food Chain Resources

Fish harvested from all freshwater sources may be contaminated by mercury and other trace contaminants such as polychlorinated biphenyls (PCBs). Most states have issued their fish consumption advisories noting areas where high contamination has been found or is occurring. While fish is a great food resource, overconsumption or complete reliance could lead to adverse health risks. Most fish, however, are healthy to eat and are an excellent source of low-fat protein, so do not let this information deter you! Eat fish in moderation as with any other food resource.

Risks from eating contaminated fish can be reduced by the following:

- fillet the fish, remove the skin and trim all fat
- do not eat fish eggs
- broil, grill, or bake the fillets instead of frying or microwaving
- do not eat or reuse juices or fats that cookout of the fish.

You can treat saltwater fish in the same manner due to the same reasons. However, almost all saltwater fish can be eaten raw. Saltwater fish are safer to eat raw because the oceans' water temperatures help to kill parasites and bacteria.

Frogs in the United States are generally safe to eat. Typically, people eat the frog's back legs because that is where you will find the most meat, and they discard the rest. You should be aware of the differences between frogs and toads since toads can be poisonous without showing indicators that you would see in frogs, such as brightly colored skin. To tell the difference between frogs and toads, remember that frogs have smooth skin, while toads will have bumps on them. Frogs also have longer, narrower faces, while toads have shorter, wider ones. If you watch a frog capturing its prey, you will notice that it has a sticky tongue that extends easily. By contrast, a toad will have to catch its game in its mouth.

Snakes are another food option to be considered. Whether venomous or not, snakes are a viable meat source that must be handled with care. Venomous snakes can, of course, cause a variety of medical issues should you get bit. Non-venomous snakes have bacteria in their mouths, which can also cause infection. Carefully remove the head and bury it, and gut and skin the reptile. Clean your hands after discarding the skin and entrails.

Common Snapping Turtle
Photo Credit John Dosch

Turtles of several different kinds are located in fresh-waters which are suitable for food. The most popular is the snapping turtle. These can grow to be very large, and care must be taken when harvesting them to avoid their powerful beak. Terrapins are smooth bodied turtles that are generally much smaller than snappers. All are good for the iconic dish, turtle soup, but the snapper is the most highly prized and is easily found in most ponds or streams in North America. Because turtles spend their time in the water among fish parts and are generally dirty and host various bacteria, a vigorous scrubbing is required after dispatching one for food. Begin by removing the bottom shell plate, gutting the animal, discarding the innards, or using it later as bait for other things. Skin the turtle meat you wish to use, then parboil to soften it before cooking. It can be fried or made into a soup relatively easily.

Worms are the lowest of our water's edge resources because they're generally considered bait for the critters preceding them. That said, a single worm can provide one calorie, over 50% of which comes from protein. Not much one at a time, but the handful of worms can provide some short-term nutrition.

The 5 Mid-Chain Resources

Insects- the estimates of numbers of edible insect species consumed globally range from 1,000 to 2,000. These species include 235 butterflies and moths, 344 beetles, 313 ants, bees and wasps, 239 grasshoppers, crickets and cockroaches, 39 termites, and 20 dragonflies, as well as cicadas. While most insects are safe raw, they are more palatable after being cooked. Boiling or roasting in leave kills any bacteria, as well as renders the proteins more digestible. Remove beady heads, hard carapaces, wings, barbed legs, and antennae to reduce the "crunch factor," ease swallowing, and eliminate any parasites. With a grasshopper, twist off the head—the guts should come with it—before swallowing the abdomen. Don't eat bugs covered in fuzz. (Bees and wasps are safe to eat if you remove their stingers.) Beware of brightly colored insects; they're usually poisonous, and avoid disease-carrying species including flies, mosquitoes, and ticks. Any bug that emits a strong odor should also be avoided.

Lizard meat is full of microorganisms, including several parasites and bacteria that can cause food-borne illnesses. Improperly handling carcasses or raw meat can lead to cross-contamination. So, safely-prepare the meat and cook it thoroughly; otherwise, the potential risks will outweigh many of the rewards you hope to enjoy. Most species are not poisonous, and they also tend to have lean, nutrient-rich meat.

Rabbits have long been a staple of the survivalist's diet. Not only are they relatively easy to harvest with a throwing stick, but they are also easy to snare and trap. Rabbits are generally safe and healthy. In rare instances, they can be infected with Tularemia as with other mammals such as ticks, dogs, and rodents. According to the Mayo Clinic, Tularemia is a rare infectious disease that typically attacks the skin, eyes, lymph nodes, and lungs. In humans, symptoms of infection can include fever, chills, headaches, exhaustion, swollen or painful lymph glands within 5-14 days after contraction. It can be treated with antibiotics if diagnosed early. Whenever harvesting rabbits or any animal for food, for that matter, check for signs of illness, ulcers, spots on the liver, and other abnormalities. If anything is off, dispose of the animal, wash your hands well, and try again.

Rodents are eaten in much of the world and even raised for food is still developing countries. From guinea pigs and nutria to rats and mice, rodents provide a reliable food source that's easily attainable. Traps are generally the best means of capturing rodents, including simple sticky traps and the standard mousetrap. Rat Traps can be easily modified to work well for not just rodents but rabbits and squirrels too.

Squirrels are essentially the rodent of the trees, and as such, traps and snare poles work well for harvesting. Projectile weapons such as arrows, spears, and atlatl darts are also very effective at reaching them higher off the ground but require constant practice to maintain proficiency. Cane and bamboo blowguns can also be utilized to significant effect. Regardless of the method, take the same precautions as previous animals when checking for illness or abnormality before consuming.

And remember, the larger the animal, the more preparation, skill, and resources required to trap it!

The 5 Tracking Signs

Game Trails

Game Trails are the highways and sidewalks of the woodlands. These are the best areas to gather information on the type, size, quantity of animals, frequency, and travel directions. So much information is available along a game trail that resting alongside one in pursuit of the game will almost guarantee a meeting should you pay attention to the signs.

Prints

Whitetail Deer Print

Paw and Hoof Prints will tell you the type and variety of animals you have in your area. Look for a track trap such as soft dirt, sand, or gravel to get a good print indicator, then make your trapping and hunting assessment based upon what animals are active in the area. Like game trails, the prints themselves can give you a wealth of information. Signs such as how many, how big, where from, where to may all be derived from a single area. It's important to know standard track identifiers, so you don't think you track a wolf when in reality, it's the neighbor's dog.

Scat

Whitetail Deer Scat

Scat or poop is another great sign to look for that can tell you the general health of an animal and what they are eating, which may key you into other resources in the area to exploit. Steaming scat is fresh. Soft, moist scat is recent, and firm scat is a day or so older. The drier and more weathered, obviously, the longer the duration since the animal passed through. Check scat carefully when you find it for resource indicators and to get an idea of how often animals are passing by.

Fur or Feathers

Fur or Feathers will often show you locations that an animal is nesting, frequents, or crosses often. These are good spots to often set traps. Fence lines are great spots to find fur as it often gets trapped in the wire as various animals climb over and under the fencing. Look for holes or drops in the wire top and bottom to see where larger game such as deer or hogs may be crossing.

Chewing's (Food stores or remnants)

Black Walnut, squirrel chewing's

Chewing's show us where the animals are eating. Good spots to look for these are fallen trees and logs, stumps, and other elevated flat surfaces. Animals like flat tables just as we do, so when nature provides one, they often take advantage of it by eating on it. You can see what they're eating and how often they frequent the area to eat. A sign like this may key you into other resources available you have not yet realized while also giving you another indicator of animal type and frequency of visitors to an area.

The 5 Survival Tools

These five tools may be used to trap or hunt lower and mid food chain resources with great effect.

The Minnow Trap

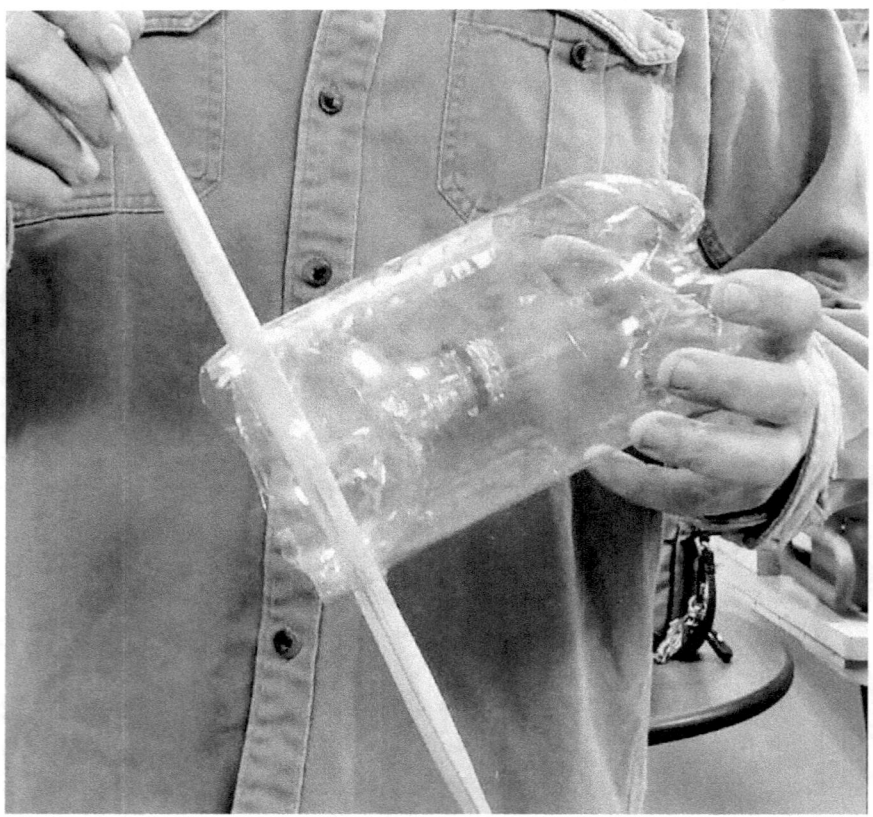

2-Liter Minnow Trap
Photo and model by Jamie Burleigh

You can easily make the minnow trap from various trash bottles you may come across in the woods. Cut off the end with the cap, remove the camp, invert it, so the cap now faces inside the bottle, and then secure it by cutting slits and tying, with barbs of wire or from thorns or just cut two holes, one on top and one on the bottom that goes through both plastic pieces and run a 3ft long stick through it. Not only will the stick keep it secure in a current, but it will also make it easier to place in deeper pools of water. Bread, pet food, chewed nuts and corn, and even entrails work as baits.

THE GOSPEL OF SURVIVAL

Figure 4 Deadfall Trap with Ranger Bands

This trap configuration has been around for ages, but it was Jamie Burleigh who figured out how to use Ranger Bands (Heavy Rubber Bands) on one instead of carving a lot of notches. After all, in a survival scenario carving and other fine motor skills diminish in a true emergency. There are only two carve points on this trap, a 7 notch and a squared edge, these are macro carving techniques easily accomplished.

All you need are three sticks of about finger diameter and sized according to the prey you wish to trap. On the center stick, which is the upright, create a sharp corner. On the bait stick, the pointed one, create a number 7 notch that will rest on the sharp corner. Then the fulcrum, which holds the deadfall, you can carve a flat if desired, so it rests better under the fall, but it's optional. Band them together tightly, and you're all set.

Bird Snares

Snares were used during Biblical times to catch birds.

Psalm 124:7 We escaped like a bird from a hunter's trap. The trap is broken, and we are free

You can set snares to capture around the foot or leg, the body, or around the neck. This will largely depend upon your target animal; more often than not, you'll get a neck or body snare as you'll often be forced to rely upon string-based cordage in a survival scenario unless you're able to procure some thin wire. Be sure to check photo and mirror frames when in a suburban area as they often are hung with wire, which is perfect for survival snaring!

In the Ojibway Bird Snare shown here, you drill a hole through a stick and run your snare line through the hole to a weight. Place a small branch perch into the hole just enough to keep the snare from being pulled through the hole by the weight. Once a bird lands on the perch, it triggers the snare, and it catches the feet. Be careful, though; if your weight is too heavy as my first few were, you'll break legs off birds. Use a small stone, tree nuts, or stick as the counterweight.

THE GOSPEL OF SURVIVAL

Shepherds Sling

The Shepherds Sling is a projectile hunting weapon that can also be removed from the staff and be used by hand. This weapon takes quite a bit of practice, but it is quite devastating once you figure it out. Choose a straight staff that's no taller than chin height. Sharpen a blunt tip on one end and 1" below the taper, carve a V notch circumferential to the staff. Now create a leather or heavy canvas pouch that will hold the projectiles. This pouch should be the length and width of your hand, fingers together. Directly attach it to the staff with cordage. On the blunt taper, place a loop that will connect to one side of the pouch. On the opposite side of the pocket, the cordage will attach to the V notch.

Once attached, the pouch should hang no lower than one hand-span from the bottom of the staff to somewhere in the middle; this will be determined by personal preference over time. Test the throw to make sure the loop comes off the blunted tip easily with each throw. Projectiles should be about small potato to fist-sized; they can be stones like David threw at Goliath (1 Sam. 17) or golf balls, blocks of wood, or whatever you can find. Rounded stone's throw amazing! This weapon can easily take out the small game, and if a head shot were possible, it could likely kill a larger animal such as a deer.

Slingshots are another great sling option and are a more accurate, lightweight alternative for harvesting small game.

The Hunting Gig

A hunting gig is an excellent tool for frogs and water's edge game and fish. All you need is a stick that's taller than you. At the heavier end of the stick, split it into four sections, then sharpen each barb you have created. Put some spacer sticks between the barbs to keep them spread apart, then tie them into place so that when the spear is used, it stays together.

When deploying this tool, you do not throw it; you stab and maintain pressure on the animal you hit to pin it to the ground. Animals will often wiggle out of or off the barbs if it wasn't a direct hit, so follow the shaft down to dispatch the live animal with your free hand. Hopefully, you'll have a knife or stone in it to make it quick. This tool is excellent for spearing rays and lobsters along coastal regions as well. You could attach slingshot banding to create a Hawaiian sling spear, but this is best used while swimming in open water with larger fish.

Photo and model made by Jamie Burleigh

14

Rescue Essentials

No training in wilderness survival can be complete without covering the fundamentals of how search and rescue teams operate. This information will enable those in a survival situation to aid or avoid such search or rescue efforts as dictated by your circumstances. Basic Search and Rescue consists of three primary topics: Search, Rescue, and Survival/ Patient Support.

Search

Search information begins with the theory and philosophy of searching for a lost subject and proceeds into the skills and resources, concluding by applying specific search tactics, including how to perform the land search.

Rescue

Rescue, at this level, is not intended to teach you how to perform any type of recovery necessarily, but to educate those who will probably be involved in a rescue situation. I will present some of the equipment and terms used so you will be able to identify commonly used equipment. Rescue is a highly specialized field of study with technical specifications in numerous areas ranging from rope rescue to low-angle, high angle, air, moving water, swift water, white water, wilderness, and urban, naming only a few areas of specialty. At the very least, you should seek training on how to assist in packaging a subject in a Stokes basket and SKED for wilderness pack-out, as these are the most common basket types across the country among volunteer agencies, and you should know how to signal for rescuers to find and assist you.

Survival & Support

Having a basic understanding of wilderness survival as making a temporary shelter, making fire, and maintaining your own and a patient's core body temperature is critical. You may need to provide patient care until other Search Team members, or EMS arrives on the scene.

Laws about Search & Rescue

In all states, the local division of emergency management is required to have:

- A state SAR plan
- A state SAR Coordinator
- Resources for Searches
- Date with regard to searches
- Also, most counties in every state are required to:
- Have a county SAR plan
- Have a county SAR Coordinator(s)

Designate agencies in the county to conduct searches and rescues in the county, independent SAR Teams, or local Fire Departments. These county activities are often organized by the county emergency management director or the highest elected official such as a County Judge Executive. Please check your state and county laws for specific information related to SAR Laws and Team development.

Good Samaritan Laws, generally speaking, only applies to those not involved in an organized rescue squad or other agency. Thus, as an individual, you voluntarily rendering aid to another would be protected to some measure by such laws. However, if you are actively engaged in a SAR deployment and are part of the team, you would not be covered and would be expected to assist at the level your training dictates.

The Importance of Ground Searchers

Of the types of resources utilized for SAR efforts, such as dogs, aircraft, and satellite images, nothing takes the place of a ground-pounder. The lone search technician that provides actual intelligence on clues, terrain, and information that can prove whether a subject is actually in the area or not.

The Crucials

- Search is a real emergency!
- The Subject may need emergency care
- The Subject may need protection from self or the environment
- The Subject may be responsive for hours or even days
- An urgent response lessens search difficulty
- Search is a classic mystery that requires you to look for clues that lead to a lost subject

Freelancers

Freelancers have some SAR training or interest yet have either no formal team affiliation or appropriate agency under which to operate. They can be anyone from the eager bystander, team member from 'another department' to those that wait for things that catch their ear over the police scanner. Freelancing is not well received in the Search and Rescue world. Showing up to a SAR emergency without being requested could lead to you being removed or arrested by law enforcement. If your plan includes responding to SAR emergencies, it is best to be formally affiliated with an existing SAR Team in your county. If your county does not have a SAR Team, find out the agency responsible for conducting search and rescue within the county and following up there. In most cases, that agency will be the local volunteer fire department.

Author's Experience:

When I became interested in Search and Rescue, the nearest SAR team I could locate was over an hour away. I still joined and completed my basic training with them but never responded to an incident. It wasn't until a year later that I could track down the local agency in my area responsible for SAR activities, the Fire Department. When I joined the fire department, I had no interest in fighting fires but merely serving on the search and rescue team. But to join, I was required to at least complete Basic Fire training. As it turned out, I thoroughly enjoyed the fire training, became an asset to my department, and top it off, I was the only person in the department with any actual SAR experience. This dual qualification enabled me to take advantage of all sorts of free courses that have helped me in many areas of my career in and out of emergency services.

Clue Awareness

Clues are facts, objects, information, or some other evidence that helps solve a mystery or problem. Search team members must search for clues in addition to the lost subject. Because there are always more clues than subjects, the detection of clues reduces the search area, and the information gained from clues may give you information about the lost person's location.

- *Be clue conscious!*
- Clue seeking is a significant job of the field searcher
- Clues can be found, discovered, stumbled upon, etc.
- Good clue seeking is learned and practiced frequently to develop and maintain skill level
- Opinions are based solely on the information available; not by gathering information to support an opinion

- Clue seeking helps us solve the problem (finding lost subjects) by gathering all the facts and information possible
- Significant clues may provide the basis for essential tactics and actions in the field

Clue Generators (The Lost Person)

Virtually everyone that passes through an area leaves evidence of some type. A common problem is not the lack of clues, but determining which of many possible clues relate to the search and are valuable. A detailed subject profile enables searchers and managers to connect a particular indication to the subject or not.

The 6 Elements of Clue Oriented Search Theory

- The Subject or Clue Generators
- The Clues themselves
- The search area where clues are located
- The searchers or clue seekers
- Chronological order of events as they relate to the search
- Search methods and tactics used to locate clues

There are four messages that a lost subject can convey that a searcher must be able to detect during a search event:

- Present Location
- Previous Location
- Destination
- Total lack of clues
- Have a plan to deal with any clues found; how Incident Command deals with clues found will be presented to searchers in the briefing

4 Clue Categories

1. Physical- footprints, cigarette butts, broken vegetation, discarded items, overturned rocks
2. Recorded- summit log, trail register, boat or ATV rental
3. People- witness, family, friend, people in search area
4. Events- flashing lights, whistle, yell, etc.

The Importance of clues

It's crucial to search for both clues and the lost subject

It's essential to look side to side, down to up, and even behind you to gain a different perspective of the search terrain

Another way to locate the subject is to blow a whistle or call their name and wait to listen for some response. This must be coordinated through command, so EVERYONE on the team goes quite to listen.

If the clue can be related to the lost subject, you may be able to discover:

- Direction of Travel
- Physical sign or mental condition
- LKP- Last Known Position
- *Signs*

If the clue found is in cold weather and includes discarded articles of clothing or equipment, it may indicate that the subject is suffering from hypothermia. If the clue is located in the summer and contains empty water bottles and clothing, the subject may be suffering from hyperthermia and dehydration. A series of clues can be linked together to tell a story and determine a direction or possible refuge place. An indication such as a fire or shelter can indicate the subjects' behavior or knowledge of survival techniques. If the fire is still warm, the subject may not be far off. It's vital for searchers to continually look for signs that the lost subject is trying to communicate to them.

Signs that are intentionally recognized in groups of three are:

- Gunshots

- Fire

- Whistles

- Stacked Rocks

- The following may not be in groups of three:

- Pyrotechnics (Flares, Rockets, smoke generators, etc.)

- Direction of travel arrows

- Subjects with knowledge of survival techniques may utilize ground to air symbols or emergency codes such as S.O.S. or three X's on the ground.

- Some subjects may leave behind clothing or notes along their path of travel

If the clues are properly reported to the Incident Command, then the command staff can work with the relatives of the lost subject to determine if the clues are those left by the missing subject; the subject's actual travel or condition may be determined, and new search area assigned. With the understanding of what common clues now are and how they are processed, you can leave a lot of them to maximize the potential of being found or rescued.

Search Techniques

There are three methods for determining how or where you should search.

1. *Theoretical Search-* this area is determined by locating the Last Known Point (LKP) or Point Last Seen (PLS).
   Takes into account elapsed time from the time the person went missing until the search area is determined.
   Figures out how far the lost subject could have traveled.
   Establishes a maximum distance within a 360-degree radius or PLS or LKP.
   Example: If the lost subject traveled at three miles per hour and has been missing for two hours, that is a radius of 6 miles in every direction from the PLS or LKP. It would take a small-town population to cover that much terrain at an 80% POD over ten hours!
2. *Statistical Method-* this area is based on past searches using information from similar age and condition subjects.
   It limits the search areas based on age, distance traveled, and condition of past lost subjects of similar age and types that have been found.
   While this method is an improvement over the theoretical method, experience search managers also utilize deductive reasoning to determine which areas to search first.
3. *Deductive Reasoning* – the search area will be limited or expanded based upon factors such as barriers to the lost subject's travel.

Rivers, lakes, cliffs, or other areas where subjects are not likely to go are balanced against things that may attract the subject to alter their paths for easier travel or places of interest

- If someone went hunting, where's the best hunting spot?
- If someone went fishing, where's the best fishing spot?

- If someone went hiking, where are the best trails?

Patterns

The initiation of search tactics takes place at the same time as establishing the search area. Search tactics are categorized as:

Passive- Confinement and Attraction; you make the subject come to you

Active- You find the subject

Passive Techniques may include:

- Smoke
- Lights or Fire
- Sirens
- Whistles
- Horns
- Loud Speakers

Confinement Techniques may include:

- Point control at road and trail intersections
- People coming out of an active public search area are asked about clues they may have found
- People going into the search area are asked to keep an eye out for clues and evidence of the lost subject
- Running roads and trails with ATV's, mountain bikes and on foot maintains a workable perimeter and search vein activity

Day and Night Searching

Your vision is different in the daytime than at night, and that difference can profoundly affect your search capabilities.

How vision reacts to daylight:

- Pupils constrict
- Colors and fine details are seen
- Visual acuity is at an optimal level
- Images are perceived towards the center of the field of vision
- Scanning requires concentration; a set routine should be used (up and down, side to side)

How vision reacts to darkness:

- Pupils dilate to let more light in, meaning you will need to use peripheral vision at night, and it will make your eyes longer to adjust to the darkness.

- Your vision will be improved as you look around instead of focusing on an object- you'll look around to perceive an outline or catch movement.

- Scanning requires concentration, use the same techniques as day scanning, but view the object off-center in your field of vision instead of straight on

- It takes at least 20 minutes for your eyes to adjust to the darkness

- Avoid night blindness by not depending on the beams of bright flashlights and by not shining lights into the eyes of other team members; also, do not look at the flashing lights of response vehicles

- Look for shapes, shadows, and contrasting movements

Night Vision Goggles
Night vision goggles (NVG) are light amplification devices that do not work in total darkness. If you are in the deep wilderness with a thick canopy or in a cave, they are merely extra weight to pack. Additionally,

they burn out when other searchers introduce reasonable light. Less expensive civilian models are becoming more popular and have their merits, but generally speaking, they're all too expensive and do not perform well enough for SAR use.

Thermal Imaging Devices

Thermal imaging devices detect heat sources and do not rely on light sources. They also work better for SAR applications than most NVG's available to civilians. That said, the light emitted from the screens does nothing to help searchers' eyes in the night, and it can at times be challenging to distinguish between a warm body and a warm, wet pile of leaves. Most Fire Departments carry handheld FLIR (Forward Looking Infrared) devices on their apparatus, so take advantage of them should you feel the need if they become available.

Hazards of Searching at Night

- Falling off Cliffs
- Falling into holes or dry creek beds
- Eyes can become injured from tree limbs
- Bears, Snakes, Feral Hogs, etc.
- Bad Weather conditions
- Trip Hazards (Rocks, Logs, Vines, etc.)
- Becoming lost or disoriented yourself in unknown lands
- Fear of the dark- becoming panic-stricken
- Being unprepared with improper field gear

The Lost Subject

When you find a lost subject, Notify the Authorities!
Use the Acronym L.A.S.T. When searching for a lost subject:

- L- Locate: Notify command of the search team and the subject's location

- A- Assess: Assess the subject's condition and administer first aid if needed
- S- Stabilize: Stabilize and secure the subject for extrication
- T- Transport: Transport the subject/ patient to safety

If YOU ARE the lost subject, make a plan to L.A.S.T.

- L- Location of your area should be made easily identifiable. Make a mess, cut down trees, and leave signs everywhere all pointing to you.
- A- Assess your equipment, health, and situation. Enact survival training protocols as soon as you realize you are lost.
- S- Stabilize any injuries you may have incurred if at all possible. Control bleeding and splint bones where needed.
- T- Think about ways you can signal for rescue and what clues you have left to lead rescuers to your present location.

SAR Packaging
Stokes Basket

The Stokes basket is a wire or hard plastic litter designed for use over harsh terrain, slopes, and wooded areas to protect an immobilized patient from further injury during extrication.

Backboard

The backboard is a rigid board with handles, made of durable plastic material that is resistant to wear. They are a floatable device and are X-Ray translucent. The spine-board or backboard is mainly used by hospitals, sports events, ambulance services, and outdoor activities for safe patient handling in the event of an accident.

Packaging

Packaging refers to the process of securing a patient into a Litter to keep them in a stabilized position for extrication. Typically taking the form of nylon webbing, packaging secures a patient so that even in the event of the litter being turned upside down, they will not move during transport. Packaging also includes padding areas of the body that may be injured or prone to injury from prolonged immobilization in a litter.

Demonstrating a proper Litter Package so the patient remains on a backboard

Preparing a Litter for Transport
Appoint a Litter Team Boss

Guide/ Trail clearing personnel should get ahead of the litter team and clear trail and mark paths

Reserve litter bearers should follow the litter to rotate in to carry when one becomes tired

Lifting the Litter

- A nylon shoulder strap should be attached to the litter and adjusted should the rescuers hand slip from the litter rail, so the patient does not fall

- Litter bearers all face inwards and kneel on knees closest to the subject's feet

- Bearers place both hands on the litter rail a comfortable distance apart

- Litter bearers lift with legs and not their back

- Litter Boss gives the command: "Prepare to Lift," and bearers indicate whether or not they are ready

- "Lift" command is given when all are ready to lift and proceed.

- Lift smoothly without jostling the patient

- Normally patients are carried feet first toward their travel objective unless going uphill, in which case they will travel headfirst.

- Carrying the Litter

- The litter boss gives the instructions to move in an indicated direction

- Litter bearers walk out of step with one another to avoid discomfort

- If terrain becomes too steep for good footing, the litter should be lowered and low angle rescue equipment should be employed

- If a litter bearer becomes unsure of or uncomfortable with their footing or ability to continue, they should speak up and ask the Litter Boss to halt.

JASON HUNT

The Smoke Generator

The smoke generator is the wilderness standard for revealing your location in the deep wilderness. A plume of thick smoke coming from nature catches the eyes of Rangers and anyone else in the region, allowing them an opportunity to pinpoint where you are. On an overcast day, when the sky is full of clouds, black smoke will be vital to creating enough contrast to be visible. Rubber, plastics, and accelerants will provide colored smoke. So, locate trash, tires, and the like to create dark smoke. On clear days, when the sun is bright, and few clouds are in the sky, white smoke will work well. To create white smoke, burn living plant material and leafy, green tree boughs. You can create a lot of smoke quickly, with a reasonably small amount of green materials, so have plenty on hand to keep the smoke generating as long as necessary to signal. Smoke generators can be placed on the ground in a cleared area where wildland fires are not a significant concern. Otherwise, you should build smoke generators on a tripod, which keeps the fire above the ground or water if necessary. Create a tripod, build a platform in the center on which the fire will be built. Then, hang green boughs over the top of the tripod so that it sucks air in from under the fire and blows heat and smoke out the top. This is also a great technique to punch through low-pressure systems, which often prevent smoke from getting above the canopy line.

If you would like additional training with lectures and skills demonstrations, please check out the Modern Survival Wilderness Skills course available at CampcraftOutdoors.com

15

Bracing for Winter

"Pray that your escape will not take place in winter or on a Sabbath."
~ Matthew 24:20

Jesus was teaching about the time of the end of days before his return. You are aware that there will be a time of calamity upon the earth, one that his followers would need to bug-out (flee) from, and his instruction to them was to pray (plea) with God that this time did not take place during a time they would not be prepared for it. The Sabbath day was and remained to be a day of rest for us weekly, and Biblically it's on Saturday as this never changed in scripture and was the day Jesus and his followers observed their rest from weekly labor. Church tradition created by man changed it to Sunday; regardless, it's a day we worship and remain low key, often recouping from the week's events. But there are other Sabbath days too, which is what this verse speaks to, such as God's Festivals of Passover, Pentecost, and Sukkot. At times, the first and the last days of these festivals are also Sabbath days where believers did no work. They were set aside for church fellowship and worship. A flight during these days would certainly be one which those still observant to Biblical cycles would be unprepared to endure. Practically speaking, there are other times of rest when we let our guards down as well. When we go on family vacations, weddings, funerals, shopping, seeing movies, and other recreation times, all of these may also be substituted for times in which we're not prepared to escape danger.

Of course, winter-time is a time of hardship where animals den up and move far less often, trees and plants are unavailable for full usefulness, and the environment creates hardship through wet, mud, snow, and cold. For someone living off the land to survive, it isn't easy to plan and prepare to endure harsh winter months. My family and I celebrate only the Biblical holidays of the Bible. On these days, Passover, Pentecost, and Sukkot, we have an annual training cycle of preparedness to strive for but, while we're prepared and understand the times, we would be hard-pressed to switch gears to bug-out during these times. For those of you ensnared by the traditions of the mainstream church- imagine having to bug-out on Christmas morning; this would be a time for which you would likely not at all be prepared, and enduring it would be quite difficult. We must brace ourselves for such a time and prepare accordingly, especially if we have larger families.

When it comes to winter survival, most think about being warm, and for a good reason. In as little as fifteen minutes in cold or wet weather, the body can begin displaying hypothermia symptoms, including shivering, chattering teeth, and decreased fine motor skills. If not addressed, the body will continue to spiral into a deeper state of hypothermia, leading to becoming unconscious, frostbite, and potential death in as few as three hours in more extreme weather.

#1: Know how to dress
Nothing is worse in the winter than walking around with wet clothing or clothing that doesn't keep you warm. Clothing is a type of shelter and is your first line of defense against adverse weather. The key to dressing correctly in winter is in the layers you choose. Dressing in layers allows you to remove or add clothing to thermo-regulate; you certainly want to avoid sweating if at all possible, so having a layer or two to remove to keep you cooled off is a great way to stay dry and keep your body in check. I typically dress in three layers when in the Eastern

Woodlands. These layers include a moisture-wicking base layer comprised of wool undergarments, a mid-layer consisting of a fleece top, bottoms, and an outer shell, typically a wool blanket shirt. I'll also have some moisture-wicking socks with wool socks over those, depending on my footwear and location. Of course, I have wool gloves with mittens for more extreme weather and always a wool hat of some sort.

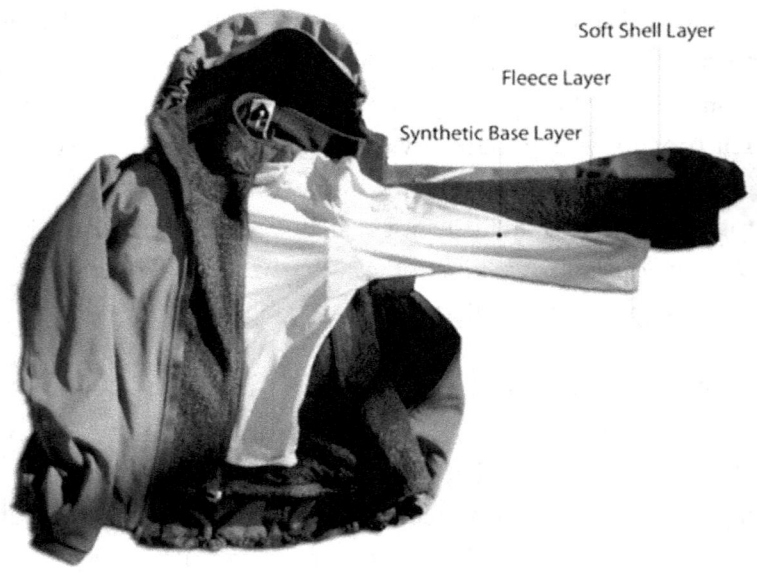

Wool is my preferred garment because even when it's wet, it retains about 70% of its insulative ability. Not all wool is created equal; some may irritate your skin more than others, so investigate different types of yarns such as alpaca, camel, and cashmere before discounting it altogether. As far as footwear, if it's not below 30 degrees, I'll generally wear leather boots that have been properly waterproofed. However, once temps drop into the '20s, I'll typically wear a Muck style boot or heavier leather Guide boot with Gore-Tex.

 # 2: Own Fire

Once you know that you're dressed in proper layers, fire becomes your best friend in the winter. Not only will fire warm you and cook your food, but it will also melt snow and ice, giving you clean water to drink. An adequately stocked winter fire kit is an absolute necessity. You cannot depend solely on a Bic lighter for all your fire-starting needs because they break and fail when cold. Have several sure-fire ways to create a raging fire capable of drying out marginal or wet tinder materials and wood you're likely to find. I carry a ½" x 6" Ferro rod on myself whenever I'm out, but I also have a fire kit.

When it comes to survival tools, two is one, and one is none. This concept is critical when it comes to fire. My basic fire kit contains the following items:

- Backup Ferro Rod
- 2 Lighters
- 2 Sticks of Fatwood
- Flint & Char Cloth
- Chaga (Tinder Fungus)
- Hemp Twine
- Canvas Cloth
- Waxed Fire Starters in Tin
- 6x Magnification Lens
- Friction Free Bow Drill Block

That might seem like a lot, but it all fits easily and nicely into my hip pouch or roll-top tinder bag. These items give me many different options for starting a fire and the ability to create more fire starters should I exhaust one option. For example, the tin that carries my waxed fire starters allows me to create charred cloth or charred natural material such as punk wood I might come across. The flint I have is meant to be struck off the spine of my carbon steel knife, allowing me to save the weight and space a striker would take up. The friction-free bow drill block eliminates one troublesome piece of the bow drill kit, increasing my odds of success when forced to make friction fire off the landscape. Whatever items you select for your fire kit, please make sure you know how they can be used multiple ways so that the lack of fire will not be why you're in a survival situation.

3: Make a Cozy Shelter

A good night's rest is vital in a survival situation, and it becomes even more elusive in the wintertime. The cold extremities, cold spots on your back, the call of the bathroom at 2 am when you just really got warm, all things that you can generally avoid if you will only take the time to shelter correctly. Conduction sucks heat away from your body and into the cold ground as you lie on it. Convection occurs when the cooler air circulates around your body again, wicking away heat. God forbid you from being wet when the wind blows as it will suck heat away 25 times faster! By combating these two forms of thermal action with our shelter's construction, we will have a more comfortable and restful night's sleep.

To prevent conduction, place several inches of compressed material between yourself and the ground on which you plan to sleep. This compressed material can be anything natural such as leaves, boughs, or other debris. Another thought is to take two or three 55-gallon drum liners and fill them with debris that makes a mattress. Then bring an emergency space blanket (Mylar) and construct a lean-to where the reflective side faces toward the inside. Lastly, drape a sheet of plastic, such as a simple painter's drop cloth, over the entire shelter. I like clear plastic as it makes it easier to keep an eye on your fire, but any color will work. By draping the plastic over the lean-to, you create what's called a super shelter. You are preventing convection by covering the shelter, preventing conduction with your mattress, and with the addition of a log fireplaced one step in front of your shelter. You take advantage of radiant heat, which turns your shelter into a greenhouse more or less. We have achieved temperatures of 100 degrees Fahrenheit inside shelters built this way in the dead of winter. Just be sure to leave a ventilation hole in your plastic; it will become suffocating hot otherwise!

 # 4: Eat well and Hydrate Often

You are just as likely to become dehydrated in the winter than in summer. It's only a slower onset of dehydration due to the ambient temperature. When everything around you is damp, wet, and cold, your brain fails to process your need for hydration at the appropriate time. It's not uncommon to not drink most of the day, and once you do drink, you typically want heated beverages and drink a lot of them, which keeps you up going to the bathroom all night. Set yourself on a hydration schedule- drink at regular intervals whether or not you feel like it. This process will maintain a steady-state of hydration and keep you from staying up most of the night watering plants. When you eat, ingest foods high in protein, fat, and carbohydrates. Carbs get your inner fire stoked, and the fat and protein draw that out for a more extended period. One of the camp favorites we have in our classes is called the foil wrap. You wrap your food in foil, toss it into the fire for about 45 minutes, and presto, you're ready to eat a nutritious hot meal.

To make a foil wrap take: 1 potato cut to preference, a handful of meat such as chicken, beef, or venison, 1cp broccoli, 1 cup carrots, and some onion, season everything heavily with salt, pepper, and garlic powder, and toss in a couple of big dabs of butter. Wrap in at least three layers of foil and toss onto the coals for about 45 min to 1hr. Cut open the foil and eat!

By properly preplanning all your outings, you can avoid a survival situation altogether, take the time to gear up properly, and practice your skills regularly. By doing this, the worst you will come to expect will be an inconvenient camping experience. With the essentials covered, we'll now expand upon them and other essential details of winter-time survival and camping skills.

Weather Forecasting

Cirrus Clouds: Thin and wispy, they are made of ice crystals on the leading edge of a warm front. Cirrus clouds show a coming change in current weather conditions.

-- U. of Illinois Cloud Catalog --

Cumulus Clouds: Are Puffy, fair-weather clouds. When thickened and towered (Nimbus), they create Cumulonimbus clouds or storm clouds. High winds and an anvil shape signify a building storm.

THE GOSPEL OF SURVIVAL

-- Photograph by Ronald L. Holle --
-- U. of Illinois Cloud Catalog --

Stratus Clouds: Fast-moving and low, usually accompanied by strong winds, are those that move through during a strong/severe storm front.

Lenticular Clouds are caps that appear over mountain peaks and signal that strong, cold winds hammer upper elevations. They warn of rain in the surrounding area within 48hr.

Halo's around the sun or moon generally indicate rain. A tight halo signals rain within a 12hr period. A wide halo would mean rain within a 24hr period or signal ample moisture in the air. An open side on the halo reveals the direction from which the weather front is moving in.

The following ambient air temperatures with corresponding wind gusts can lead to frostbite within 30 minutes:

- 5°F with 30mph wind gusts = -19°
- 0° with 15mph gust = -19°
- -5 with 10mph gusts = -22°
- -10 with 5mph gusts = -22°

With wind-chill in mind, let's move into ways to identify the onset of winter-time medical complications that are common to outdoor activity.

Winter Self Aid

Hypothermia

Hypothermia results when core body temperature drops below 95° F. A body temperature of 90°-95° is considered mild hypothermia, whereas anything under 90° is severe. Mild to moderate hypothermia can be treated by moving the patient to a warmer location, out of wet clothing, and into a dry environment. Carbohydrates fed to a hypothermic patient will aid in warming them from the inside. Do all you can to promote heat entrapment until the patient regains a "warm" feeling. In the case of a severely hypothermic patient, you must handle them gently as rough or abrupt movements can induce cardiac arrest.

The Author demonstrating hypothermia recovery after water immersion

If breathing is undetectable, first perform 3 minutes of rescue breathing before any action. Remove clothing and bundle the patient with as much dry insulation as possible, insulating them well from the ground with at least 4 inches of compressed materials under them. Place warm canteen bottles under their arms, around the neck and groin area, and finish with a vapor barrier such as a tent fly, drum liner, or trash bag to trap what heat is remaining in the patient. These actions will aid in actively warming the blood as it circulates in the body. Continue treatment even if the patient appears dead! Do not force food or liquids into the patient and evacuate as soon as possible.

Frostbite

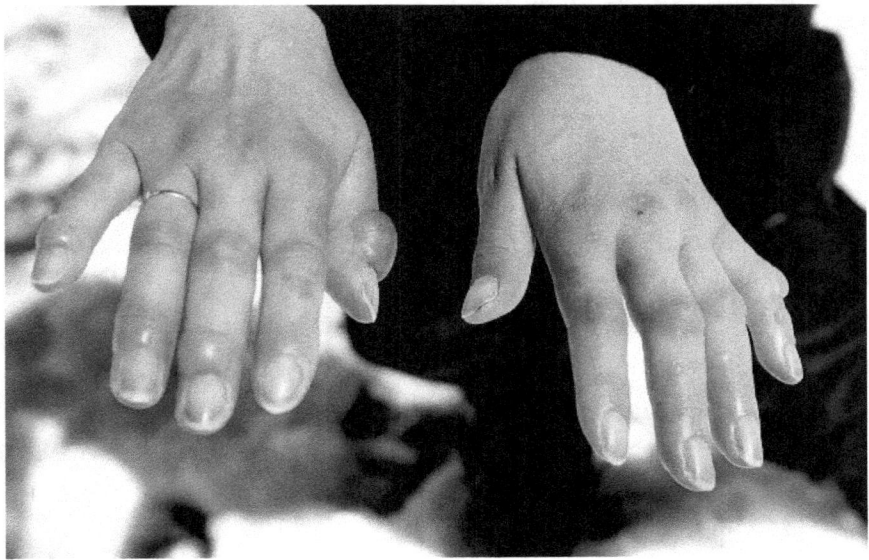

In that case, circulation withdraws from the surface and the extremities because the vital organs have higher priority. Then the temperature in the extremities can drop as rapidly as 1° per minute. Knowing that we lose skin sensation at about 50°, the skin is not yet frozen. To test for actual freezing, dent the skin with your fingernail; if it remains dented like wax, it's frozen with superficial frostbite. If you cannot dent the skin, then the underlying tissues may also be frozen. In the event of superficial frostbite, rewarming the area is recommended in the field. If, however, deep tissue frostbite has occurred, it is fruitless to rewarm the site if you cannot remove the patient from the cold area into an area they can be kept warm. Patients can walk on frozen feet, but it's excruciating. Moreover, damaged tissues quickly refreeze in subzero weather.

Wind Chill

Wind chill dramatically increases the risk of frostbite. Other contributing factors include:
- Hypothermia
- Alcohol consumption
- Smoking (Causes blood vessels to constrict)
- Tight boots (Impairs Circulation)
- Fatigue (slows heat production)
- Wet skin (Cools 25 times faster!)

Contact with icy metal can cause the skin to freeze instantly, especially a full metal fuel container. Petroleum fuels can chill far below the freezing point of water, and they too can freeze on contact, so prevent exposure by wearing gloves and taking precautions. If the skin is getting numb, the circulation is beginning to withdraw. You may start to place your hands into your armpits or shake them vigorously to warm them. It's challenging to rewarm your feet; this is why knowing how to make a fire in extreme conditions is a necessity. Portable hand warmers are also beneficial for staving off frostbite.

If you or someone in your group freezes an extremity or is exhibiting signs of frostbite:

- Immerse the extremity in water 104°-108°
- Do not massage the extremities, but allow the patient to try to move them.
- Continue warming up to 30 minutes or until the skin is red and pliable.
- After removing thawed digits, separate the fingers or toes with loose, sterile dressings and handle as little as possible.

THE GOSPEL OF SURVIVAL

The goal of rewarming is to restore circulation as quickly as possible without damaging the tissues. As the tissues rewarm, their oxygen demand increases, so they will die unless circulation is restored fast enough to meet this demand. Radiant heat (from a heater or fire) is often too slow to remedy severe frostbite by itself. In contrast, water transfers heat about 100 times as fast as air and quickly brings the chilled flesh up to temperature, at which time the blood circulation will return.

Chilblains

Chilblains result from repeated exposure of bare skin to wet, wind, and cold; they cause red, itchy, tender, and swollen skin and usually appear on the fingers. Chilblains typically heal by themselves within 1-2 weeks and can be avoided by keeping extremities warm and dry. Topical steroidal creams may aid in the relief of burning or itching sensations.

Immersion Incidents

The Author post immersion, heading to start a fire

If a person has immersed in cold water in ambient temperatures of 72° or less, you should take hypothermic treatment precautions. Treat by removing wet clothing and drying the patient- wring out clothing or replace it with dry clothing if available. Cover the patient with insulative material or wrap in an emergency survival blanket, which is known to reflect as must as 95% of the body's natural heat when placed against the skin. Block wind from the patient, make a fire and monitor the patient's condition. Give warmed liquids as able to tolerate.

Keep your Water Bottle from Freezing

Freezing your drinking water during wilderness travel can become a real issue for those not used to working or hiking in temperatures below freezing (32°F). In single-digit temps, your drinking water can freeze in just a few minutes if not protected in an insulated wrap of some sort. Additionally, in below zero temperatures, locally sourced water freezes up, which means you may have to chop through thick ice to access whatever water may still be available. This process is potentially dangerous and physically taxing, which burns up precious calories which will cause you to need to eat more to maintain your core temperature.

Here are some helpful tips to help you keep your drinking water usable at all times:

- *Do not bury your bottle in your backpack or haversack.* Stowed this way allows it to become too cold as your pack contents often do not provide enough warming insulation. Also, you will be less likely to drink from it as often as you should.

- *Place a stick or plastic spork inside your bottle.* Doing this will increase movement in the bottle as you travel, which will help prevent ice from developing too fast.

- *Insulate your bottle.* You can use wool socks, reflective insulation, or place hand warmers around the bottle during extended travel periods, and it will all slow the cooling process. Also, consider carrying hot water, which will cool down slowly as you travel, or use a double-walled insulated container specifically for hiking and woodland travel.

- *Drink on a schedule.* Cold and wet weather trick your body into a false sense of hydration due to ambient liquid in the air and environment. You need to drink more frequently when it's cold as you're just as likely to suffer from dehydration in the middle of winter as you are in the heat of summer.

Winter Food Considerations

We all know that as soon as the weather gets cooler, we start wanting to eat more. We pack on the pounds to get our winter bodies into shape to tackle the colder climate. The average person in cold weather (40°F or below) requires 3500-4500 calories daily or 2 – 2.25lb of food. In extreme cold (below 0) or when exerting themselves for extended periods, these requirements can easily be 4000-5000 (3.25-4lb) calories, per person, per day. It is said that the average man engaged in the expedition of Lewis and Clark consumed 9lb of meat daily! That is roughly the equivalent of 31,500 calories or what today's average man would consume over two weeks- imagine that per day!

For our purposes, we'll use estimates here for two people for three days at 3500 calories per day, which would equal 12lbs of food. After-all, going outdoors is more fun with a friend. Having some food and drink every hour will maintain warmth and strength. Eating high-fat meals every few hours will keep the body operating at an optimal level, thereby keeping it warmer longer. Simple sugars such as candy, hot cocoa, etc., are like fire-starters. Complex carbs such as oats, sweet potatoes, etc., are the kindling, with protein & fats being the fuel logs to sustain the fire for a long time. So, some hot cocoa with a breakfast of oats, bacon, and eggs is an excellent start to the day. Follow it with a snack such as a piece of fruit or some trail-mix a couple of hours later. A hearty lunch includes some whole grains, meat, and fats; another snack.

Finally, a dinner that contains fats, protein, and some complex carbs will be a great way to maintain your core body temperature throughout the night.

Backpacker meals such as those freeze-dried or MRE-style foods are not the best to rely upon as a sole food source while winter camping. However, they are okay to work into your real food rotation to make packing a bit easier when you don't have conveyance, such as a canoe, ATV or horse. However, when transportation is not an issue, break out the wannigan (camp box) and cast iron and plan to eat real foods to get the most from your excursion.

The Food Vault

The Food Tin Bag or Food Vault has been used since at least the 1930s. It can be found in the old Boy Scout manuals and is something we replicated many years ago as it just made sense for the type of trips we regularly engage in. Over the years, my instructors and I have used this system across the United States in all seasons, and it's proven to be an excellent tool as it's just a great way to carry a variety of food or non-food items. You can bring your fire kit, then a smaller food supply, and it keeps everything dry and organized in handy metal containers, which enable you to cook, char, or signal depending on your needs. Here's how we jam-pack this full of calories for winter excursions because, again, calories are ultimately the name of the game when it comes to maintaining warmth in a winter survival scenario.

Food Tin Bag from Campcraft Outdoors

The tins we use in this kit are 16oz tins. Although you can press 1lb of goods such as bacon, lard, or dehydrated meats into the containers, these are fluid ounces. The point of this for winter travel excursions is to pack it with as many calories as possible with high-quality macros to produce the most energy for maintaining your body's core temperature.

Sample load-out that we use:

- Tin 1: Steel Cut Oats: 1,213 calories (2 cups)

- *By mixing in sugar or flavors, you can bump this up.*

- Tin 2: Pancake Mix: 1,157 calories (2 cups)
    - *Can be made into stick bread, biscuits, etc.*

- Tin 3: Trail Mix: 1,413 calories (2 cups)

- Tin 4: Dry Pasta: 1,688 calories (2 cups), Instant Potato Flakes would be another option coming in at 1,012 calories for 2 cups.

- Tin 5: Jerky: 1,860 calories or Spam: 1,411 calories, or Bacon: 749 calories- by packing lard around the bacon, you can gain as many as 115 calories per tablespoon. *Store bacon and/or lard in a baggie inside the tin to prevent seepage or get a German butter dish. These are locking tins with a leak-proof plastic liner.*

- Tin 6: Cheddar Cheese: 1,832 calories, Lard: 3,698 calories

**you can mix lard into pancake mix or oats easily to make cookies.*

You can pack as much as 11,029 calories into these tins should you choose Lard as the primary foodstuff in tin #6- even by choosing 8oz of lard and 8oz of cheese, you've got plenty of calories to eat well over a weekend winter camping trip.

Sleeping well in the cold

JASON HUNT

I spent three nights in Northern Minnesota one winter sleeping in this shelter. The daily high never exceeded -5°F, and nightly lows averaged -15, with one night getting to -25. It was roomy and fairly well insulated, and with the aid of my fire, I was quite comfortable every night. When it comes to battling conduction and convection, look at your arm. At wrist depth, you have enough insulation to get you through chilly nights. Think cool summer, early fall, late spring. At elbow deep, you have enough for cold nights. Late fall, early winter, and spring. That will work well to about 32 or so degrees. Armpit deep is what you need when the temperatures are below freezing. Remember to compress it and wallow around in it to make a lovely nest. In my Minnesota shelter, I had material waist deep, which I then compressed.

The quality of a survival kit is determined by how much it can help you when you need to sleep. If you can sleep well at night, you have it made."

~ Mors Kochanski

Gear

The right gear certainly makes a difference. We've already mentioned insulation layers, and these are important in all sleep situations, including hammocks. The only time you would want to omit that would be at the hottest time of the year. The clothing you wear is essential. Loose and layered to trap or release heat. The blanket vs. sleeping bag dilemma usually comes next. The fact is that a queen-size high-quality wool blanket, like a 6-point Hudson's Bay Blanket, will permit you to sleep comfortably down to about 40 degrees. After that, you need more ground insulation, more significant fires, or coal beds to make them work. But they can and do work below freezing. Sleeping bags are the way to go otherwise. Wiggy's brand is some of the best for the money and will keep you toasty warm.

Some helpful tips for adding warmth when needed:

- Hug a Hot Water Bottle
- Sleep on, or hug hot stones
- Make a Coal Bed
- Use a Wiggy's Lamilite Sleeping Bag (Dries when wet in winter)
- Layer sleeping Bags (Fleece liners, etc.)
- *Sleeping bag ratings are based on the lowest temperature survival rating, NOT COMFORT. Always choose a bag for at least 10° lower than expected temperature.*

16

Woodsman Skills

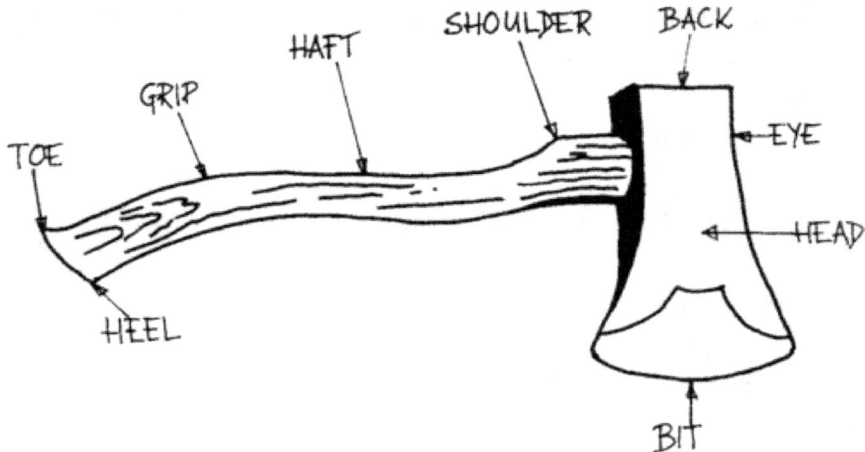

The ax is perhaps the most widely recognized tool of woodsman around the world. It only makes sense that in the study of survival skills, axemanship be discussed because the skills for processing wood for tinder, kindling, fuel, structures, and projects for the camp and the homestead transcend 'survival' and were considered life skills, especially before 1920. Because we're focusing only on the basics of Winter Survival, we'll look at how to safely take down a tree and then process it into fire materials. We'll also examine using it for fire craft. The more you practice with your ax, the more comfortable you will become with it- many use axes, in the same way they would a knife.

The 4 S's of Axe Safety

These 4 S's were developed by Ben Piersma of Ben's Backwoods. These safety mechanisms apply equally to all bladed tools.

1. *Sharp*, a dull ax, is a dangerous ax as you have to work too hard to get it to bite into the wood. This dullness can lead the axe to easily slip or skip out of your work, thereby increasing the risk of a potential injury. Sharp tools accomplish their intended purpose.

2. *Stability*, a stable platform to work from such as a wood anvil, stump, a proper body position, or another secured log is essential for safe tool use. It protects the tool from damage when processing and the user from missed or erroneous strikes with the ax. Logs bouncing around or moving too much while your working drains your energy and are simply unsafe.

3. *Slow Down*; most hand tools work at one speed, slow. You need to slow down and let the sharp edge do the work. Slowing down permits you to work longer with less fatigue and allows you time to find a safe rhythm to work. You will slowly get comfortable with the tool and will be able to work faster, but most often, trying to work harder and quicker will wear you out and create the potential for hazards. A steady pace of work is preferred, limiting injuries, limiting your exertion, and keeping a check on your bodies' core temperature.

4. *Safe Follow Through*, if you fail or forget to employ steps 1-3, a safe follow-through will mitigate a dull tool from skipping back into you or another bystander. Every time you are using an ax, you need to ask yourself where that sharp blade will go if it skips out or cuts straight through the intended work. Rotten wood, Frozen wood, Super dry hardwood, etc., all can and will act differently with your tools. The surprise of cutting straight through that log in one blow is not safe if your foot is on the other side of it.

Chopping

When you chop a log or downed tree, chop at about a 45 or so degree angle. Anything more may result in the ax glancing off the material you're working on.

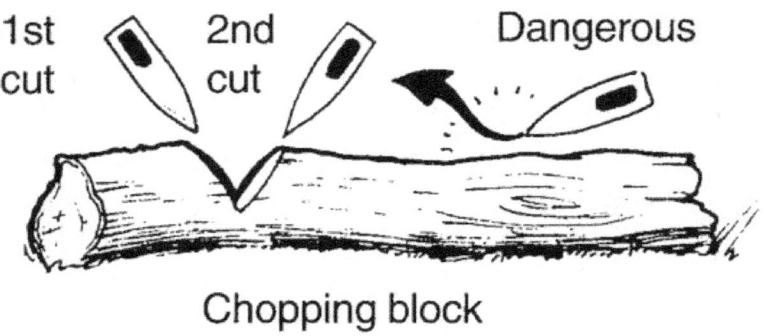

Chopping block

Felling

When felling a tree for survival purposes, we would rarely need to fell one any larger than 6 inches in diameter. When felling smaller trees for fire and shelter use, it's safest to work from your knees as a way to eliminate the threat of over-swings into your legs or feet. This skill also enables you to use more of the tree by getting a strike lower on the trunk.

Limbing

Limbing is the process of removing branches from a downed tree. The easiest way to a limb is from the tree's base to the top, cutting the under portion of the branch nearest the trunk, so they do not split into the main trunk. Always use the trunk of the tree as a physical barrier between you and your ax. Move around the tree whenever possible, instead of trying to step over as it's easy to trip over a branch or take a poke in the eye from the same, that with a sharp tool in hand is not a good mix. Slow down, work safely. Limbing downed trees is one of the faster ways to procure firewood in an emergency.

Splitting & Wedges

If you have to split a more extensive log with a small ax, utilize hardwood wedges in the wood grain cracks. If you do not have a noticeable gap, create one with your ax. By using wedges along with your baton, you will find you can split larger logs much easier.

Sawing

There are two primary types of take-down models, modern and made of metal and plastic, and traditional, made of wood. Both have their pros and cons to consider. Both will use the same blade style with two blade options, dry wood (deadwood) or greenwood (live wood). The dry wood blade (peg tooth) is intended for cutting through dry wood and is a single shape of a tooth, meant to cut on both the forward and backstroke and is the most commonly used in survival and bushcraft. They do an adequate job of cutting green wood but do not carry an anti-corrosion coating on them, which means they rust quickly. You may elect to carry one or both with your saw; in my experience, however, the dry wood has served me well for years at a time with minimal upkeep.

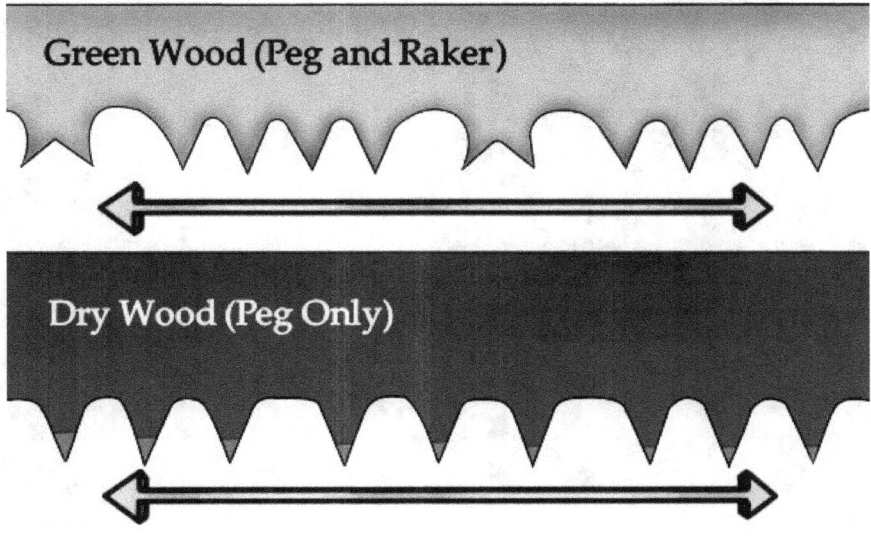

Saw Kerf & Set

The term "*kerf*" is used to describe the thickness of the cut woodworking saw blades make in a piece of wood as it cuts through it. The "*set*" is the lateral inclination of a saw tooth along an edge. Over time, the kerf of your saw may be broader or tighter due to extended use of the blade- this often means the set of some number of teeth has been compromised and may need adjustment. Usually, a saw set is used, but you can make a field adjustment using a standard nail. Look down the length of your saw blade to identify the misaligned tooth or teeth, then mark them.

By laying the blade flat against a stump anvil, take a nail tip and place it against the tooth needing adjustment and give it a smack in the direction it needs to move with the back of your ax. The teeth can break, so use care and do not overstrike them. This technique will make a field-expedient set for your saw to keep your tools functional while afield.

Winter Sheltercraft

The shelter is one of the most crucial survival skills, right up there with fire actually, as a properly insulated and well-built shelter will enable you to go without fire, even in cold conditions. The secret to shelters without a fire lies in the amount of insulation used for them. I refer back to the graphic from Chapter 10, which notes the approximate depth of compressed material needed to protect the body from conduction, the ground sucking heat away from the body.

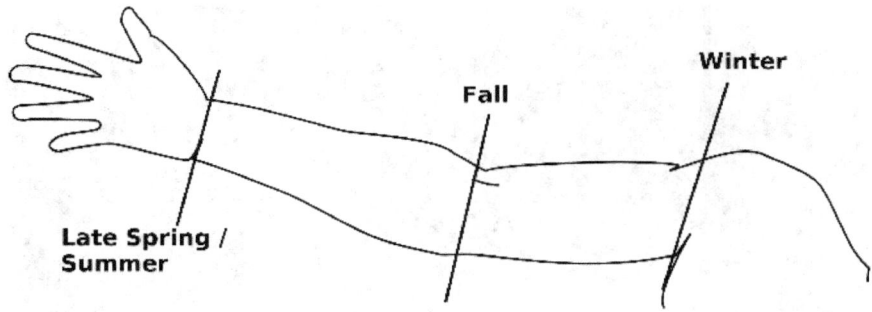

Notice in winter months, you want armpit depth of compressed material called *browse*. Browse is natural material collected off the landscape, such as leaves, pine needles, grasses, etc., that can create insulation. Dry browse is ideal, but you could use wet so long as some sort of barrier is placed between it and you, such as with a drum liner or other plastic barrier we call G.S.I.- Ground Substance Isolation. This G.S.I. creates a vapor barrier, a layer of protection between you and whatever browse you collect. Drum liners work well as an improvised mattress that you fill with browse. We call these browse beds, and the benefit to the drum liner is that the G.S.I. is built in. The bag serves as the barrier and aids in keeping your material from spreading out too much in the night. A frame around the bag is usually helpful as the bags are slick and tend to move around when sleeping on them.

You can also create a nested style browse bed if conditions are dry. The nesting material will soak up any moisture throughout the night; the more, the merrier as these browse beds are very warm and block the wind. The student in the above photo is compressing his material as he goes.

THE GOSPEL OF SURVIVAL

In the North-woods, browse beds are often called *raised beds*. This student laid a foundation of springy saplings across a firm foundation of 5" diameter logs to stay above the snowpack. Browse is then laid atop the foundation to create a comfortable outdoor mattress. A fire with this style of browse bed, along with a tarp overhead, makes for a very cozy winter shelter set up. You can further extend the usefulness of this shelter style by attaching plastic to it. By covering the entire shelter in plastic, ensuring an opening on one end for air exchange, you create what Mors Kochanski called the *Super Shelter*.

JASON HUNT

The long-fire in front of the shelter provides evenly distributed heat across the front of the plastic sheeting, which heats the air captured within the shelter. One end of the shelter is closed entirely, with the opposite end being left loose, facing away from prevailing winds, so air can be exchanged and for entry and egress. Condensation within the shelter becomes an issue as the fire dies down through the night. To combat condensation, you could use a thin fabric such as a cotton shemagh across the shelter's tarp side, inside, of course. This material will soak up the majority of condensation. Alternatively, if you had it available, you could use parachute material as Mors taught in his Canadian Bushcraft courses. By covering the shelter with parachute material, then plastic, the issue of condensation is eliminated.

How to Wrap in a Wool Blanket

Yes, even wrapping up correctly in a wool blanket is a skill! Doing it in a manner like this creates multiple layers of fabric under and over your body, which traps more heat, thereby creating a sort of mummy bag. For best results, you should use a Queen size (6 point) blanket or larger. When not available, place two twins together, having them overlay each other around your core to get the needed leg coverage.

Step 1, lay diagonally across the blanket.

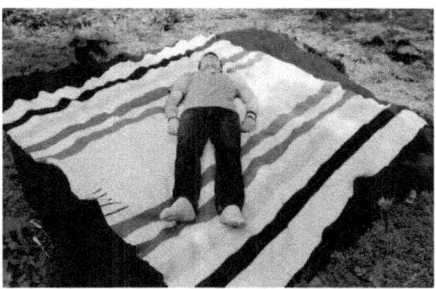

Step 2, cover your feet with the bottom corner of the blanket.

Step 3, take one corner of the blanket and wrap it over top of your body and tuck it underneath.

Lastly, wrap the remaining cover over the top of your body, again tucking it underneath yourself. Use the top corner as a head cover if needed.

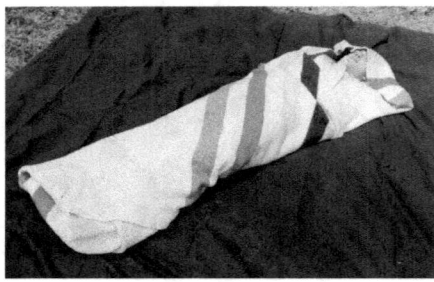

By using a wool blanket in conjunction with proper insulation and shelter techniques, you'll be well equipped to sleep warm all winter.

> *He gives snow like wool; He scatters frost like ashes.*
> ~ Psalm 147:16 (NASB)

Winter Fire Skills

Before delving into the fire skills that we use most often in the winter months, we should first discuss fire kits designed for winter emergencies. It's common for most people to take along a lighter, Ferro rod, and perhaps another method of creating fire, such as a magnification lens. However, cold-induced hazards ranging from exposure to full water immersion must be considered when the potential for cold weather exists. The standard lighter loses pressure at 32°F, which means that it will not light until it's warmed up above that temperature. In a genuine emergency, your fingers or hands may be too cold to function properly due to the onset of hypothermia, which can occur in as few as 15 minutes, with frostbite occurring in as little as 30 minutes in more extreme conditions or high winds. While carrying your lighter in an interior pocket close to your body can remedy this pressure issue, you must have the mindset to remember this simple nugget of information. Alternatively, you must know how to go to your backup fire starter immediately should your lighter be inoperable for any reason. Striking a Ferro rod off the spine of a knife, which is the common practice most of the year, may now become more difficult should we use tools or techniques that require fine motor skills.

It would be best if you guaranteed flame in the winter, so we recommend fire starters, fatwood (resin-rich pine), and anything else that will give you an edge. Be it a road flare or butane lighter- do what makes you most comfortable- but carry at least three ways to guarantee fire for yourself.

The Cold Arm Soak

Now, we're developing a winter survival mindset. We're attempting to train our mind and body to deal with the stress affecting it under pressure. We begin this by soaking our hands up to the wrist for 5 minutes. Soak your hands, palm up in a cold creek or bucket of well-prepared ice-water. Feel the initial stages of pain, burning, and what feels like swelling until it goes away, and you adjust to it. Now, at the end of 5 minutes, make a fire as quickly as possible in a prepared fire lay. Once you're successful over a handful of attempts, move on to soaking your arms up to the elbow. This time, soak for 10 minutes and repeat the fire-starting exercise.

THE GOSPEL OF SURVIVAL

Water Immersion Exercise

The water immersion exercise is one that requires a safety net, especially when training solo. It's only done in class with medical staff and evac to a warm spot available. Safety is always #1 in training; with that said, you can do this in a kid's pool in your yard with a hose or a big yard puddle. The point is to get soaking wet in your clothes in the wintertime, then rewarm yourself so that you may self-rescue. At the basic level, this means being able to warm up and dry out enough to walk back to your vehicle, get back to the house, or, at worst, stay out overnight for one night.

We'll have students walk/swim across a pond as a final exercise to determine their readiness and reaction to icy water in classes. They have the option of going clothed or putting clothes in a drum liner to float across. To date, no one has ever taken longer than 5 minutes to get a raging fire- nothing like a little motivation to get warm again! This training helps better prepare you for the worst-case situation of falling through ice into water. When it's that cold, and you're in an area with an ice thick enough to cross, you should be equipped with a set of ice escape picks. Ice picks for self-rescue are worn through the sleeve of your outer garment so that the spikes hang out near your hands. This rig enables you to deploy them quickly should you ever need to. The sharp points gain you a purchase in the ice to help pull you out or at the least break through thinner ice to get to a shallower area.

The 1 Stick Fire

This is the process of taking a log and creating your tinder, kindling, and fuel from one piece of wood. By splitting a round log, you will be able to get past the outer barks, which will be wet or snow-laden, to find dry wood in the center of the log. You can process this dry wood to create a fire that will dry out your outer wood layers. Baton through the wood with your axe with the intent of increasing its surface area by splitting it into about 30 or so smaller pieces.

Once you have the wood processed, select 4-5 nice, straight pieces free of knots to create feather sticks. Use your ax to create feather sticks.

THE GOSPEL OF SURVIVAL

Upon completion of the feather sticks, use your ax and Ferro rod to ignite the feather sticks, along with any dry bark tinder collected from the log you harvested to achieve a sustainable fire.

Winter Fire Lay

Fire lays for winter activities are essential, and there are many methods of setting up a fire to stay warm through freezing temperatures. Here, we will focus on the Swedish Sandwich Fire (Nying in Scandinavian) since we have already covered the emergency fire and long-fire techniques. The traditional Finnish rakovalkea (literally "slit bonfire"), or "Nying" in Scandinavian languages, is constructed by placing one log atop another, parallel, and bolstering them in place with sturdy posts driven into the ground. Traditionally, whole unsplit tree trunks provided the fuelwood. Tinder and kindling are placed between the logs in sufficient quantity (while avoiding the very ends) to raise the upper log and allow ventilation, thus creating the gap. The tinder is always lit at the center so the bolstering posts near the ends do not burn prematurely.

The Nying has two excellent features. First, it burns slowly but steadily when lit; it does not require arduous maintenance but burns for a very long time. A well-constructed nying of two thick logs of 6ft in length can warm two lean-to shelters for a whole sleeping shift. The construction causes the logs themselves to protect the fire from the wind. Thus, exposure to smoke is unlikely for the sleepers; nevertheless, someone should always watch in case of an emergency. Second, it can be easily scaled to larger sizes (for a feast) limited only by the length of available tree trunks. In the Eastern Woodlands, smaller diameter trees are most often used as nighttime temperatures often do not reach near-zero very often. It's common to split larger diameter trees in half to use a single tree to conserve resources.

For additional information on Winter Survival skills, please check out our online or on-site courses on the subject at CampcraftOutdoors.com

17

Backwoods Hygiene

"Although you wash yourself with lye, and use much soap, the stain of your iniquity is before Me," declares the Lord God."
~ Jeremiah 2:22

One of the most poorly managed skills of the nominal woodsman is that of hygiene. For some reason, many are under the impression that keeping clean, sanitary and even smelling "good" are not attainable goals while camping; thus, people naturally relax the rules for these issues. However, when these rules become lax, people begin to have poor camping experiences. Illnesses related to food-borne contamination, conjunctivitis (pink eye), irritated or burning feet (athletes' foot), smelly odors, and that uneasy greasy feeling anywhere there's a fold on the body.

Many a spouse, and I suspect, many an alpha male at some point, have remembered at least one camping experience and rated it as good or bad based primarily upon how clean they felt. If you're unable to get clean, you cannot feel "good," not entirely at least. There are, of course, those on the opposite end of the spectrum that are germophobes. Some invest a good portion of their camping funds into devices to keep them clean, such as pop-up shower stalls, camp soaps, toilet papers, foot powders, propane water heaters, and all else related to camp hygiene and comfort.

George Washington Sears (Nessmuk) said in his book Woodcraft & Camping, "*We do not go to the green woods and crystal waters to rough it; we go to smooth it.*" One of the things I made a point to learn how to do early in my career was smooth it while in the woods. I mean to make every outdoor experience enjoyable by smooth it, regardless of how little equipment I carry. This purpose led to figuring out innovations in equipment and natural resource use, which was done by book research and practical experience in the field. With my background in wilderness medicine and the great enjoyment I get cooking over the campfire for a group of hungry woodsmen, I naturally drifted toward methods of first keeping my hands clean.

Keeping my hands clean, even when I didn't have soap or sanitizer, was important because I use the restroom or outhouse daily, and at times I deal with caring for others' wounds. I also cook for people- so safe food handling skills are a necessity. I then became concerned with keeping my feet in better condition due to the miles we would put in during our regular outings and general body and tooth care. The following techniques I'm going to describe do not rely on hard to find natural resources, nor do they require any modern invention to create. Anyone can perform these techniques anywhere they find themselves in the backwoods with or without minimal gear.

Once you begin putting these techniques into practice, you'll soon realize that you can most certainly forgo packing the majority of your store-bought camp hygiene items. This practice saves weight and space in your pack and allows you to stay hygienic in an actual emergency. Dedicated woodsmen have practiced these skills for centuries.

JASON HUNT

Hand Sanitation

You can find the earliest mention of soap used in Babylonian tablets dating back to 2800 BC. In 1500 BC, we learn the Egyptians used soap-like plant substances mixed with various oils to bathe. The Native Americans, specifically those in the Southwest, utilized the soap naturally occurring in plants such as Yucca, Soapberries, Buffaloberries, and Saltbush. However, my survival method does not rely on plants or trees that you may have to search for and correctly identify to utilize, but on the simple ash from around your campfire. The World Health Organization lists ash, sand, and even dirt as preferred methods of hand sanitation whenever soap is not available in post-disaster scenarios[11]. When the time comes to cleaning your hands, whether after using the bathroom or for any other reason for needing cleaner hands, collect the white ash from around your fire pit, rub it over your hands because ash is alkaline. The ash disinfects, and should you have any wounds on your hands, it will help clean them. When a thorough scrubbing is needed, wet the ash and add some powdered charcoal to work as a scrub.

Foot Care

When putting mile after mile on your feet along the trail, nothing feels quite as lovely as airing them out near a crackling fire in the evening hours. The fire's heat helps dry out your sweaty feet and soothing the joints. But, what about the next day when you put the same socks on for another day's work or those times when your feet have been sweating all day and smell so bad a goat would become ill? Once again, the hardwood ash from your fire is the answer. While sitting near your fire, coat your feet in the ash and rub it in. Make sure to get it between your toes, too; this foot powder will not only eliminate bacterial growth and odors but freshen your socks and serve as an antibacterial agent in your boots throughout most of the day.

Body Sanitation and Odor

The human body has natural oils it releases, which help protect our skin from the elements by moisturizing, protecting it from the sun by essentially creating an oily bark over time. Modern soaps are detergents that eradicate all traces of oils from the body for periods, drying the skin, which causes so many to add moisturizers back into the skin through various lotions. Odors are caused by bacterial growth in areas the skin folds or does not get a lot of air exposure, such as the feet, armpits, groin, and butt.

These areas are often not exposed to the air for obvious reasons, so bacteria have a warm place to colonize. Our detergent-based soaps eliminate these colonies. Then we use antiperspirants that help limit the sweat in these areas by plugging the pores with aluminum salts that melt as they heat, creating a temporary gel usually boosted with an aromatic perfume to mask the residual bacterial odor. Deodorants work by either making it too salty for bacteria to grow or killing bacteria should the deodorant contain chemicals. Antiperspirants are typically applied only under the arm, whereas deodorants may be used anywhere bacterial growth leading to odor may occur. You can clean yourself and eliminate body odors a couple of different ways:

The Smoke Bath

This tried-and-true method eliminates the bacteria on the bodies' surface, eliminating most odors. This method is nowhere near as good as bathing with water, but it is a suitable alternative for removing general odor from the skin or clothing. Create a fire and burn green boughs of pine or similar greenery to produce a cloud of thick, white smoke and position yourself so that you can waft it over you without having to breathe it in.

Body Wash

If you know a few tree species, you can create a very effective means of cleaning yourself by producing a toning body wash. Trees higher in tannic acids such as Tulip Poplar, Oaks, Hickories, or Aspen work the best. The tannin they provide aids in tightening the skin's surface with an astringent effect that is not only soothing but will aid in the relief of minor burns and other irritations. To create a body wash, remove some of your selected tree's outer and inner bark and boil in water until the water turns a dark color, then dip a rag into the solution and use it to wash. Simple and effective.

THE GOSPEL OF SURVIVAL

You could also consider adding finely crushed charcoal or wood ash into this decoction in those times you may require some grit in your wash to exfoliate or remove stains or stubborn dirt. The addition of ash or charcoal will significantly increase the wash solution's effects and dry the skin a great deal.

Mouth Care

When it comes to cleaning your teeth in the woods, I do not recommend chewing up a stick to scrub the teeth for a couple of reasons. People must know how to identify trees and plants to understand which ones they may be allergic to and produce the desired result. This skill often requires additional research and field experience the average person does not have. Another reason against twig brushing is that it's dangerous and may lead to tooth and gum damage. One fragment in the gum under your tooth will ruin your trip! It's simply not worth the risk in most cases as you can either go a few days without brushing until you get home or take a toothbrush or two easy enough. If you are one that decides to carry your toothbrush but forgets your toothpaste for whatever reason, you can utilize the same decoction of tannic acid from trees we use for body wash as a mouth rinse. Swish it around in your mouth, brush your teeth, then swish again and spit. It will eliminate odor and bacteria and leave your mouth clean and dry. It's also great for tightening the gums, although it will not taste terrific!

Another option is to create a paste of pulverized charcoal. Charcoal is highly abrasive and will scratch the enamel on the teeth, so it should be used sparingly and not long term. But these two methods will certainly take care of general cleaning and odor care while on lengthy trips. Throughout the centuries, Woodsmen have been utilizing these same techniques, so there's no reason we should not continue using them simply because we have modern options.

There's much to be said about the smell of smoke, trees, and earth elements on the body. It grounds us in nature a bit more, releases us from the burden of modern society, and relieves us a bit of expense and effort when buying and carrying additional hygiene items that, in reality, are not required to smooth it while in the backwoods. All you need is a rag, toothbrush, the ability to make fire, and the willingness to learn the resources nature provides so you might make the most of them.

Methods of Soap Making

In a 2006 article published in the London Medical Journal of Inflammation, the researchers cited a wide variety of Yucca health benefits. Studies have shown that yucca has properties that protect against sun damage, perhaps even better than many available sunscreens. Yucca can be used to treat a variety of skin conditions ranging from dandruff and balding to sores and cuts, arthritis, sprains, and general infections. Add to this the numerous internal benefits when eaten as an edible and its survival uses for tools, fire, and cordage; this is one plant to become very familiar with and fond of.

To create soap from Yucca, you need to crush the leaves with a stone or other blunt object to release the saponins. Saponin is the substance that makes the foaming action when added with a little water. Take the crushed leaf and douse with water and rub briskly between your hands to create a rich lather and use it as a hand, body, or hair wash. You can also use it to wash dirty dishes and laundry as needed. Various types of yucca are used as ornamental plants nation-wide and grow wild through much of the South-west and South-east.

Cold Process Soap

Cold process soap is made by combining oils and sodium hydroxide lye. That causes the chemical reaction of saponification. The benefit of this process is that it allows you to select the soap ingredients a bit more carefully and add them right away into your mix. This technique is a popular option for those that frequent farmers' markets and create designer soaps. It's not very labor-intensive and it is very easy to do while in the field. This cold-process is what I use most often as it permits me the option of changing ingredients quickly without recalculation while providing me with a consistent end product that's smooth and more similar to store-bought soap. While I do use heat, it's only to liquefy the lard.

Truthfully, it generates enough heat on its own, and I do this purely for effect! Oils such as olive oil, coconut oil, etc., do not require outside heating to saponify. I use lard because it gives a more traditional appearance and texture, and I most often make Pine Tar Soap for classes and events; here's the recipe I use:

Ingredients:

- Sodium Hydroxide: 8.5oz
- Water: 26.4 oz
- Lard: 4lb
- Pine Tar: 1lb/ 16oz

Directions:

Add lye to the water in a glass or heavy plastic container. Stir as you pour it in slowly and continue to stir until lye is fully dissolved. Allow the solution to cool until you can hold your hand to the side of the container or until it's roughly 120°F. As this solution is cooling, melt 4lb of lard over the fire, then add in your pine tar. Remove from heat immediately as soon as the fat melts.

Once your lye solution is at the appropriate temperature, slowly add it to your oils (lard and tar) and continue stirring it in. Keep stirring the concoction until it begins to thicken into a cake batter consistency. This batter will be quite hot and may sting if it gets on your skin as the lye can burn you. Have white vinegar to stop burning on hand or flood the affected area with soap and cold water.

Once the batter is nearing a very thick batter, you can place it into a mold. I use a standard wooden soap mold that holds 5lb of soap. I then allow this to set up and cool for at least 5-7 hours, after which I cut it into bars. I store the bars flat on a shelf for a couple of weeks, which allows time for the soap to cure, after which it's safe to use. If possible, flip the bars over once weekly to ensure event time to air on all sides of the bar. It is not always necessary to wait a couple of weeks before using a cold process soap, but I have found that it's too acidic for those with sensitive skin. If you have rawhide for skin like I do, then you can use your soap after a 24-hour cooling-off period.

Hot Process Soap

This process is very similar to the cold process but uses external heat to generate the chemical reaction needed for saponification. Suppose you plan to use traditional wood ashes to obtain your lye. In that case, you will need to cook it over a fire, along with your oils to achieve saponification, after which you would then add your additives such as fragrances, colors, etc. Hot process soap creates a more rustic soap and has been used for thousands of years. To create lye water, collect hardwood ash (Potassium Hydroxide-[KOH]) into a bucket and pour rainwater or another water free of heavy metals through the ashes. Water should be allowed to pass through the ash bucket and recaptured into another vessel so that you may run it through many times. Generally speaking, running water through the ash solution several times is required and takes about 2-3 hours in my experience. Once you can float a chicken egg or dissolve a feather in the water, you have lye strong enough to make soap. At this point, you only need to transfer the solution to your cooking vessel along with your selected oils.

You will need a soap calculator to create your recipes. I recommend those from www.soapcalc.net and www.soapguild.org/lye-calc.php

Woodsman's Hygiene Kit

Let's be honest; no one likes to be funky while they're in the woods. End of the world or not, wilderness hygiene isn't just about getting rid of your stink – it's crucial for your health and well-being, as well as that of your fellow campers. Poor hygiene can lead to urinary tract infections, nasty rashes, GI illnesses, dental infections, and several other preventable diseases. It can be challenging to stay clean in the wilderness, but being dirty is a choice. For the sake of your health (and those of us who have to smell you), you should regularly take advantage of the simple skills shared in this text to maintain a base standard for good health and hygiene. With that in mind, let's look at a Woodsman Hygiene essentials kit- this kit is what you should take with you camping or training, while you should use the techniques discussed in this text to supplement your equipment.

- Shemagh – This lightweight, the multi-use cloth can serve as a wash rag, bath towel, and any other hygiene use you can think of. It dries fast in fair weather and should be dried in the direct sun whenever possible to kill any bacteria. It can also be boiled in a pot to sterilize between uses. I am a huge fan of the shemagh which is an Arabic word that also described the Biblical Tallit (prayer shawl). My shemagh actually has knotted tassels on them, which I also use as tie-outs on hot summer days to create shade.

- Victorinox Classic- this little knife provides tweezers, a toothpick, a nail file, a small blade, and scissors which can be used for trimming your nails as needed. Alternatively, you could include some nail clippers with a file.

- Toothbrush- this makes life easier and is safer and more effective than other methods of cleaning teeth.

- Toothpaste- this again is safer than making char-coal tooth powder and can be used daily whereas field-made powders should be used sparingly.

- Soap- this may be in liquid or bar form as desired, but I like to have the option of really cleaning my hands and myself as needed. Soap can also serve as a shampoo and is great in cutting the oils after contacting poison ivy.

- Alcohol Wipes- these are handy for quick cleaning and disinfection of minor wounds.

- Comb or Brush- I like a comb due to its smaller design, but having something to tease out ticks, detangle hair, and aid in making oneself feel better is a great morale booster. Also works great on getting food out from beards.

- Q-Tips- I use these for cleaning excess wax or debris from my ears and have on occasion used them for removing debris from under my eyelid and cleaning out deep wounds.

- Medicated Powder or Anti-Chafe Stick- when it's wet out and you've slogged over miles of rough terrain, chafing can become a real problem. A medicated powder or stick for chafing is essential and can be used on the feet and under the arms as needed.

- Sunscreen/Lotion- repeated burning is not good for your skin, nor your eyes. Having some sort of sun protection is vital in all seasons. Sunscreen also serves as a lotion for dry skin due to overuse of ash or charcoal washes.

- Deodorant- This is purely a comfort item. If I'm leading classes with strangers, I'll often have it. If I'm with friends or alone- I never have it! Ash or medicated powder under the arms works just as well.

This image is my actual hygiene kit- the primary technique I have used for bathing has been the oak/poplar decoction bath. I like a warm-bath before I retire at night to soothe me to sleep. Add some lavender from the woods, and you'll most certainly get a rested night's sleep.

Campcraft Outdoors Accessory Tote carries it all

18

Wilderness Self-Aid

Pre-Emptive self-care

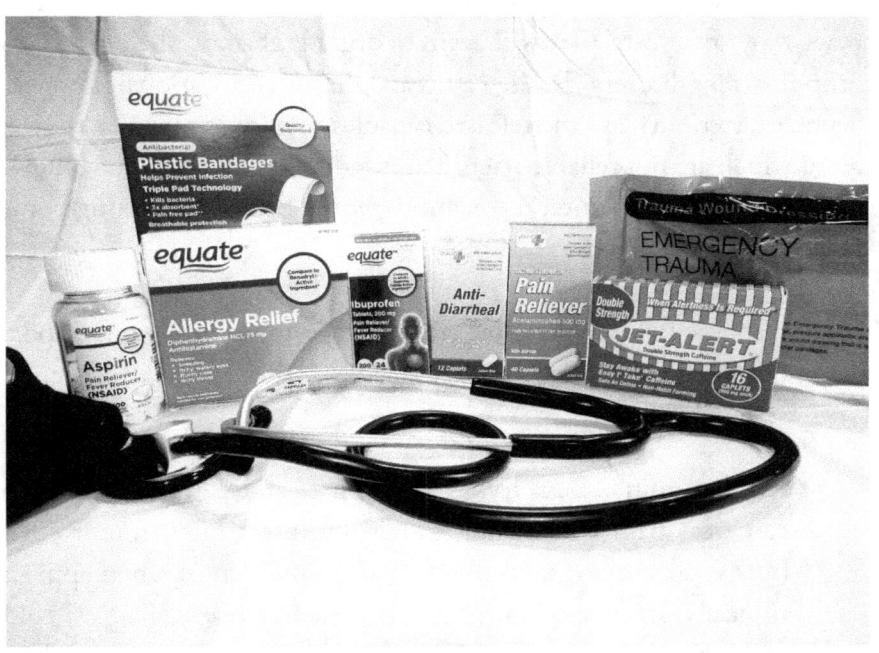

Imagine, if you will, an actual survival or collapsed society situation. How long would it take for you to begin suffering from caffeine withdrawal? What if you had diarrhea or a severe seasonal allergy? While you can undoubtedly learn wild-land resources to deal with these sorts of ailments to some degree, the average person does not take the time to learn all of this information. Those who do take a nominal interest in herbal remedies do not make it a part of their daily lives. Thus, preparing for such issues well in advance only makes sense for the average person. Not only will the following products help you circumvent common problems associated with the initial shock of off-grid living, but they're likely items you already have in your home and that you can quickly obtain, at least at this point, without a prescription. Long gone are the days when you can go to the junk drawer to pull out that stash of antibiotics from the illness you had years ago. Restrictions on pain medications and antibiotics have caused physicians to stop giving as much to their patients as they used to. So, save what you do not need or use now! If stored in a cool, dry place, medications will not lose their potency for at least five years. After five years, they will begin to degrade at a rate of about a 10% drop in strength every decade (10 years). Some medications, however, degrade faster, such as time-released capsules and liquid capsules, the latter of which are not reliable after their intended expiration. The following list of over-the-counter medications would be a good starting point to always keep on hand.

- Caffeine Pills: To stave off withdrawal symptoms of coffee, soda, tea, etc. as they become less available or unavailable in an actual system collapse

- Antihistamine: Benadryl, Dramamine, and Diphenhydramine can treat pain and itching caused by insect bites, minor cuts, burns, poison ivy, poison oak, and poison sumac when applied topically. In its oral form, it can treat hay fever, allergies, cold symptoms, and insomnia. They also make pain relievers work better, such as Acetaminophen and ibuprofen, Vicodin, and Percocet.

- Claritin: A non-drowsy antihistamine alternative

- Anti-Diarrheal: Immodium, eases pain, gas, and inflammation of the digestive system. If blood is present in diarrhea with a fever, it's a sign of a toxin in the body, and diarrhea is the body's way of removing it.

- Rehydration Aids: Gatorade, Pedialite, Jello all serve as electrolyte replacements and should be administered at half strength, diluted with water.

- Anti-Nausea: Anavert, Dramamine, Phenergan, Promethazine all perform very similar functions and can treat allergies and motion sickness. They can also be used as a sedative before and after surgery and medical procedures, control pain, nausea, and vomiting. One recent study showed cetirizine (Zyrtec) to be 90% as effective as the prescription drug Zofran for controlling nausea.

- Acetaminophen: Tylenol for pain and fever reduction

- Ibuprofen: Aleve, Advil, for the reduction of inflammation
    - When Acetaminophen and Ibuprofen are combined at the rate of 1000mg Acetaminophen and 800mg Ibuprofen, they mimic the effects of Vicodin without the narcotic side effects. Administer every 8 hours, not more than three times daily. Be cautious about the total dose of Acetaminophen. It is present in a lot of other OTC drugs.

- Aspirin: Can be used to treat pain, fever, headache, and inflammation. It can also reduce the risk of heart attacks.

These items are in addition to specialized products related to hygiene, dental care, eye care, etc. If you wear glasses or contact lenses, stock up several eyeglass repair-kits, toss them about your various outdoor bags and supplies and perhaps include as recent a prescription of extra contact lenses as possible and possibly the older pair of prescription glasses. Any specialized dental needs should be added to the list, whether it be denture adhesive or dental wax.

Bushcraft First Aid Tips

The 5 B's of Bushcraft First Aid is a concept that we developed during my time at The Pathfinder School. We wanted a system that would address the five most common issues facing outdoorsmen and ways of treating these issues from our survival kit.

The 5 B's are:

1. Bleeding
2. Breaks
3. Burns
4. Blisters
5. Bites & Stings

The following tips will address each of the 5 B's and permit you to add to your field skills knowledgebase.

Bushcraft Tip #1: Homemade Sugardyne

Over 4,000 years ago, on ancient Egypt's battlefields, soldiers used honey and animal fats to treat the wounded with excellent results. With the advent of modern sugar technologies, which replaced honey due to its wider availability and ease of transport, and current oil availability for cooking, honey and fat have primarily been left to the primitive past. The combination of sugar and oil has been proven sufficient to heal battlefield wounds, ulcers (bed sores), gunshot wounds, and burns. Sugar was later added to povidone-iodine and marketed as Sugardyne during both world wars.

THE GOSPEL OF SURVIVAL

The addition of povidone-iodine was found entirely unnecessary, and physicians again started testing the power of sugar and found that powdered confectioners' sugar and standard cooking oil provided the best, most cost-effective treatment.

To make: mix 3-parts confectioners' sugar with 1-part cooking oil of choice (olive or coconut being ideal). Mix until uniformly smooth and store in an airtight jar. The material will last indefinitely and will be shelf-stable.

Caution! Because sugars bind with calcium, adding Sugardyne before bleeding has stopped will prevent the formation of blood clots, thus worsening bleeding. So, do not use Sugardyne on a wound until the bleeding has stopped entirely.

JASON HUNT

Bushcraft Tip #2: Salve Around Breaks

"Is there no salve in Gilead? Is there no physician there? Why is there no healing for the wounds of my people?"

~Jeremiah 8:22

After any bleeding has been controlled, you can apply medicated ointment called *Cerate* (Sair-ate) also called *salve* (pronounced: sah-v) into a wound or around a suspected break to aid in healing and pain management.

Medicinal Herbs used for salves

THE GOSPEL OF SURVIVAL

To create a salve, select your herb of choice; for this recipe, we will say Yarrow (ACHILLEA MILLEFOLIUM), known for its ability to stop bleeding. Simmer your yarrow (or other herbs) in an oil such as olive oil, coconut oil, or even animal fat (I have used raccoon fat!) for at least thirty minutes, although some prefer several hours. While the oil is hot, begin to add in flakes of beeswax, do not add too much, or you will have a block of wax, which we'll get to in a moment. Allow the mixture to cool until the desired consistency can be reached. You want it similar to a petroleum jelly consistency or perhaps a little firmer in warmer climates. That's it! You can pack wounds with this, which will significantly aid in bleeding control and healing. Now, I would recommend also making a medicated block of wax with this method. It's just a hard salve, and you can use this block as a dental wax should you lose or injure a tooth. You can also apply it to all your tools to protect them from rusting and be used on your boots or fabrics to waterproof them.

Medicated soap and wax cake made in the field

Bushcraft Tip #3: Burn Field Care

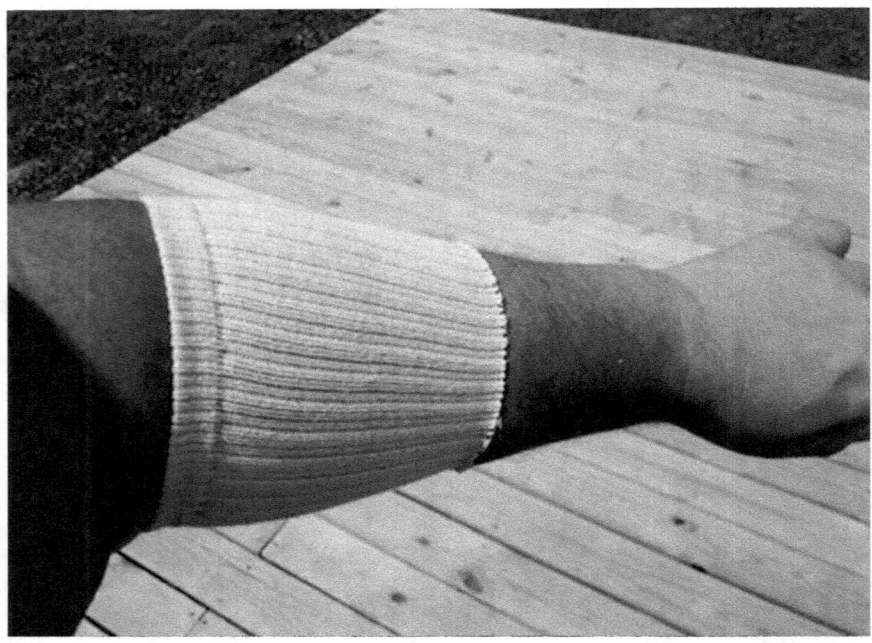

Not all burns require immediate medical attention. Anything with a 5% or less total burn surface area may be field treated for up to a few days before more definitive care should be sought; this does not include burns to the hands, face, groin, or feet.

Step 1: Wash the wound thoroughly with soap and potable water.

Step 2: Remove loose debris and peel away dead skin (which may be painful). Alternatively, trim dead skin back with some scissors.

Step 3: Drain fluid-filled blisters if present to prevent closed-space infection.

Step 4: Apply an antibiotic ointment or soothing salve to the burn or burn dressing, which will prevent the dressing from sticking while promoting healing.

Step 5: Use a cotton sock as a bandage over the burn dressing. Cut the end of the sock off to create a circumferential wrap when possible.

Step 6: Change the wound dressing once daily; however, a wet or sticky wound dressing, one that has been saturated, should be changed more often as needed until dry. Vitamin E and Aloe will significantly aid in healing and should be applied to wounds that have begun healing to hydrate newly forming skin.

Bushcraft Tip #4: Survival Blister Kit

Using cotton to dress a blister

Looking at the items within our 12-piece survival kit- here are some ways we can treat blisters.

1) Repair needle: We can easily sterilize our needle with a lighter and then use it to lance a blister for draining.

2) Water bottle: We can use the water bottle as a cold pack to cool down the blistered area and, of course, to aid in cleaning the area by pouring

water over it. If you carry a water filter such as a Sawyer Squeeze, you can generate enough pressure to perform forceful irrigation if needed.

3) Cotton material: You can use your cotton material to create dressings- once coupled with your Duct Tape, you can create effective Island dressings.

4) Cerate: This is your antibiotic ointment. Learning to make salves will enable you to create a wide variety of applications.

Do not apply duct tape directly onto a blister once it has formed, as it will merely make the blister worse. At best, you can use it as a precaution to areas you generally get blisters, but you must apply the tape before work begins to be marginally useful. If you apply tape directly over the hot spots in your feet, you may end up with an enormous blister as the tape will still move- thus, the blister will be as large as the tape you use to cover the hot spot.

For additional information related to Bushcraft First Aid, please consult my book titled Bushcraft First Aid, coauthored with Dave Canterbury. You may also take advantage of our online and in-person training course on Bushcraft Hygiene and First Aid by visiting CampcraftOutdoors.com

19

Enduring Trouble, Together

What is Tribulation? In its purest sense, the word we read as tribulation in the Bible means trouble, affliction, and oppression according to both the Strongest Strong's Concordance (Greek word 2347) and the Webster's New World College Dictionary. The time is soon coming in which anyone calling themselves a Christian will be oppressed, afflicted, and troubled.

Matthew 24:4-8: *"Jesus told them, "Don't let anyone mislead you, for many will come in my name, claiming, 'I am the Messiah.' They will deceive many. And you will hear of wars and threats of wars, but don't panic. Yes, these things must take place, but the end won't follow immediately. Nation will go to war against nation and Kingdom against Kingdom. There will be famines and earthquakes in many parts of the world. But all this is only the first of the birth pains, with more to come."*

We are now living in the birth pains of the return of the Messiah Jesus. We have witnessed institutional Christianity's travesty in the world today, with some of its most prominent leaders revealed as sexual deviants, thieves, and liars. Yes, these are the people Jesus warned us about, those that claim to be Christians yet live the life of a sinner; these people have misled a great many. We have been witnessing an ongoing war in the Middle East for the last two decades. We have indeed seen the famines taking place in Haiti, Africa, and even here in the United States due to the ongoing COVID-19 pandemic. Lastly, we have witnessed a dramatic increase in earthquakes globally, many of which are hitting the United States' central part.

Again, Jesus has told us that these signs are only the first of the birth pains with more to come. As you may realize, a mother giving birth generally experiences a tightening of the uterine muscle called a contraction, also known as birth pain. These contractions can often go on for many weeks, some typically unnoticed, but as the time for delivery draws near, these contractions increase in intensity, frequency, and duration. Jesus tells us the next series of birth pains to watch for, beginning in Matthew 24:9-14.

"Then you will be arrested, persecuted, and killed. You will be hated all over the world because you are my followers. And many will turn away from me and betray and hate each other. And many false prophets will appear and will deceive many people. Sin will be rampant everywhere, and the love of many will grow cold. But the one who endures to the end will be saved. And the Good News about the Kingdom will be preached throughout the whole world, so that all nations will hear it; and then the end will come."

This tribulation period is what we are on the verge of witnessing; a crackdown on outspoken Christianity (*Newsweek*, January 4, 2018). Most recently, various governments nationwide have been issuing bans on religious services and gatherings and have even issued fines to churches and pastors[12]. The world-wide COVID-19 Pandemic has wrought havoc in world affairs despite its 99.8% survival rate. This social engineering via a contrived pandemic has enabled the globalist government to enact their Great Reset of the global economy[13]. This global economic reset includes the social paradigm and how people interact with each other in public. We are now catching glimpses with each wind of change between the wheat and the tare. We are on the precipice of being jailed for preaching the gospel in public.

Plain and simple, tribulation exposes unbelief and promotes true belief. A trial is a tool utilized to see whether we fear God or man. Time and again, it has been used in a wilderness survival atmosphere- think of the desert of the Exodus, the wilderness wanderings of the prophets, and Jesus' frequent retreat to the wilderness to seek His Father's face amid oppression, to name only a few. Again, the warning is clear; when the time comes to go to the wilderness, we cannot hesitate. We have a clear result of this hesitation outlined for us in Genesis 19. Jesus has told us that in the end times, we should not only pray that it doesn't come at a time when we are not prepared (winter or Sabbath), but that our women not be pregnant (which would make it difficult) and that it will be worse than at any other time in history! The purpose of surviving or enduring until the end is so that we can lead as many souls to Jesus as possible during these precarious times. This leading begins in our home. So, how do we start training our children, loved ones, and friends in these skill sets?

Teaching Youth Survival Skills
We may begin equipping Children with the core survival skills such as making fire, shelter, and boiling water as a family bonding activity. In time, we turn it into a test of their resolve, forcing children to come face to face with the harsh realities of making a fire without a lighter or perhaps constructing a shelter in the rain. Will they give up, or will they press on? This practice develops their survival mindset and allows us as parents and guardians to teach about personal awareness and survival psychology regardless of their decision.

What if, for example, you, as the leader of the family, became ill, injured, or worse yet do not make it through the initial crisis event- what will the children have left to depend on besides the gear you have amassed? Knowledge weighs nothing, so the more they know now as youngsters, the less equipment they'll become dependent upon as adults. While the skills are fun, the reasons for the skills are topics that many parents seem to have trouble conveying to their children. I do not understand this. If they are your children, then why is there a problem communicating information to them? I know how to talk to my kids; I treat them as I would want to be treated now, and as I would have liked to have been treated when I was a child. So, I articulate my concerns with the world to them as best I can regularly. When I see something in the news that alarms me, they all hear about it and, yes, with all the gory details. When we watch a movie together, and there's an important lesson in it, I often pause it, talk about the lesson and how it applies to us, and we move on. It's our daily routine. The good book tells us to train up a child in the way they should go so that when they're grown, they will not depart from the path we've shown them (Proverbs 22:6), and that is a wise methodology.

If you've done your part as a parent, they will share your concerns and develop an awareness of these same issues. Is there fear involved? It depends on your family dynamic. If you appear afraid of a situation, kids are very keen on reading your reactions. If you are conveying fear to your children, it will, in turn, make them afraid and perhaps harder to wrangle back in during an actual crisis event. However, suppose you use the situation as a teaching moment. In that case, even though you may be afraid, you share rational intelligence about what you as a family will be doing to overcome the obstacle—thereby instilling confidence and faith in your endeavor. This ideology will replace fearful reactions with purpose-driven, problem-solving reactions.

So, how do we approach teaching survival skills to our kids? We Educate (Tell them), Demonstrate (Show them) and have them Imitate (Do it themselves). It's not that much different from teaching adults, really, save for the fact that children, for the most part, often lack the physical strength to perform specific survival skills and often require consistent reinforcement of a concept before they get it for themselves. For example, striking a ferrocerium rod off the back of a knife's spine is a learned technique that takes a fair amount of manual skill and strength to perform. I've seen many adults fumble with this technique for quite some time before learning how to adapt to overcome their limitations. With a child, you may need to point out a few solutions to get their mind working on how they can adapt to compensate for their lack of strength or inability to perform specific movements. Perhaps a broken file, the spine of their pruning saw blade, or another device may better suit them for the task- figure a solution together to get them thinking about options and resources.

Additionally, if you've never let your child hold a knife before or trusted them enough to carry one outside, you cannot expect them to be able to use it to strike a fire-steel the first or the fiftieth time during a crisis event. Practice makes better, and above all, patience and love should be given by the boatload! We want our kids to learn these skills and the last thing we want to do is give them a terrible learning experience with us while doing it. While there will be discouragement, we must instill a can-do attitude and continuously remind them to persevere and

NEVER give up, for their life or that of another loved one may one day depend on it.

Gear for Kids

Not all Ferro-Rods are created equal. When selecting Ferro-Rod for yourself or your child, you should get the largest one available. The old mini-rods on the side of a big bar of magnesium (Dones mag-bars) are not your best choice. Mag-bars require too much prep time and require too much manual dexterity to use correctly. Most people don't even know how to scrape off the magnesium properly, so avoid them unless you have been trained on them. In like fashion, the popular fire-steels with plastic handles are often too small to be of long-term use, and the handles always end up flying off. The scrapers that come attached rarely do an adequate job in taking off enough molten metal to light a fire with marginal or damp tinder, but they work well as a backup.

THE GOSPEL OF SURVIVAL

Knife Selection for small hands

Get your kids a decent knife, one that will withstand the rigors of a survival situation should it be encountered. I offer the following recommendations, which can be adapted to fit your child's age and abilities. The Mora 511 would be a suitable choice for those under age 13. You can usually pick one up for around $7, and they are razor sharp and hold an edge well. They come in carbon or stainless steel, but they will not strike a Ferro-rod off the spine out of the box. They will require you to take a file across the spine to sharpen it to a proper 90-degree angle. Alternatively, plan on adding a scraping device to your child's kit. Use a heavy rubber band (ranger band) to attach a Ferro rod with a scraper to the case, and you're all set. The handle of this specific knife design provides added protection so little hands won't slide up onto the blade should unnatural force be applied or the knife becomes wet. For those ages 13 and older that need a more robust knife capable of realistic survival tasks off the grid, I would recommend the Mora Bushcraft Black. The Bushcraft Black, which retails for about $40.00, has a heavier carbon steel blade capable of being struck by flint to throw sparks, is very sharp, and again holds an edge well.

Safety

Next, we move into proper fire lays for heating, cooking, boiling water, and survival. Please explain the differences between Tinder, Kindling, and Fuel, finding it off the landscape, and finding natural accelerators such as fatwood. It's also a good idea to stress the importance of always carrying "sure-fire" with you at all times in case of an emergency. This process would naturally bring us to Ferro rod striking techniques, which are discussed in Chapter 7. Then, after the use of the fire-steel is covered, consider alternative ignition sources ranging from lighters and solar sources to batteries and primitive techniques.

Shelter & Water Skills

8yr old Cecile Fiscus 7:38 on her shelter, fire and water boil

The shelter would be next on the list of priorities. The simple lean-to survival shelter using an S.O.L. Utility Blanket available from Adventure Medical Kits is the first step in teaching shelters that will immediately increase one's odds of survival. It would be best if you taught the appropriate knots and alternative uses of the survival shelter and what to look for in natural shelter sites. The primary importance is staying warm and dry when it's cold and calm and covered when it's hot; these two sentiments will help maintain core body temperature and stave off hypothermia and hyperthermia, at least in the short term. Last but not least, discuss water purification. Filters such as the Sawyer squeeze are the easiest for kids to use. Boiling water, however, remains the most reliable for most conditions.

Now, reinforce the skills you teach

All of these skills, once they get a handle on them, should be timed. Yes, TIMED! Your goal is to have your youth perform each skill set- Make a fire, Build a Shelter, Boil 32oz of water in no more than 5 minutes per skill for a total of 15 minutes. Fifteen minutes is a crucial element because that is approximately the amount of time it takes your body to begin exhibiting symptoms of hypothermia (by lack of finger dexterity) and hyperthermia (by becoming dizzy and light-headed). By enforcing this timed dynamic, situational awareness is developed, hard skills mastered, and fear eliminated as they're able to perform skills quickly and effectively under stress. By starting with these necessary skills, you'll not only prepare your children for stressful times but have a significant bit of family fun doing it.

Teaching loved ones and friends

Leading adult outdoor classes is one of the most gratifying experiences one can take part in. You have the opportunity to soak in God's creation, develop bonds, and impart skills not enjoyed by the majority of modern society. But how do you run a class? The most significant indicator of a real outdoor educator is their willingness to learn by doing. This ancient Biblical principle is often overlooked, "Be a doer of the will of God, not just a hearer that gets tricked easily" (James 1:22); they delve into their learning environments through experience-based initiatives. When they read about skills or tools from history, they experiment with them (experimental archaeology), and through their experimentation, they learn skills by experiencing them first hand.

Experiential education, in a nutshell, is learning by doing combined with reflection. This type of education is the best method to pass on tribal knowledge; it's been done this way for millennia. As you pass on your skills from one to another through personal contact with friends and family, learn to teach effectively. It's in that vein that I offer these tips to help you understand the basics of effective outdoor leadership.

These tips have been adapted from the Association of Experiential Education's guidelines for educators and are pretty much the standard for professional outdoor leaders.

1. Use Direct and purposeful experiences.
All change and growth have some sort of experience at their origin; our job as instructors is to place our students as close as possible to that origin. Why? Because this process can be the most productive for lasting positive change over other learning methods such as books or videos. Students may read about or watch videos on making a five-minute fire, but until they see the preparation period involved, learn the fire lay, then do it for themselves; it's all been theory. By directing their actions toward making the five-minute fire, they learn through the experience of gathering material, then processing that material, and ultimately lighting the fire. So, each step of our curriculum must reflect purpose toward a more significant end-result. Random skills thrown in "just because" rob students of direct and purposeful experiences.

2. Challenge Students.
The most remarkable change occurs when a person is placed outside of their comfort zone and into a state of dissonance (the need to resolve the discrepancy that caused their discomfort), where there are degrees of perceived risk. They must think hard to regain equilibrium. Thus, we should strive to place our students in an environment and in situations where the level of risk- both real and perceived- fosters a motivating attitude to change and retain the changes. For example, when I tell students to soak their arms in an icy creek in the middle of winter then make a fire in under five minutes, they think it's insane, unsafe, and initially, they refuse. Colleagues have even told me that it's too hardcore of an exercise. The stress levels peak during this event; there's often some cussing, internal angst, and arguments with partners-

the perceived risk is significant. However, once they do it, often well under time, they've been motivated to make this achievement their new low standard of what's possible and usually never go back to their old ways.

3. Allow for Natural Consequences

Natural consequences occur from the setting, situation, and circumstances of the class without human interaction. The ramifications of decisions made by students provide realistic, immediate, and often, individualized feedback. When appropriate, utilize natural consequences to match a student's choices or behavior, thereby providing a basis for growth. This technique can apply to something as simple as failure to pack an item on the pack list. The student's decision to watch television the night before class instead of getting the last thing they needed resulting in their inability to complete an assigned task. Thus, immediate, individualized feedback results.

Conversely, artificial consequences occur if an instructor anticipates or responds to a student's action, causing an artificial consequence to modify the natural result. Such as the instructor giving the student the item they failed to pack. We modified the natural result by providing a solution that did nothing to instill lasting change. If we forgot an essential item in real life, while in the field, we'd have to make do without or improvise; why should it be any different in a class should one fail to pre-plan appropriately, especially when it's all written out for them? It's one thing to replace broken gear or upgrade cheap or even the wrong type of equipment, but failure to follow a list results in a natural consequence that the student must deal with. Critical thinking exercises are a great way to gauge team dynamics

It would be best to avoid artificial consequences more often than not because we want changes that come through classes to become student-based rather than instructor-determined. Lasting student-based changes begin at a place appropriate for each person and progress as each student's pace to an outcome that meets their needs. Students make personal investments in choosing the type, level, and value of their class experiences in this process. Student-based changes have future relevance because they help resolve problems in the current class and attain a new equilibrium. Still, they will also prove helpful in improving daily life. In this example, they will not depend on others to provide their needed equipment in the field, will learn to make do without or improvise, and they'll pay closer attention to details.

4. Synthesis and Reflection are used as elements of the change process. Sometimes change is not an automatic result, and this is where synthesis and reflection can internalize proposed changes in the student. This process is accomplished through campfire chats, debriefings, individual or group discussions, journaling, or drawing. As a professional outdoor instructor, you should encourage this creative process in your students' work and learning to deepen the experiential process.

5. Encourage Personal Responsibility. Students are compelled to become personally responsible for outdoor experiences. The activity itself draws them into action; they should not be forced to participate by you or other leaders, nor should they be motivated by reward. Experiential teaching applies methods and activities that encourage personal involvement and personal responsibility, especially challenge by choice, to give students power and control over their learning. It's the student's responsibility to complete their assigned tasks and thereby the class, it's not the instructor's job to make them or do it for them.

6. Active Engagement. Outdoor classes require problem-solving, curiosity, and inquiry, and they are followed by synthesis and reflection. Students can deal with new situations by applying what they have learned and applied from previous problems. This active process requires students to be self-motivated and responsible for their learning and growth. Your job as an instructor is

to facilitate this responsibility based on each student's individual needs and abilities.

4 Learning Styles

We can break down learners into four distinct categories. You must have at least a precursory understanding of these four learning methods. It will enable you to quickly diagnose students' learning difficulties in classes and address them rapidly, thereby avoiding frustrations for all involved. Educators call this the VARK model, VARK is an acronym for Visual, Auditory, Reading, Kinesthetic (Hands-on).

1. *Visual* learners process information through charts and graphs and prefer images to explain concepts and ideas. They like to see things done instead of only hearing how they're done.

2. *Auditory* learners receive spoken information the most readily. They like lectures and discussions and process information by talking it through.

3. *Reading/ Writing* Learners prefer written words. They like written instructions and processes by writing notes. They often enjoy reading and writing assignments and process through writing things out.

4. *Kinesthetic* Learners are hands-on learners. They prefer concrete personal experience and process information by recreating and practicing.

By including all four learning styles into your training curriculum, you will reach all your students more effectively.

The Campfire Counselor

Some of our greatest breakthroughs can happen around the campfire. Peter the apostle betrayed Jesus while sitting at a campfire (Luke

22:54-62), and while this act was prophesied only hours before by Christ himself, Jesus would later use this same campfire scenario to reconcile Peter to the Kingdom (John 21: 1-19). Meal-time and story-time are often the most productive times while at camp from a spiritual perspective. It is your time to share your testimony and journey with Christ along the trail of life. With these simplistic leadership skills, you can create a discipleship ministry, youth group, or survival group. By teaching all the skills you have learned from this book, you have all you need to provide fundamental training in the four areas of Modern Survival, which are wilderness skills, winter skills, bushcraft hygiene, and urban survival, the latter of which we will now examine in greater detail.

20

Urban Awareness

You may be asking yourself why you need training in Urban Survival. People have been living well in the resource-rich urban landscape for thousands of years. You may live in the city or suburbs of an urban environment yourself. After all, the United Nations reports that as of 2017, 55%, or 4.1 billion people, live in an urban environment worldwide. Urban areas include towns and suburbs with high population density per square mile with access to commercial buildings, bridges, railways, roads, and multiple housing types. Urban areas are, of course, resource-rich having a variety of materials readily available, ranging from shops and stores to kitchens, office buildings, and construction sites.

These higher populations and resource options dictate a change in the order of your survival priorities; safety is of greater importance since heat or fire, water, shelter, and food are often available in abundance. While wilderness survival focuses on the rescue of self or others to get back to civilization, Urban Survival is about remaining unnoticed as you gather what's needed to survive and stay in a safe location. In this field book, I will first address how to prepare your home to bug-in as safety and security begin at home, then we will work our way toward bugging-out which takes us into more wilderness-like skill sets.

Situational Awareness

Simply put, situational awareness is the ability to know what is going on around you—paying attention to where you are, who's around you, and what's going on at all times. In an urban environment, this is vital as there are so many dynamic factors that come into play at any given moment. Moving cars, trains, multiple buildings, sightlines, and masses of people may all come into play during a crisis. In an age where most of us are focused on continual media, be it from a phone, tablet, or ear-buds vying for our attention, practicing continual situational awareness is a skill sorely lacking in society.

I like to play with my family as we go out to reinforce their situational awareness. As we enter a restaurant, I may ask what color the car was nearest the door or how many people did we pass as we walked to the table. The more I can do to keep my wife and kids thinking about their surroundings, the better off we'll all be as I may have missed something. Should a crisis occur, I'd rather have several pairs of eyes scanning for resources than just my own. Alternatively, I also like to point out people from the room to my wife and children so they know who to avoid and who to make an example of should the need arise (we call this the Jack Reacher theory). The 'Jack Reacher Theory' is just something my kids coined after watching the movie Jack Reacher starring Tom Cruise. In the movie, he has to fight a handful of opponents, and beforehand he notes that he will not have to fight them all because he will make such a devastating first blow that only the true friend of the guy he hits first will defend him while the others scatter. The reason this scene made such an impact on my kids is that I have applied this in a few actual fights and I have taught it to them since they were quite young. It was part of my self-defense training and I learned it in part from readings of ancient ninja and samurai. Here is some samurai wisdom from Kawakami Gensai (lived 1834-1872) who was a noted master swordsman and assassin of the late Edo period.

Gensai instructs:
"*When entering a room where a social gathering is taking place, pause and observe. Assess those not taking part in conversation or drink. The one*

or two who hold silent, yet whose eyes are in steady motion, circling the room; these are the most dangerous men to deal with. Those holding center in conversation and festivities, brandishing expensive attire, or lost in drink, are the weak. To eliminate your mark, be vigilant of the dangerous men. In enacting your movement and in taking a position, stay close to the weak on approach to the target. If recognized, quickly eliminate one of the vulnerable to stun the crowd momentarily. Then immediately, without pausing for a breath, kill your mark and make your escape. Only engage the dangerous, if necessary. Retaining anonymity is essential."

This leads us into our modern OODA Loop decision-making process. This process allows you to direct your energy to win a situation and survive. OODA is a continuous cycle that involves feedback from your environment and your actions. OODA stands for Observe, Orient, Decide, Act.

Observe is the process of seeing and absorbing input from your environment, your situation, possible threats, including feedback from your actions or inactions.

Orient is processing the inputs you observed and comparing them to your previous experiences, cultural traditions, genetic heritage, and new information, then analyzing and synthesizing them to formulate your options.

Decide is choosing the best course of action given previous inputs.

Act is putting your thoughts in motion. Action is a test to see if you are getting your desired result. You observe the results of your action and the loop repeats itself.

Being situationally aware will keep you out of trouble and stay ahead of the OODA loop. Thus, in playing awareness games, you continuously observe available resources in the surrounding environment, orient or figure out things to do with those resources and then decide how to use them to your advantage best when it's time to act. Colonel Jeff Cooper developed the situational awareness color code, which adds nicely to the OODA Loop. It is the mental process for alertness based upon your surroundings:

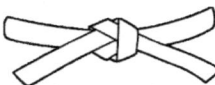

White: When you are in a White state, your mind is off, and you are completely relaxed. You are unaware of what is going on around you. Unless you are asleep, you should strive to not be in condition White.

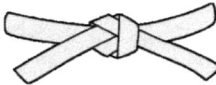

Yellow: This is a relaxed state, but you know what is going on around you. You are paying attention and are not entirely caught off guard by people's actions. You are entirely aware of your surroundings.

Orange: You have identified something that could be a threat. Action is not required yet, but further attention is needed. Until proven otherwise, the perceived threat is on your radar. Do not become so focused that you develop tunnel vision. While in condition Orange you should be working through the initial stages of your OODA loop. This what-if game plays out in your head and lets you identify exits, cover, and concealment for plans of action.

THE GOSPEL OF SURVIVAL

Red: is the change from a possible threat to an actual threat. At this point, you are in action. Depending on your situation, your weapon is out; you may be leaving the area, verbally confronting the threat, seeking cover, or possibly shielding others.

> *"...Son of man, see with your eyes, hear with your ears, and give attention to all that I am going to show you; for you have been brought here in order to show it to you. Declare to the house of Israel all that you see."*
> ~ Ezekiel 40:4

Awareness is a Biblical concept and aids us in preparing to endure the things we may not always be prepared for.

Should I stay or should I go?
At some point in our OODA Loop, we'll identify the need to hunker down or get out of the current area during a crisis. This thought process brings with it its own unique set of challenges. Before delving into specifics, let's briefly examine some thoughts should we decide to remain in an urban area.

- People have always been able to survive in an urban setting. Wars have been fought in cities while the population continued with their lives.
- Staying in a familiar location with known area resources keeps you more independent for a short-term situation and buys you valuable time in a longer-term condition.
- Stealth and operational security become extremely important.
- The first places for order, medicine, or utilities to be restored will be urban areas of higher population.

- The worst fighting and most chaos will also take place in urban areas.
- Urban areas will serve as operational bases in major disasters, which would mean an increased military and police presence with large influxes of displaced people from the region.
- Rioting, if present, may be limited to a specific area within a city and may or may not pose a life threat.
- Those most dependent upon public services (housing, food, etc.) live nearest the public centers; when these services cease, they will have to search for sustenance.

In cities across the nation and around the world, in the Spring and Summer of 2020, we witnessed mass protesting over racial injustice and inequality. We also noticed how local television news and social media could distort and disrupt events on the ground during these events. According to the Associated Press Stylebook, which sets reporting guidelines for news agencies around the world "Use care in deciding which term best applies: A riot is a wild or violent disturbance of the peace involving a group of people. The term riot suggests uncontrolled chaos and pandemonium."

Thus, according to the media, a riot may now include vandalism, looting, assault, and wanton endangerment (an action likely to cause bodily harm to another person) as a "Mostly peaceful protest." By continually reporting this "peaceful" narrative and showing armed riot response by law enforcement agencies, further violence erupts, and a louder outcry of injustice prevails despite the opposite being reality. It's hard for the average person to make an informed decision on when to leave the area or remain to shelter in place due to this double-minded reporting.

When people are saying, "Everything is peaceful and secure," then disaster will fall on them as suddenly as a pregnant woman's labor pains begin. And there will be no escape.

~ 1 Thessalonians 5:3

Before making the decision to stay or go, first, create what is called a PACE Plan. P.A.C.E. stands for primary, alternate, contingency, emergency.

Primary: Your primary plan should always be to stay home. We also call this Bugging-In or Sheltering in Place. Home is where most of your loved ones are, your food, supplies, and other essential gear. You are also the one most familiar with your home's layout, yard, and neighborhood. So, defending it should you have to is in your favor.

Alternate: Ideally, an alternative to staying home would be to go to another Bug-in Location. Perhaps you have a cabin in the woods or a small cottage you could go to for several days until the danger has passed. Maybe a relative that lives out of town has space for you- or perhaps you have a family camper you could hook up to get away until the danger has passed. In any of these situations, you will have ample opportunity to stock your needed supplies in advance of any such emergency. This alternate location is somewhere you could get to by vehicle. In the best of circumstances, you'll have multiple locations in opposing directions since you never know where disaster may strike. Along planned travel routes, you could even place caches for specialized equipment. Maybe in a nearby town's storage area, buried in a friend's backyard, or even along a country road. Whatever alternate plan you develop, it is yours to understand and use. Make sure it will work for you and make certain you create a map so other family members can use it if you are not available.

Contingency: This plan would follow the previous procedures, but a vehicle is no longer available as a resource. You may not be able to drive for whatever reason, or perhaps the area has become non-permissive, requiring you to move with haste in stealth. You will follow your same travel routes on foot to your planned alternate bug-out locations.

Emergency: The emergency plan is your worst-case scenario. It would be best if you fled with whatever you can carry due to immediate danger. You are now a refugee. Running on foot is a Bug-Out in its most primal form.

Historically, refugees who remain in urban environments lose access to necessary survival equipment, like firearms, knives, and tools to make them utterly dependent upon those in control. Never be forced to become a refugee; develop a solid PACE plan.

Passover, the Bug-Out Model

As we've discussed in this book, the Old and New Testament Biblical Passover events took place in Urban Environments. Let's look at it now from the perspective of an urban survivalist. The Passover discussed in the Biblical book of Exodus occurred after months of severe civil unrest. The unrest was in the form of plagues upon Egyptian society, crippling the entire nation's economy and day-to-day life. Pharaoh ordered over one million people to flee their homes and land in the middle of the night. Men, women, and children had to flee their homes. The Hebrew families took all they could carry, including unleavened bread and livestock, on their escape. They traveled overnight approximately twenty-five miles before their first encampment (Sukkot). They traveled over the next seventy-two hours until they crossed the Red Sea- all the while evading capture by the army that was chasing them.

This Passover became an annual Rehearsal (Practice) commanded by God for all time (Ex. 12:14). We are to prepare our homes for escape be-

THE GOSPEL OF SURVIVAL

forehand- cleaning them from the evidence of living in them (Ex.12:15). We are to be prepared to flee, be fully dressed, shoes on our feet, staff in hand, and eat quickly (Ex. 12:11). In the New Testament, we see this same pattern. He instructed his disciples to prepare Passover's feast in an appointed place (a clean home). As they ate the meal, Jesus forewarned of his impending capture and death, offering Himself as the body and blood of the lamb given for the forgiveness of all mankind's sin. Upon conclusion of the meal, they fled to the Garden to pray and keep watch.

Once in the Garden, Jesus reprimanded his disciples for not being watchful, admonishing them to keep watch with him, lest they be tempted by "the enemy". The impending capture weighed so significantly upon Jesus; he sweats blood due to the stress of what was to come. Because no one watched with him, the guards captured Jesus just as He foretold (and as appointed by God the Father). His disciples acted in their teacher's defense by attacking a guard and cutting off his guard's ear. But it was too late, God appointed Jesus to die for humanity as the Prophets foretold, and so he did as his disciples fled around the city in secret. Seventy-two hours later, Jesus rose, only to find his disciples in hiding, at which time he sent them on a new mission to the world. Thus, we see in the Passover, escape, and capture in a bug-out situation. We are to practice Passover every Spring to remain prepared for the coming of the Messiah Jesus.

From these passages of scripture, we can glean some things beyond the command to practice this holiday every year.

1. Live simplistically and pack light. Keeping our homes clean and in order, it keeps us from having to search for things. We're to have our essentials at hand always.
2. If the family is going with us, we can carry more gear. The equipment needed to sustain children and pets can be burdensome for a sole individual.

3. Don't depend on friends to help you when everyone needs help. You're ultimately responsible for yourself/your family unit.
4. If you must fight your way out, it may be too little too late. It would be best if you had left sooner.

Reorienting Priorities

In previous book sections, we've discussed Survival's 5 Smooth Stones- or survival priorities. This section has already mentioned how these priorities will change due to the lack of a nearby wilderness interface. Let's examine the five areas of focus and how drastically they change for the urban landscape. We'll delve further into each of these areas with specific skills later.

Safety: While always a top concern, security may now include the use of hot and cold weapons (guns and knives), homeopathic first aid, alarms, and warning systems, and escape and evasion protocols to maintain personal safety and security. While glossed over in wilderness skills, they become of greater importance now due to the increased potential for conflict due to a diverse population.

Water: Easy to find, but not always safe to drink. Depending on the type of emergency, it may be possible to continue to obtain water from the tap for some time. However, tap water may still require purification. Having alternative methods to make water safe for consumption without only relying on boiling is of primary importance. A high-quality water filtration system that removes waterborne pathogens and chemicals will solve most urban water filtration issues.

Shelter: Easily found, but not always easily defended. Service buildings, sheds, outbuildings, and abandoned areas will all serve as temporary shelters, but look for multiple exits with a lower chance of encountering other people.

Food: Required for constant movement. Initially, during a crisis, food will be abundant. However, in as little as three days, certain types of food can become scarce. Within three weeks, it will be virtually nonexistent. Get it while you can.

Fire: Fire gives off light and smoke, which alerts people to your position and can cause unnecessary risk to your life. In an urban area, fire risks from surrounding buildings and debris may be high. Warmth should be sought through proper clothing, insulative shelters, and chemical warmers whenever possible (hot hands).

The Minimum State of Preparedness

We've discussed much of this in Chapter 4, but adapting it to urban survival, we much know the risks for our area. While some weather-related disasters are seasonal, others are not. Fires, Floods, Earthquakes, Pandemics, and power outages are all risks that face everyone.

Have a Plan. Understand how to shut off the utilities to your home, meet if the house is no longer safe, and have alternate routes to get to or leave your home. Have a back-up method of communicating with loved ones.

Refrigerated foods begin to spoil in as little as four hours. Have a plan in place to circumvent this obstacle. FEMA recommends a 2-week shelf-stable food supply for each family member at the minimum. I regard FEMA recommendations as to the barrel's bottom, so take this for what you will.

If you have pets, make sure that you include them in your plan as a family member.

Remember to have back-ups of any necessary prescriptions and, if possible, back-ups of your important documents and prescription eyeglasses.

Essential Supply Kit (Per Person)

72hr Kit

- Small Tool Kit that includes lighters wrenches for utilities and a can opener
- Weather Radio
- Lanterns & Flashlights
- Phone Chargers with Emergency Phone if possible
- Extra Batteries
- Duct Tape
- Roll of 3mil Plastic Sheeting or a Tarp
- Rescue Whistle
- Wool Blanket
- First Aid Kit
- Toilet Paper
- Map of Area
- Change of Clothing
- 3 days of Food
- 3 days of water (3 gals.)

These essential supplies are geared more towards the storm and natural disaster emergencies such as earthquakes, wildfire, snowstorms, power outages, etc. We recommend keeping critical supplies in a tote if possible. So that should you be forced to vacate due to said emergency, each individual could grab their tote and have what they need for at least three days. Having multiples permits the ability to barter items or allow flexibility in what's packed in the tote. For example, your children would not require wrenches for utilities or other tools, so they could instead pack snacks, games, or another personal item.

Food & Hygiene Supply Kit Recommendations (2+ weeks)
These recommendations are for a long-term emergency such as a power outage, flood, pandemic, or hurricane. Designed for staying home, you would still have access to everything in your house. Again, these are the minimum recommendations.

Please do not put all of your eggs in one basket when it comes to food storage. Investing in nothing but MRE's will result in bloating, gas, severe fatigue, and intense constipation after eating them for a few days. According to the U.S. Surgeon General, MRE's are for fighting men that require energy to stay in the fight for up to 21 days. At this time, they would return to base to receive another form of nutrition. Food diversity is a necessity to maintain good health physically and mentally. If you don't already eat it regularly, don't store it! When you hate rice and don't know how to cook dry beans, buying hundreds of rice and beans pounds means this foodstuff will likely waste. It's perfectly acceptable to only store things you know you will eat regularly, including your Chef Boyardee Ravioli.

Honey, Vitamins, Minerals, Dry Milk, and Protein Powders are vital to good health over the long term. The majority of emergency foods are high in sodium and preservatives to give them a longer shelf life. By supplementing vitamins and powders, which also have long shelf stability, we add variety to our diets. Food combinations aid us in processing those higher-than-average amounts of other preservatives. Also, consider adding fiber supplements to your stored foods via a powder or capsule form. Fiber will ensure you do not have any bowel obstruction and maintain good health.

At a minimum, keep a two-week supply of hygiene items per person in your family. Hygiene items include toothpaste, sanitary pads, shampoo, soaps, toilet tissue, Kleenex, and everything else that falls under your regular hygiene routine. Cleaning supplies for the house such as bleach, surface cleaners, glass cleaners, etc. Georgia Pacific recommends that a four-person household keep 17 double rolls or nine mega rolls to last approximately 2 weeks.

The 2-week food supply per person in your family that you create should, again, be composed of ordinary things you eat. Your essential emergency supplies, those from the storm prep tote, should not be included in this calculation. Also, have multiple methods to purify drinking water. Purification methods should consist of Sawyer style filters and chemical decontamination methods such as unscented bleach and iodine. It would be best if you also considered storage containers such as Water Bags that fit inside the tub and other means of collecting large amounts of rainwater. Store and use municipal water for as long as you can.

And lastly, have a two-week supply of general first aid and medical supplies available. Anti-septic washes, alcohol, hand sanitizer, band-aids, tourniquets, burn gels, and itch creams. A well-stocked home first aid kit is a staple.

We have now been under a national quarantine period for the past several months due to COVID-19. In many states, mandated travel is essential only, such as work, medical issues, or supplies. Everyone in America became a prepper for the first two weeks of the quarantine, which nearly crippled the supply chain. As panic buying has eased up, people are more concerned about the long-term economic effects of their employment. The "new normal," as the government calls it, is nothing more than a police-state, which we must now learn to negotiate.

While the preceding 2-week guidelines may have certainly eased your burden at the onset of the COVID19 pandemic had you had them, they are minimum for a reason. Things change, and all emergencies are dynamic and changing until they resolve. With this in mind, let's examine ways to achieve practical self-reliance so we might master the art of bugging-in which should be primary in your PACE plan.

Practical Prepping

Preparing the Elderly

Preparing for an emergency situation is a difficult task. It is a task made even more challenging when elderly people are involved. Maybe your parents have recently moved in with you for care. Alternatively, they may live nearby and you want to include them in your family's survival plan should a natural disaster or other emergency situation occur. In either case, planning now for the added challenges of caring for your loved ones during a crisis will pay off when the plan is put into action. During a disaster is not the time to begin thinking about survival.

If you already have a survival plan in place you are already one step ahead. Additional provisions can be included to help the elderly loved ones in your life. Elderly people present a unique set of challenges that are often not considered when creating or modifying a survival plan. It is essential to understand these components now so adjustments can be made allowing for everyone's survival.

1) Medication – Your elderly family members will often be prescribed medication essential to their health. These prescriptions can range from blood pressure control and other heart-related illness to even more severe diseases. The American Red Cross recommends having at least seven days of medication available at all times. Even more, would be ideal. In the event of an emergency, pharmacies may close or be inaccessible. The supply chain can also be interrupted, meaning that it is no longer available during the crisis.

2) Mobility – Your loved one's mobility may be compromised by age or a medical condition. Those in your care may need canes, walkers, wheelchairs, or other mobility devices in the event of a disaster. These devices can be large and cumbersome to transport. Realizing that these devices are required for movement means making considerations for them when designing a survival or evacuation plan. Even people fortunate enough not to rely on these devices to get around will surely be less agile than some of your younger family members. Hopping over a small picket fence in the backyard may seem like a no-brainer for you and your children. Still, it may present a significant obstacle for an elderly parent.

3) Personal Devices – Eyeglasses, hearing aids, and dentures may easily be forgotten during an emergency. Overlooking such essential items will make survival difficult at best for the elderly. Consider how you will guarantee that these items will be available when needed. Ideally, an extra set of all required personal devices can be kept in a safe place with all other survival gear. If this is not possible, figure out a way to guarantee that the items will not be left behind.

4) Other Medical Equipment – In addition to the minor medical equipment already mentioned, some people also rely on additional devices for survival. Oxygen tanks are a big one as the supply of oxygen can be severely limited during a survival situation. So, plan on storing extra oxygen tanks in a secure location that is easily accessible. Take the necessary precautions to ensure safety as compressed oxygen is extremely flammable. Pacemakers are another possible consideration. Although a pacemaker cannot be replaced in the field, realizing that they are susceptible to electronic disturbances may affect evacuation plans or even self-defense initiatives.

5) Driving – As people age, their ability to operate a vehicle safely diminishes. Many older people do not drive. If they live with you, make sure there is enough room in the car for everyone during an evacuation. If the family member(s) live somewhere else, figure out how they will travel and make provisions to assist them if necessary. Try not to rely on public transportation as it may become rendered useless during an emergency.

6) Pets – Do you or your elderly family member have any pets? Since older adults are already at a disadvantage during a survival situation, taking pets should be considered carefully. Most disaster shelters will not accept pets (except service animals). Plan to bring the pets if possible or give them the very best chance of survival.

7) Specialized Caregivers – Many older people have caregivers that may help with various tasks such as administering medication, checking blood glucose, and assisting with catheter insertion. During an emergency, these tasks may have to be completed by a member of your family. Someone must be familiar with the medical procedures required for each individual and take the time to learn any specialized techniques needed in the absence of trained medical staff.

The key to understanding the exact difficulties you will face is making an honest assessment of everyone's abilities.

19 Items to add to your Home Kit
Many things should be in everyone's home emergency readiness kit, as we've already discussed. The following items will allow you to survive when travel is not possible. When you need to shelter-in-place; even if you evacuate your home and head to a safe secondary location (bug-out), have these additional items part of your PACE plan.

A 30-day food supply: Non-perishable food supplies for each household member or in your survival party. It could be quite a haul. We'll get into a budget strategy in a few.

A 30- day water supply: at a minimum, this means one gallon of water per person per day, and this does not include water used for cooking. Some medications require ingesting with juice or milk. Plan for this if you or your loved ones are on any of these medications. If you can't store a 30-day water supply, purchase a water filter such as the Berky Filter. If your plan includes leaving home, get a personal filtration device for each member of your group, such as the Grayl Geopress.

A Portable battery-powered radio: Make sure to also include extra batteries for the device. The radio will alert you to changes in the situation and possible emergency response presence.

Flashlights and Chem Lights and extra batteries: In low light conditions, chem lights will provide the light necessary to set up equipment, administer medication, and provide medical treatment if required while maintaining a low profile. If elderly family members have poor eyesight, a flashlight will allow them to move around more safely.

Family First Aid kit – Having a well-stocked first aid kit will allow you to treat minor wounds during a crisis. Taking a first aid class is beneficial for learning more advanced first aid techniques.

Sanitation and hygiene items: The basics include toilet paper, hand sanitizer, and soap. But include shampoo, deodorant, toothpaste, and all your other regular hygiene items. For elderly family members, also consider adult diapers (if required) and denture paste. Again, a 30-day supply is an initial goal.

Alternative cooking: Multiple surfaces permit your options when it comes to food preparation. When power may not be available, consider Coleman fuel stoves, propane stoves, and even alcohol stoves. Plan on at minimum a 30-day supply of fuels so that variety will permit for more comfortable storage options.

Extra proper clothing: should not be much of an issue while bugging-in, but everyone in the family will need spare clothing. Try to pack at least one outfit for each possible weather condition (warm, cold, rain, etc.) that you may experience. If your elderly parents do not live with you, ask if they have spare clothes that you can pack in the readiness kit.

Blankets: Blankets provide warmth and padding from the ground or other hard surfaces. Remember that the elderly are more prone to hypothermia, especially during stressful situations.

Cooking utensils: Packing necessary kitchen supplies will make food preparation easier during a crisis. You may prefer paper plates or compostable flatware over those requiring washing.

Rolled Plastic: Plastic sheeting is a multipurpose tool that will enable you to winterize your home, create a decontamination room during a chemical attack, patch your roof in a storm, or create an improvised shelter on the run.

Barter Items should the friends or neighbors come calling. You always want to maintain peace and normalcy as long as possible, so helping a friend or neighbor with a tool or meal can go a long way in a stressful situation. Ramen Soup mixes go a long way and are cheap; big-box store "survival" tools such as knives, fire-starters, etc., typically found in gift packs, are also affordable and look like a great help. Alcohol and other vice items are also a great way to get things done in a pinch.

Photo ID: Make copies of the photo identification for everyone in the family. Store these in the kit for use later. Passports included.

Cash: Store some money in the kit as well. Ask your parents if they will contribute to this fund as well. Having cash on hand is always a good idea because electronics may fail in an emergency, rendering your credit cards useless. Also, consider coins or valuable jewelry that could be traded for supplies if necessary. Cash will lose value during a crisis.

Special Needs Items: Special needs items include medications, batteries for hearing aids, and eyeglasses. Be sure to fully understand the medical requirements of any elderly adults in your family. Include medication they take daily as well as those that they only need on occasion. Keep at least a 30-day supply of all drugs stored in the readiness kit.

Cell phone with charger: Having a non-smartphone is a great way to communicate in an emergency. They do not rely on internet services to operate.

Whistle: The shrill sound of a whistle can be heard for miles. Using a whistle can signal emergency responders to your location. Elderly loved ones can also use it under medical duress if you are not in the immediate area.

Extra set of car and house key*s*: Leaving these items stored in a readiness kit means that you will not have to waste time looking for them in an emergency. Also, keep a spare set of keys for your elderly parents' home if they do not live with you.

Police Scanner: While you have power or while attached to your battery backup, a police scanner will keep you up to speed on what's going on around your town. Here you can gather intelligence on when you may need to consider a bug-out.

THE GOSPEL OF SURVIVAL

21

Urban Kit Development

Gear carried in an urban scenario must meet individual needs based on the distance to travel, terrain, weather, lifestyle, and skill level. Urban survival kits should be lightweight, not leave an imprint, and should blend in with the area or people you find yourself. Tactical clothing, morale patches, and the like are obvious identifiers. The national average commute is 16 miles one way to work. That is quite a long distance to travel with a heavy pack of gear. If you are in shape and traveling light, that's usually a 5hr walk. Can you do that now in an emergency with 30lbs of gear? Fitness is the most overlooked aspect of survival training and skills. Stay functional; you don't need to be a cross-fit athlete, be able to jog, crawl, and navigate obstacles with a light load on your back.

Thinking like a smuggler will also be beneficial. Understanding that you can pick up specific tools along the intended path of travel or make them on the run is a skill in itself. Learn to utilize or recreate standard tools from everyday items (we'll cover this more in Fieldcraft). The area you travel through may be non-permissive (secured), so expensive survival devices may be confiscated. Think ahead and be ready to ditch what you must only to recreate it later.

Urban Kits are based upon the Emergent C's, but tiered:

- Tier 1 is EDC Gear
- Tier 2 is a shoulder bag or day pack

THE GOSPEL OF SURVIVAL

- Tier 3 is a Bug Out Bag
- Tier 4 is a Vehicle Kit
- Tier 5 is an INCH (I'm Never Coming Home) bag

"No one owns life, but anyone who can pick up a frying pan can own death"

~ William S. Burroughs

The Tier 1 Kit

Wallet (Fresnel and E & E inside), lighter, sharp bottle opener/cordage, Legal Blade

Tier 1 is an everyday carry (EDC) system that will serve you in lifestyle, emergency, self-defense, escape, and evasion. It should be concealable and comfortable enough to carry on the body daily.

The kit should include:

- Knife
- Lighter
- Handkerchief

- Wallet: cash, id, cards, Fresnel lens + change
- Phone
- Two key-rings on climbing grade carabiner (self-aid and defense)
- Firearm with reload
- E & E Kit if in high-risk kidnapping zones (cuff key, lock picks, razors, shims, saws, chem light)

Pro Tips

Two is one, one is none. This military adage applies to your EDC. You don't want to be without these items if possible. Imagine, if you will, a primary knife on your waist, but a second, perhaps a razor knife hidden in your boot or jacket. One of these knives should be a ditch knife, one that could be easily ditched if confiscated, broken, or lost.

Cash in your wallet, and also a couple of $100 bills hidden in the sole of your shoe. Cash will still work during the initial onset of a crisis. A lighter in your pocket but a Ferro rod on the pull of your jacket zipper. Think outside the box here and consider a social lubricant to gain access or gather intelligence. A 50ml (airline size) bottle of alcohol or pack of smokes can open many doors with locals. A prepaid Tracfone is also an excellent tool so long as it's not connected to your personal information. Your Escape and Evasion (E & E) kit should be multiplied and well-hidden to permit as many opportunities for use as possible. A necklace, sewn into your pants, hidden in your belt, or a bracelet. Handcuff keys, shims, micro saws, and a chem light will permit several methods of escape from illegal detention.

The Tier 2 Kit

Photo courtesy of Anthony Awaken Photography

Tier 2 equipment features larger core survival equipment that's too difficult to carry at all times. Carry these items within a sling, shoulder bag, or day pack. Again, the carry bag must fit your lifestyle, be of average appearance, and match your local environment. You could think of this as a light haversack load out.

Tie 2 Kit Items:

- Fighting Knife or Machete
- Full Fire Kit
- Stainless Steel Water Container
- Paracord and Bankline
- Small roll Gorilla Tape
- 2 Drum Liners
- Headlamp and Flashlight

- Multi-Tool/ Sillcock Key
- Shemagh/ Triangular Bandage
- IFAK
- Personal Medication
- Phone Charger + Extra Battery
- Tool Kit (Lock Picks, Wrenches, Bolt Cutters, Wire Cutters)
- Snacks and drink mixes (hydration and caffeine)

The Tier 3 Kit

Photo courtesy of Anthony Awaken Photography

The Tier 3 kit is a traditional Bug Out Bag in a medium-sized (20-26L) backpack. This kit is further building upon previous tiers by providing further kit redundancy and new options.

- Poncho added to cover category along with functional rain gear.
- Red lens option added to the headlamp (mandatory for urban)
- Safety pins and sewing kit added to cloth & sail needle
- Cerate should include a complete First Aid kit with multiple Tourniquets

- Dust Mask, safety or dust goggles, and leather gloves
- Complete change of clothes including footwear
- High-calorie foods for energy

Pro tips

The Bug Out Bag is not to make or keep you comfortable, but mobile. Food is a necessity for continuous travel, as is hydration. The contents of a bug-out bag will enable you to travel largely uninhibited from the need for hunting, trapping, or scavenging. Your primary objective with this kit is to travel from an unsafe area to a safe location, hopefully, your alternate bug out location.

The Tier 4 Kit

Tier 4 is a vehicle kit that will contain oversized, heavy-duty gear too heavy to carry. A vehicle may be subjective; conveyance may be more appropriate. You may transport tier 4 tools in a shopping cart or any other type of carriage or sled.

Kit items:

- Recovery & Service gear to keep vehicle operational
- Tent, Sleeping Bag, cold weather gear, extra boots, socks, and blankets
- Pioneer tools such as felling ax, bow saws, shovel, rope, sensible tool kit
- High lift jack with a tow strap and come along
- Long Jumper cables with 12v air compressor/charging system
- Robust First Aid Kit (Family Size)
- Long Guns, ammo for hunting/ defense- but not so expensive that it could not be abandoned or disabled
- Camp/tent stove with food and water

Tier 5 Kit, The INCH

Tier 5 is the I'm Never Coming Home Bag. It is unreasonable to believe that anyone can live solely off the land in modern times with society's infringement. In a dire emergency, it's simply not feasible. So, this kit level is added or collected to establish your new or alternate bug-out or safe space. This is the kit you will begin to use to supplement all other preparations you have acquired.

All previously listed tiers plus:

- Essential Hunting & Trapping Tools
  - *Traps, snares, wire, pliers, bow and arrow, etc.*
- Fishing Equipment
  - *Poles, yo-yo's, hooks, lures, line, bobbers, etc.*
- Essential Firearms, reloading equipment, and accessories
- Seasonal clothing & footwear needs
- Essential wilderness living gear: carving tools, gouges, spoon knives, carving hatchets, augers, draw knives, etc.

The layers represented here combined would weigh upwards of a few hundred pounds. It's not at all practical to carry them. However, they can be staged and distributed among the caches on your pre-planned escape routes to your alternate safe house. Your PACE Plan should permit you to figure out the best solution for your family's needs.

Equipment Caches

Items that are inconvenient or impossible to carry cache off sight in a safe location. Redundant core kit items, longer-term supplies such as food, clothing, shelter, and tools make great cache items. Historically items ranging from guns, food, and Bibles are among the first to be seized. Include these in your cache. Caches played a significant role in WWII for food, equipment, communications, and in hiding people.

All caching should be an appropriate distance from home, placed along expected travel routes. What is appropriate? That is subjective; for me, it would be something within five miles. PVC Pipe, plastic drums, ammo cans, glass and plastic food-safe jars all work well for long term caches. Caches have long been buried, hidden in walls, and submerged underwater for decades at a time. It is best only to use definite, immovable landmarks to mark a cache. Making caches with rooted features will ensure your ability to locate them later, regardless of roadway or terrain changes.

Urban Shelters

When selecting a shelter located in an urban area, the acronym BLISS will aid you in site selection.

B: Blend

Blending into your surroundings is essential. When you stop for any length of time in an urban area, you create the opportunity for an altercation in a real crisis.

L: Low Silhouette

Standing out isn't something you want to do in a crisis. Maintain a low profile and do nothing to attract attention with bright colored tarps or loud equipment.

I: Irregular Shape

By irregular, I mean you want to break up your straight lines. Suppose you're in the proverbial belly of the urban landscape. In that case, looking like a pile of trash behind a building may be the best solution. Conversely, maybe you find yourself at the edge of a wood line nearing the suburbs. In that case, you may use a tarp shelter and lay several branches over it to break up the lines to make it appear natural.

S: Small

Comfort is secondary to rest. You can rest uncomfortably, and it will also motivate you to get moving again. Small shelters provide just enough to provide a sanctuary from the elements. The clothing on your back should always be your first shelter option. If you are appropriately dressed, curling up behind a windbreak may be sufficient for a few hours.

S: Secluded

Seclusion is vital for your safety. Being out of the way, hard to get, and away from foot traffic will make your temporary shelter much safer.

Bridges, culverts, doorways, and tunnels offer protection from elements. Construction sites provide ample supplies and often temporary shelters that are most often secured. Tyvek, plastic, and heavy tarps are usually readily available. Abandoned cars, buses, train cars, and boats all offer shelter possibilities.

Should you encounter encampments of homeless people, tread carefully. I spent over a decade working with homeless communities in and around Louisville, KY. Some are friendly and will do all they can to help you, even in their dire situation. There are safe pockets, but many within these communities suffer from various mental issues, drug and alcohol problems, and domestic violence. It's best to avoid them if possible as your mission is to get home or to your alternate bug-in location. Do not waste your time or efforts trying to blend in with them; do not let your guard down near them.

Water Collection

As you move, fill up your water containers from any water faucet or fountain you may be able to, for as long as you can. If you leave before the onset of a significant crisis, or if the emergency is not one that will affect the water supply system, continue to take advantage of it. When trying to access water from most municipal buildings, a sillcock key will be required. A sillcock key is a four-way wrench for water faucets.

Complete Water Kit, photo by Anthony Awaken Photography

Ready sources of water include residential toilet tanks, water heaters, and rooftop water collection cisterns. When the taps stop providing water, check the lowest pipes in parking garages, basements and crawl spaces if necessary. Cut these water pipes, and residual water will drain from the unpressurized pipe. You should filter water from these alternative sources because it is stagnant or sitting in an industrial line. Any chemicals present in the water will remain, so a filter capable of removing chemical and viral contaminants is preferable.

You can also collect water from fire hydrants with a hydrant wrench or pipe wrench. Many industrial buildings have frost-free hydrants with hose bibb attachments in their yards, much like those you would find on a farm. Even when water is not on, these hydrants still build up pressure and can provide water.

How to Carry your Water

Hydration bladders permit travel while afoot; add a bladder fill valve to fill discreetly from hoses, sinks, or other bottles while keeping the pack on your back. With the hydration bladder, add a Grayl Geopress filter, which successfully removes chemical and water-borne viruses. On the Grayl itself, I highly recommend a 100% cotton sock or bag to use as a prefilter to give your Grayl filter cartridge a longer life. Finally, put a stainless-steel mug on the bottom. Doing this will not only protect your Gray filter but enable you to boil water should you need to.

How to procure your Water

Think tactically. You don't want to be exposed any longer than you need to be to purify your water. Drink whatever remaining water you currently have as you approach the new water source. Now you are hydrated and prepared to take advantage of your new water source. Whenever possible, collect water at a low point; hopefully, you will have some water movement or flow. Position so that you have cover to your sides and back if possible. The bend of a stream or drainage is sufficient as it enables you to look up and down the stream. If you feel safe, proceed with filling your water containers. Using the Grayl system, you can purify 24oz of water every eight seconds or so. If you hustle, you could easily filter then transfer enough water to refill a 64oz bladder and the Grayl itself in as little as one minute. Do not sit at a water source and hydrate. Get your water and move away to survey the area as others may suddenly move in for the same source.

22

Prepping on a Budget

If you can reserve $5-$6 per week for your family preparedness plan, then you could have around 300 pounds of food stockpiled within one year. If you can double or triple that amount, you will no doubt be able to secure hygiene supplies, first aid, and other essentials if you follow a disciplined approach.

Week 1: Rice

Rice is a staple of the survivor's diet. But not everyone likes or agrees with it. Consider rice alternatives such as quinoa, barley, and couscous for dietary diversity.

Week 2: Beans

Dry beans store well and can be rehydrated, fried, and combined with other items to make patties. When combined with rice a complete protein with all essential amino acids is formed.

Week 3: Canned Chicken or Tuna

Canned meat such as chicken or tuna provides protein and an increased plethora of menu options.

Week 4: Canned or Potted Meat

Vienna sausages, sardines and the like can be grilled, stewed, or eaten straight from the can.

Week 5: Tomato Sauce

Tomato sauce permits you the ability to change up your rice and pasta dishes.

Week 6: Sugar

Sweet drinks, recipes, and quick energy, sugar is a must-have item in the prepper's pantry.

Week 7: Flour

Flour is a must-have item for baking. Diversify your flour every time you buy it. All-Purpose, Bread Flour, etc.

Week 8: Cooking Oil

Fat is required for a balanced diet. Canola oil is easy on the body and easy to cook with. You might also consider coconut oil.

Week 9: Pasta

Load up on your favorite type.

Week 10: Rice

More rice, you're getting some diversity so this staple needs bolstering.

Week 11: Canned Fruit

Prioritize variety here. Nutritious and sweet, this will allow you options for cooking and morale.

Week 12: Salt

Iodized salt contains iodine which is beneficial in a survival situation.

Week 13: Powdered Milk

Add this to recipes and coffee.

Week 14: Coffee / Tea

Drink mixes for electrolytes, coffee, and tea will aid in hydration and curbing caffeine cravings.

Week 15: Canned Tuna

Tuna is rich in protein and omega3 fatty acids. You can also use it as a chicken substitute and few will notice!

Week 16: Canned Vegetables

Heat and eat veggies, your choice.

Week 17: Rice

Yes, more rice...

Week 18: Beans

Mix it up every time, Black beans or Northern Beans for added variety.

Week 19: Peanut Butter

Adaptable to all conditions, nut kinds of butter are essential.

Week 20: Shortening

Crisco allows you to bake more things and makes a great candle when needed.

Week 21: Sugar

More sugar!

Week 22: Canned Chicken

More Chicken!

Week 23: Canned Veggies

Week 24: Canned Meat

Corned beef hash or whatever else you will eat for added variety.

Week 25: RICE!

You knew that was coming...

Week 26: White Vinegar

Vinegar improves recipes and can be used for cleaning.

Week 27: Beans

Lima? Navy? Get what you like to eat...

Now repeat the list.

By following this shopping plan you'll have gathered about 300 pounds of storage food. You should end up with roughly 40lb of beans, 40lb of rice, 18lb of pasta, 18lb of flour. You'll have around 30 cans of tomato sauce, 40 cans of mixed veggies with 16 cans of various fruits, and around 70 cans of mixed meats along with salt and other spices as you see fit. Add in your own vitamin packets, protein powders, and other items you regularly buy, you're well on your way to a true prepper's pantry.

Hardening the home: Preppers Home Defense

Strengthen Doors

The most common method of entry for an intruder entering your home is by forcing his way through your door. Most doors are hollow or of low strength wood. Below are some security upgrades worth considering for your Urban, Rural, or Suburban homestead.

Step 1: The Door Frame

Door frames are not as strong as the studs that line your walls. Installing thicker wood beams along your door frame will fortify the foundation for your door and make it harder to break down.

Step 2: Replace the Hinges

Change the hinges for your door to ones that are bigger and of heavier grade. The longer the screws, the better, but be careful not to use too thick of a screw, or else it will split the studs in half when you bolt it through.

Step 3: Install steel doors

Many doors are hollow and covered in some fake material to make them look sturdy. Make sure you at least have solid wood doors. Do not buy doors with windows in them because they are easier to get through.

Step 4: Strengthen door locks and hardware

Most door locks are flimsy. Make sure you have a deadbolt and make sure it is quality grade 1. Ensure the throw bolt (the bolt that comes out of the door) is at least one inch long. Adding additional deadlocks is an easy and quick solution to more security. You can install specific "exit-only" deadlocks that only allow lock and unlocking from the inside. Exposed hinges on the inside of the door should be covered too. Otherwise, you would have to screw out the screws and install non-removable pins so an intruder from the outside with a screwdriver can't easily take the door off its hinges.

Step 5: Install a peephole

You always want to be able to see who may be lurking around. You want a peephole in all of your exterior doors, but don't install doors that come with glass windows; an intruder can then open the door from the inside with great ease. You should have peepholes installed in various areas of your house. If not, at least consider installing a wireless security camera system. The best way to protect yourself and keep your property secure is to know what is going on outside. You do not want any blind spots where an intruder can hide and make you think they have given up and retreated.

Step 6: Install a metal screen door

It is very wise to have a strong metal screen door with its deadlocks installed in front of your main door. This extra barrier will deter intruders. It will also act as a safety screen so you can open your main door and have a full view of what's outside without fear of someone rushing inside. Keep in mind that garage doors are notoriously easy to breakthrough. Make sure you have some deadbolts installed to prevent someone from forcing the door open. Make sure to add extra locks and upgrade the door that connects your house to the garage. In case your garage is breached, you want to be sure this door will keep the intruder out.

Secure your Windows

Installing Steel Bars will prevent intruders from entering your windows. You can replace your current windows with more sophisticated ones that have a metal net built inside them, but this is, of course, cost-prohibitive. Bars usually the most economical option. If you do go with the bars, make sure you install them inside your window frame to make it harder for someone to have access to the panels that screw into the wall of your house. The best types of bars are the ones that go up and down. Horizontal bars will allow an intruder to use them as a ladder to climb onto your roof. Roof access endangers your rainwater collection system, chimney system, or exploits weaknesses to get in your attic. Be sure to check any windows in the attic or vents designed to keep the attic cool. Someone can surely fit in through such an opening and can also throw things inside that could affect your family or home's integrity.

Pro Tip: You can now even buy a security film for your windows that you stick over like a tint. It is very tough to pierce, and if someone tries to shatter your window, it all stays together.

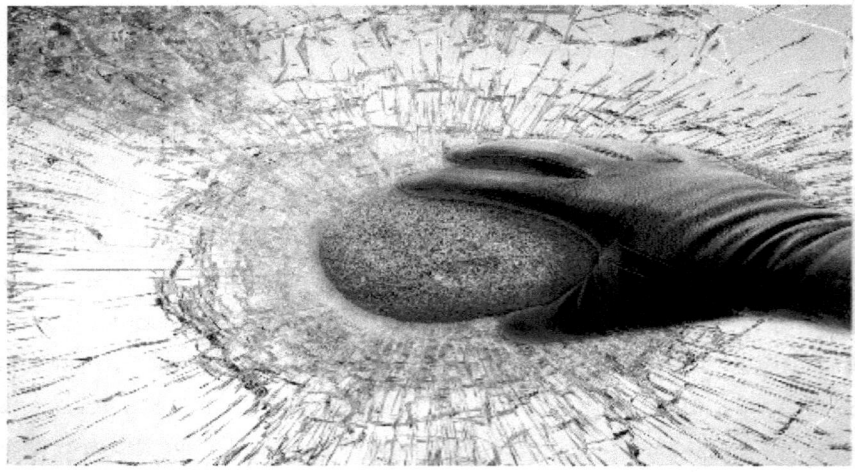

Then, of course, you can have a supply of plywood set aside for your windows. The wood used should not be OSB, but a 5/8" thick sheet of heavy plywood. Screw the plywood into the frame with Torx bits, which are less common to the average intruder. Alternatively, you could secure the boards from the inside by running a series of threaded bolts through a 2x4. The 2x4 board is screwed to the interior window frame and holds the plywood to the front by screwing down the bolt.

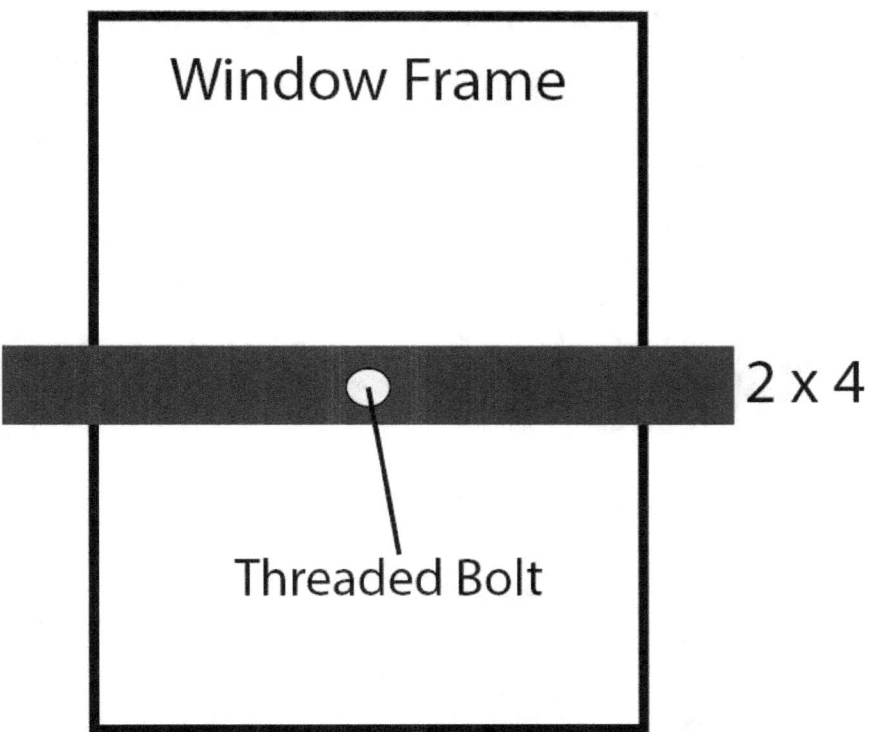

Window Break Alarms

A truly great tool for window security is the very affordable battery-powered window break alarm. You can get a variety of different designs online or at your nearest hardware store. The concept is simple. Place the device next to your window. It begins to sound an alarm if it senses any movement or a break in the magnetic sensor. Each alarm is specific, so you will know where the breach has occurred. You can choose motion-sensing types or ones that operate based on a magnetic link. The great thing is that they are pretty affordable, and you can place them on every window or door!

JASON HUNT

Now that we have covered the essentials of your Primary location in your PACE Plan. Let's look at further developing your individual first-aid and skill for the urban environment.

23

Field Craft

Field Craft refers to crafting tools and specialized survival items while in the field or operations area. Utilizing everyday items for alternate solutions is a crucial part of good fieldcraft skills. You must develop the mindset that all items you choose to carry can do at least three things. For example, I bring a steel spoon because I can eat with it, dig with it, and reflect light from it to make a fire. When applied, this manner of thought opens up a new realm of possibilities for kit development and creating tools as you travel.

Individual First Aid Kit

When it comes to an IFAK, we must recall our tier approach to our survival kits. For everyday purposes in an urban environment where gunshot and stab wounds are more likely in a real emergency, I recommend a tourniquet and some injury packing gauze at minimum. You can carry items such as these easily in a cargo or jacket pocket. It would be best if you had Personal Protective Equipment (PPE) such as safety glasses, N95 respirators, nitrile gloves, and hand sanitizers in Tier 2 kits and above. You will also have your complete first aid kit solutions for each tier of kit.

If you require additional first aid equipment as you travel through an urban area, pay special attention to BMW and Mercedes vehicles as they come standard with a vehicle first aid kit. Mouse glue traps can double as improvised chest seals. Secondary or backup tourniquets may be improvised when necessary by using webbing or drum liners. However, the kitchens in every apartment, home, and commercial space are where you can find a host of homeopathic remedies.

- Cinnamon is antibacterial and anti-inflammatory, and reduces heartburn, helps sore throats, is warming, and clears the sinuses. Use it in your water, tea, or take a small amount with some water. You may also use it topically.
- Cayenne is anti-inflammatory, helps arthritis and muscle pain and nerve pain, and is hemostatic (stops bleeding).
- Coriander is a digestive aid, calming spasms that cause diarrhea, aids in clearing E.coli, and salmonella- an anti-anxiety herbal.
- Ginger stops nausea, digestive aid, reduces pain and swelling.
- Cloves are anti-inflammatory, excellent for toothaches, and improve insulin function.
- Sage reduces blood sugar and is anti-inflammatory.
- Black Pepper warms the body, increases energy and circulation.
- Honey soothes coughs, treats wounds (once the bleeding stops) and burns, works as an antibiotic internally or externally.
- Basil is good for head colds, intestinal parasites (worms), snake and insect bites, and aids with fever, headache, and flu symptoms.
- Oral rehydration salts are vital during times of high exertion or heat.
- 6tsp sugar, ½ tsp salt, to 1-liter water makes a hydration solution.

Band-aids for general cuts and scrapes are lightweight enough to be carried. You may consider taking a small roll of gorilla tape to make heavy-duty band-aids as needed. The tape is far more useful than a handful of band-aids.

Fire and Heat

THE GOSPEL OF SURVIVAL

Fire is a dangerous element within the urban environment. While it provides comfort, warmth, and can serve as a valuable tool, fire also has a destructive side if not appropriately managed. You must ask yourself if it is a fire that you need or warmth. Fire brings smoke, light, and a scar to the location we make the fire. It is a telltale sign that someone was in a given place and gave away your position to anyone nearby. You can get warm with proper insulation, so decide carefully whether or not a fire is what you require when the time comes. Again, concealment of fire is a vital concern. There may be times when you cannot afford to have the signature of fire give away your location or activity.

Hobo Stove made by Jamie Boggs

Hobo stoves, those made from tin cans, significantly reduce the sign of fire and be taken with you afterward to minimize your perceived presence. Alcohol stoves can be built from aluminum cans quite easily on the go. However, they will require a liquid fuel source to operate. Alcohol stoves again leave a minimal sign, are portable, and are made from local trash. You could crush it after use, and it would appear as any other crushed can.

When outdoors, lowering the fire into the ground in a Dakota Fire Hole is an excellent way to minimize the light, but the wet or damp ground will create steam, which will cause wood to smoke a great deal, which is not ideal. Containment within a stove type system is always the safest method available within the urban environment. It not only reduces the fire risk to buildings, etc. but offers the best concealment option.

Candling Devices

When your batteries die, and you need to look around in the dark, trash resources once again provide many options. Tuna in oil, cardboard, grease, sharpie markers, and corn chips all make improvised candles.

Alternative ignition sources

When you're on the move collecting anything, you may need to extend your fire kit to save you from using your equipment's limited resources. This continual collecting is a prime example of a good scavenger mentality. Here are several examples of alternative fire-starting methods:

Prison Match

This one requires access to some electricity. Split a pencil down the middle to access the graphite in the center. Break the graphite into two pieces, as long as you can manage. Insert each piece of graphite into an electrical outlet or power strip. Be careful; this is dangerous! Now, loosely twist some toilet tissue into a coil, bend it over another piece of graphite, and turn once more. Now, touch the graphite in the toilet tissue across the two pieces in the outlet to complete the circuit. This touching will cause a spark and ignite the toilet tissue. If left in contact too long, it will also ignite the plastic in the outlet and potentially anything else until the graphite is exhausted.

Light Bulb Burn or Solar Ember

Once again, if you have access to electricity, you could take a light bulb's filament to ignite some tinder. Just break the glass bulb without damaging the filament. Alternatively, if electricity is not available, you can take a clear light bulb, remove the filament while keeping the bulb intact, and fill it with water. Filling with water will allow light to refract, which you can use to achieve an ember through solar magnification, similar to a magnifying lens.

Toilet tank and ceramic strikers

It can be challenging to find a "flint" rock for flint and steel while in a city. But you find toilets and ceramic mugs and tiles everywhere. Break these items to get a high-quality stone to achieve flint and steel ignition. These items are often sharp when broken, so handle them with care.

Chlorine and brake fluid

Come across some chlorine tablets and brake fluid? Well, you can make a fire. This fire also gives off noxious chlorine gas, so you should only use it outdoors. Unless, of course, you find yourself in an area where a distraction device is needed. You can use this skill for nefarious purposes as well. Powder up the chlorine tablet and pour some brake fluid over it. Within moments a chemical reaction will begin that produces heat and smoke. Have your fire material stop this mixture to achieve fire.

Water heater anodes

The anode within a water heater is made of magnesium, aluminum, and zinc. These anodes prevent corrosion of the lining within the heater. When removed from a heater that's been in service for years, they're often very brittle and covered in crud, but when scraped up, they still provide a great source of tinder material that burns hot. Recreational campers (R.V.'s) have small water heaters onboard that offer smaller, portable anodes that resemble larger Ferrocerium rods. You can collect a large magnesium pile by scraping with your knife that readily takes a spark to combust.

Non-dairy creamers

Yes, non-dairy coffee creamer is flammable. It readily takes a spark and can be used like other fire-starters.

Now equipped with several new methods to obtain fire, let's look at some techniques that will enable you to escape restraints in the event of your capture or illegal detainment. In an urban survival scenario, the likelihood of you or one of your family members being detained is high. This detainment may be for the nefarious purpose of stealing your resources or doing harm to the people of your group. Whatever the reason, understanding how to escape essential restraint devices and craft escape devices in the field is crucial.

Escape tips to be considered

In some cases, leaving or attempting to leave a trafficking/abduction situation may increase the risk of violence. It is vital to trust your judgment when taking steps to ensure your safety and be prepared to do what is necessary to ensure your safety and potentially your life. If your abductor has restraints of any type- duct tape, zip ties, rope - it's time to fight, even if it means getting shot, as your life may very well depend upon it. The savagery, being demonstrated by your abductor, requires an equally savage response.

How do we better prepare ourselves and our families to deal with potential abductions and human trafficking?

First, we educate them on the subject's realities and cite references to instances of successful or attempted abductions in our area or region. It's prevalent nation-wide. We train; we should all have dry runs at the house to identify creepy behavior and some mock abduction attempts. If we know basic self-defense, that will increase our odds of escaping immediate capture. Then, we should take steps to ensure that we understand how to escape standard restraints so that, should we be abducted, we can at least get away when the time presents itself. Basic lock-picking, handcuff escapes, duct tape restraint escapes, and zip-tie restraint escapes should all be well-rehearsed and understood, especially among our women and children. The following tool presented is something you can work into your home-based scenario training called a Personal Escape Necklace. This simple kit will permit essential restraint escape tools to be carried out of sight around the neck or as a bracelet or anklet, always ready for immediate deployment.

If capture is imminent and assured, do not fight restraints as they may roll and bind, which will make them stronger, much the same way twisted cord or rope becomes stronger- always attempt to give wrists in front of the body so that you may see and work on restraints during times left alone. Remember the adage of two is one, one is none concerning escape tools ad our layered kit approach. The more options you give yourself for escape, the better off you will be. Sew items into the folds of your clothing if you must. Again, the smuggler's mentality is in full effect in this situation.

Items needed for construction:

These items are easily located and readily available. Now is the time to secure these items and create your kit. Do not wait until the event takes place.

- 60" of Kevlar Cord
- This will serve as the main necklace body.
- Paracord Necklace Clasp
- This will serve as the release of the necklace. Strong magnets could also be utilized.
- Hand-cuff Key

- Any style you prefer, I am using a standard cuff key for this DIY model. Hollowed, more covert keys are beneficial for advanced users.
- Bobby Pin
- This will serve as the cuff shim and pick. The thin steal in windshield wiper blades work well too.
- Mini Chem-Light
- Available in the fishing section or at any party store, a glow light is great for working in low-light conditions, like the back of a trunk!
- 1/8" diameter Rubber Tubing
- This tubing will hold your tools in place on the necklace. Place them over a knot for added security which will keep them from sliding around.
- 1 Scripto brand Lighter
- The Scripto brand lighter has a carbide striking wheel which is perfect for use in breaking vehicle windows, cutting glass, and sharpening knives. This device will go on the female end of the paracord clasp to hold the necklace in place.
- 1 Small Zip Tie
- This is simply to secure the opposite end of the necklace in the male end of the paracord clasp. Thin wire or rigid tubing would also serve for this purpose.

The Build:

Step 1: Take your 60" strand of kevlar cord and tie the ends together with a sturdy knot to make a 30" long double strand.

Step 2: Remove the carbide striker from the Scripto lighter using a multi-tool or pair of needle-nosed pliers. Slip one end of the kevlar cord through the center hole of the striker and using a lark's head knot, pass the opposite end of the kevlar cord through the first section you passed through the striker. This will secure the striker to the necklace.

THE GOSPEL OF SURVIVAL

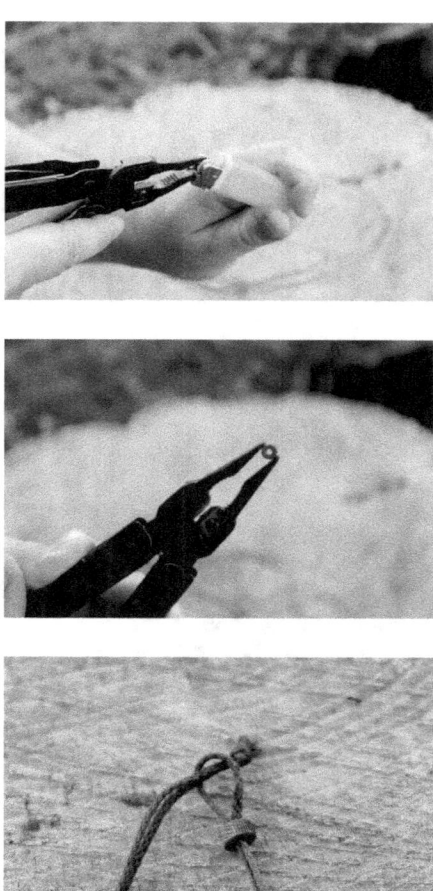

Step 3: Slide the female end of the clasp over the cord so that the carbide striker rests inside the clasp.

Step 4: Slide the tubing onto the cord. I use 3 pieces of 1/8" diameter by 3/16" long pieces. You can change this as needed to fit the items you want to carry.

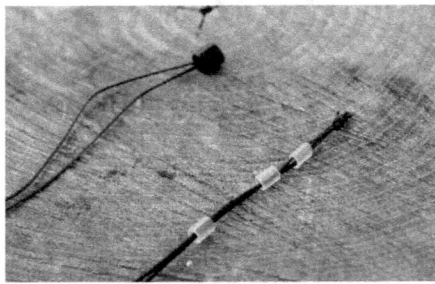

Step 5: Slide the male end of the clasp over the cord, then secure the zip tie at the end. Clip off the excess beyond the binder and seat it inside the male end of the clasp. Your necklace should now be able to clasp and unclasp easily with a yank.

THE GOSPEL OF SURVIVAL

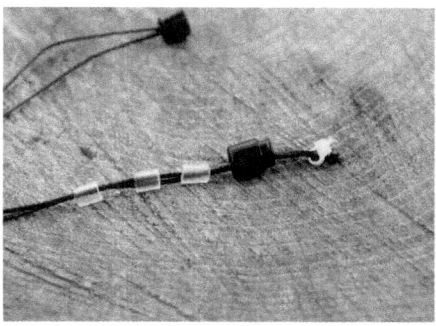

Step 6: Tie a simple knot where you would like your gear to ride on the cord. Keep in mind that you do not want too many knots that you cannot get your hands in between the cord to use it as a saw.

Step 7: Load your tubes. I install my heaviest item, the cuff key at the center, and for security, I run my bobby pin through the cuff key before placing the pin in the tube. I then add the chem light to the final tube.

Now you have a simple, effective tool for escaping a variety of illegal restraints. Practice with this tool and in a short time, it will become a regular part of your everyday carry. You can use your Escape Necklace to escape a variety of potential restraints. The necklace gives you options you may not otherwise have and reduces the need to scavenge or create immediate need escape tools. While this is dedicated to a necklace style carry, please do not limit yourself to only this option.

These necklace items are easily concealable and could be placed in shirt collars, behind labels on jeans, inside waist belts, or shoe insoles. When it comes to these items, it's better to have and not need than need and not have. Just be sure to train with the things you stow on your person so that these tools' limits are understood. To drive home the point that our families need this training, my 16-year-old daughter will demonstrate the following escapes; she's our resident expert. She teaches these and other escapes and lock-picking techniques in the Urban Survival classes at our school, Campcraft Outdoors (campcraftoutdoors.com).

Duct Tape and Zip Tie Restraints

Break the necklace free and work it in between or overtop the restraints in question, then place your feet in between the necklace cords with a clasp under each foot. Then, with a peddling motion, saw through tape or plastic restraints with great ease. This will work against a wide variety of plastic restraints; however, it will not go through any that are reinforced with wire.

Hand Cuffs

The Necklace gives you two options for handcuff escape, use the key, which makes life very easy for you, or pick or shim the lock with the bobby pin. To use the bobby pin, scrape off the plastic bubbled ends of the pin with your nail, on concrete, or if you must, with your teeth.

Dark or low-light conditions

The chem light within the necklace should be used when you need extra light to see what you're doing with your escape necklace. If you find yourself in a trunk, in a dark outbuilding or basement or anywhere else you'd rather not be with impaired visibility, pop the light to give you enough illumination to work your magic on whatever restraints you're faced with.

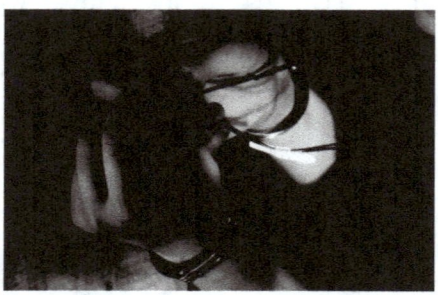

Lock-picking basics

Before resorting to picking locks, it's always best to explore other bypass options. If there's an alternate way in, explore that first; if a door has external hinges, attack those first; if a hasp with a padlock, attack the hasp. Door latches are also relatively weak and can be broken with some prying. You can create a common-man entry kit with two long wrenches, a hardened padlock, a car jack, 3 feet of chain, and a prybar. The car jack will help you to raise or press open gates or door jambs. You can use the chain to shear objects apart, lift, and use the pry bars and wrenches to attack all types' locks. The padlock will give you a way to secure the chain ends as well. Just make sure you have the key handy. The jack case in the photo is from my 2019 Jeep Renegade and it includes its own screwdriver, wheel chalk, and funnel. This entire kit is small enough to be carried in a gym bag. Add a pair of bolt cutters and little can stop you from making entry.

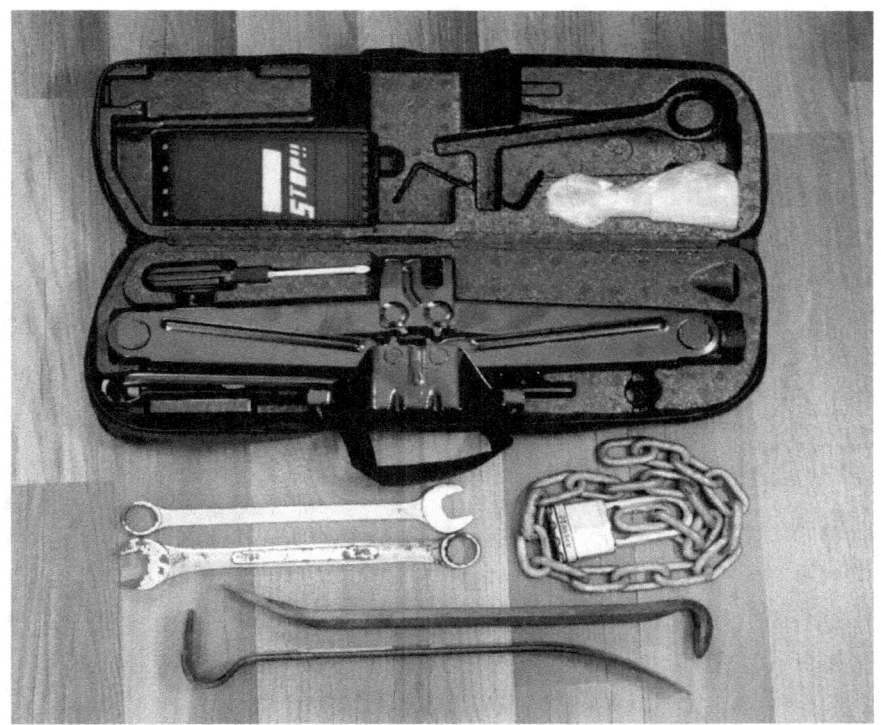

Locks

A lock consists of a body, a lock cylinder, and two-piece spring-loaded lock pins. A five-pin lock is the industry standard. The key pushes up the two-piece locking pins until the shear line allows the cylinder to turn.

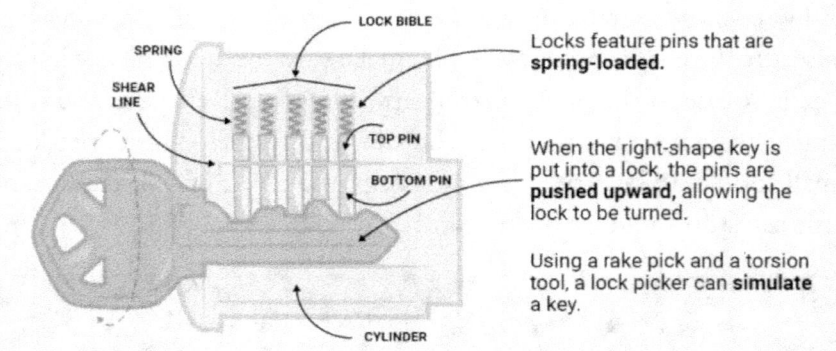

Tools of the trade

The tension wrench: You cannot pick a lock without a tension wrench. The tension wrench creates a bind on the locking pins allowing for single pin picking and raking a lock. The tension wrench is sized to fit the keyway. The tension wrench cannot interfere with the locking pins, cylinder, or the lock pick. Depending on the lock, you may need to insert your wrench in the keyway's bottom or top. A shorter wrench works best for the top of the keyway applications.

Single pin picks: A single pin pick allows you to engage one pin at a time in the lock cylinder. The pick must be long enough to reach the deepest pin in the lock, have a deep enough hook to fully depress the pin, and be small enough to index individual pins in a small keyway.

Rakes: A rake pick mimics a key by lifting multiple pins to varying heights while applying tension with the tension wrench. Rakes come in various designs and lengths such as the single, double, triple, quad Bogata, the city, snake, diamond, and ball rake.

The Single Pin Pick

Single-pin Picking is the most basic of all lock picking. Understanding single pin picking provides you with a foundation for other methods. Due to machining tolerances, the cylinder pinholes and the locking pins vary in size. This design allows applying tension to the cylinder, causing one pin to bind before the other pins touch. With a single hook pick, you can push up on each pin individually. One pin will be under pressure, and the other pins can be lifted and return freely. The pin under pressure is the binding pin. With steady light pressure on the tension wrench, push the pin until the split of the two-piece pin reaches the cylinder's shear line. When this happens, the cylinder will turn slightly until the cylinder binds on the next pin. A new binding pin is created and defeated until all the pins are raised to the shear line, and the cylinder turns freely.

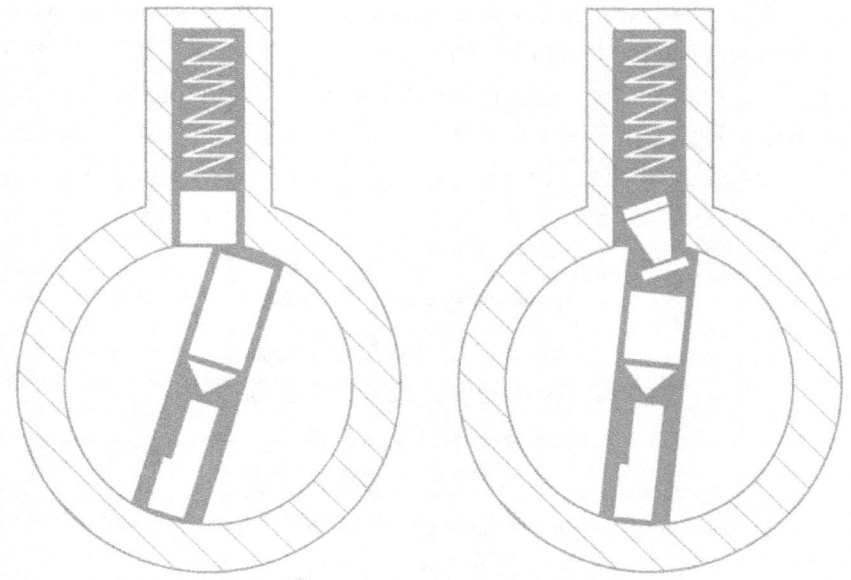

Standard Lock (Left) vs Security Pin Lock (Right)

As long a light, steady tension is applied to the cylinder, the set pins are held above the shear line. If you back off the pressure, the pins will reset, and you must start over. It is possible to over-push the pin and tie up the lock, and you will be able to feel the pin not returning under spring pressure. If this happens, you will have to remove tension, reset the clock, and start over. Some manufacturers utilize security pins. A security pin has a machined step in the middle of the pin. This step mimics the feel of a pin being pushed past the shear line, but the result is a tied-up cylinder. Varying the tension allows moving past the step of a security pin.

Lock Raking

Raking a lock is a coarse method of pushing multiple pins at variable heights in an attempt to set multiple pins at once. Rakes come in numerous combinations with varied peaks and mimics a key in the keyway. While tension is applied the rake is inserted and rocked in and out, up and down, in an attempt to try all pin height combinations. Vary the speed in an effort to bounce the pins. Kinetic energy assists the pins in reaching the shear line. Raking is faster than single pin picking but not all rakes will pick all locks. After a few minutes with a rake if you are unable to open the lock try a different style of rake or attempt to single pin pick the lock.

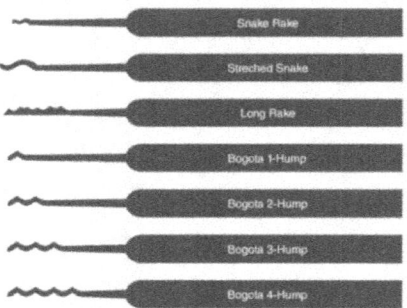

Making Cordage

Cordage and rope should be readily available in various forms in the urban environment, but there are times when making it may be necessary. You can create a strong rope by braiding together plastic grocery bags or trash bags. Once you have the cord, you can create other survival tools such as nets, hammocks, and even baskets. 2-Liter and other round plastic bottles make some of my favorite cordages, however. You can create this cordage by making a jig with a knife blade and a post. First, locate or create a post or find a sapling around three inches in diameter. Any decorative tree will do in town. You will make two cuts with a saw, one of which needs to be about 2/3rd across the face of the stump and about one inch deep. You will make your second cut to cut the corner off the remaining 1/3rd of the face. It will look like this from the top:

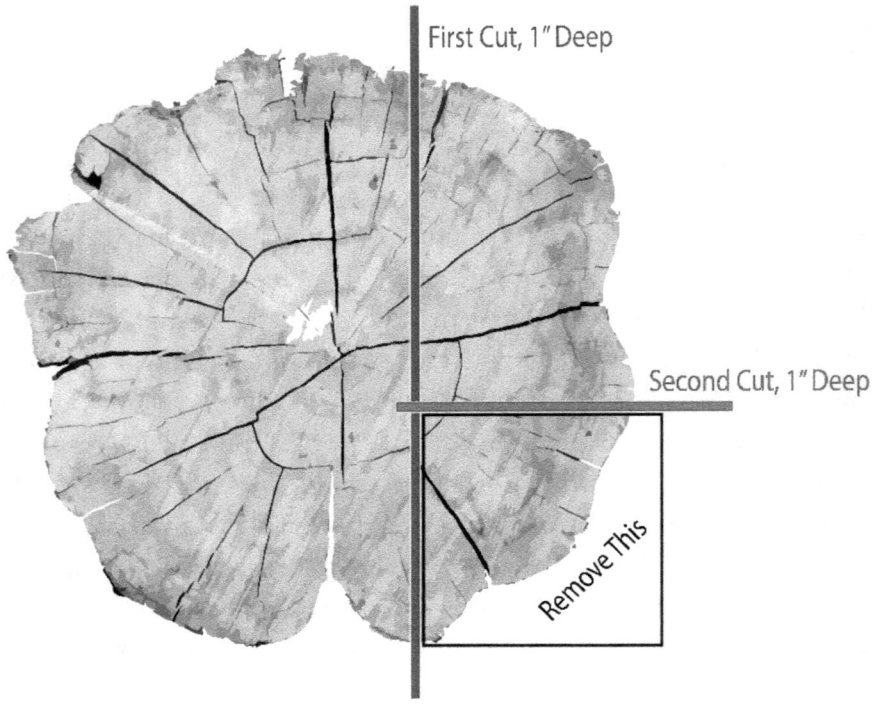

Now, insert your knife into the post at the thickness you want your cordage. The saw kerf will act as a guide for the bottles being cut. Start a section under your blade, then pull steadily to create long lengths of plastic cordage.

THE GOSPEL OF SURVIVAL

24

Urban Movement

"However, when the people of Gibeon heard what Joshua had done to Jericho and Ai, they resorted to a ruse: They went as a delegation whose donkeys were loaded with worn-out sacks and old wineskins, cracked and mended. They put worn and patched sandals on their feet and wore old clothes. All the bread of their food supply was dry and moldy. Then they went to Joshua in the camp at Gilgal and said to him and the Israelites, "We have come from a distant country; make a treaty with us."
~ Joshua 9:3-6 (NIV)

The people of Gibeon pulled a fast one on Joshua and, in the process, subjected themselves to a lifetime of service to the Israelites. This scenario could have just as quickly ended up with the Israelites slaughtering them as they had been doing with other tribes living within the borders of their promised land. There are times when the fight should, at all costs, be avoided. This was one of those times. Similarly, we must have enough awareness to know whether or not an area is permissive or non-permissive. A nonpermissive area may be hostile, patrolled, or otherwise unfriendly. Traveling through such areas should be done with caution, and camouflage and ditch kits, survival kits that can be thrown away or confiscated, are generally the best to use while in such areas.

When passing through such environments, look for common ground with those you may encounter, such as common ethnicity, sports teams, or vices such as smoking, all work to lower the guard of potential unknown aggressors. Carrying items to gift them, such as a pack of smokes, a lighter, or a small alcohol bottle, further aid in building this repour. When a repour cannot be garnered, disruption may be your best approach; manipulate the environment or the people through acting out scenarios and backstories to create a new normal based on your set of parameters. Disruption may come from a distraction device you set in advance (noise, smoke, or fire), a backstory you create with a false narrative (people being attacked 3 blocks over), or whatever else is necessary to gain you access to what you need or the area you have to cross.

Theatricality & deception. Powerful agents to the uninitiated...
~ Bane, The Dark Knight Rises

Camouflage
The ability to move undetected or conceal gear in a cache requires camouflage. There are seven principles to camouflage.

Movement, the eyes are naturally drawn to movement. Movement combined with bright colors is the quickest way to be seen.

Shape, a shape that does not fit into the surroundings, is noticeable to the eye. In an urban setting, square, straight lines are the norm and blend in. Match the shape of the environment. It would be best if you broke up the shape of your head and shoulders.

Shine, new reflective gear shines in the sun. Paint, soot, dirt, charcoal reduces the brightness. Caches should be painted a drab color to eliminate shine.

Surface, a synthetic surface regardless of color, doesn't blend into a natural setting. Natural materials or netting help blend the surface into the surroundings.

Silhouette, by back-lighting yourself with natural or artificial light, the human silhouette is instantly recognizable. Terrain will also cause you to silhouette yourself. Avoid crossing the peaks of hilltops. Pay attention to temporarily silhouetting yourself by flashlights, passing cars, or opening a door of a lit room at night.

Shadow, sun, moon, and artificial light can cast your shadow. This shadowing is of significant concern if your shadow extends beyond a corner, wall, or door.

Spacing is an invention of man. Evenly space telephone poles look normal to the eye. Breaking this human-made pattern draws the eye and is instantly noticeable. This subtlety is paramount in an urban setting where trees, bushes, houses, and cars are in nice neat rows.

Building a Ditch Kit

A Ditch Kit or nonpermissive environment kit is a no-excuses kit that is currently legal to carry. You can take this type of gear on an airplane, go to a sporting event or concert, courthouse, school, or federal building. Basically, don't carry anything that you are not willing to have confiscated on the spot. Consider that it may be easier to create key kit components past points of inspection. Carry a small enough kit that is unobtrusive. Always avoid things tactical in appearance. Attempting to get tactical defensive pens, flashlights, or nonmagnetic blades past a checkpoint and failing will cause the rest of your gear to be closely scrutinized.

The Basic Ditch Kit includes:

- A TSA-friendly version of a keychain kit.
    - A keychain kit would include a Ferro rod, a non-bladed multi-tool like the Gerber Dime, a small flashlight, 2 key-

rings for a tourniquet, an inexpensive non-climbing grade carabiner.
- Standard ink pen
- Standard rear cap switch flashlight
- Cotton bandana
- BIC lighter
- Fresnel lens
- 12 to 18 feet of bankline or non-military colored paracord
- Cash
- Credit card
- Optional if space is available: a clean metal water bottle, 2 drum liners, small 1st kit with Band-Aids, Tylenol, Ibuprofen, Aspirin, and Benadryl.

Defensive weapons are easily procured or created past inspection points. Should you desire a knife for utilitarian or self-defense capability, the Emerson-designed Kershaw is an excellent choice for ditch kit purposes. They are affordable at under thirty dollars and have a solid lock for self-defense needs. They also make a trainer version of the knife (sold separately) to practice deployment and defensive techniques so you can get the most from the knife design.

Emerson Designed Kershaw Knife with Blue Trainer

You might also consider a standard bottle/can opener. You may sharpen the pointed can opener edge to work as an impromptu blade and effective defensive weapon. Currently, bottle openers such as this are routinely not considered dangerous.

In one of my ditch kits, I carry 18 feet of Titan Survival's Survivor-Cord™, a type of 550 paracord that includes as part of its inner strands a waterproof fore starter, fishing line, and snare wire. I also carry the cord in a reflective orange, so it's not drawing any suspicious looks. I have this coiled in a cargo pocket and as part of my bracelet. When deployed in a real emergency, I could quickly run some dirt, oil, or charcoal over the length of rope to better hide the color. This cordage option permits me several different uses and advantages. My paracord bracelet includes SurvivorCord™ and standard paracord and is about 12 feet long in total. All in, I have around 30ft of cordage on me, not counting boot laces, depending on the day.

THE GOSPEL OF SURVIVAL

My bracelet includes a mini compass, whistle, and Ferro rod in the clasp. These bracelets are so standard nowadays, and I've not yet had an issue with them being flagged. I also carry a 5-cent coin knife. This knife has passed through unnoticed many times through security as it's just a regular coin. Without close inspection, you would not notice it. These are available from DSG Laboratories and work well for cutting through cordage zip ties and for utility purposes. My wallet was made for me by my wife several years ago. In it, besides my cash and cards, I have a mini handcuff key stashed in one of the edges. You can empty the wallet and still not feel or find it without intense scrutiny. Finally, I carry a 100% cotton scarf and, post COVID-19, a face mask. Do you notice multi-layered cloth face masks have pockets? You can also use those pockets to store some escape and evasion tools, cash, or medication.

Alternatively, a ditch kit may be a Survival Tin. Within these small tins, you can carry a lot of gear for various uses ranging from urban needs to fishing and first aid. I have even seen a 24-inch-long bucksaw blade wrapped around the interior of one of these tins. By keeping all components in the container and having a band around it, you can toss it to the side to be picked up later.

Weaponology

> *"But now, he said, "take your money and a haversack. And if you don't have a dagger, sell your cloak and buy one!"*
> ~Luke 22:36

Jesus warned his disciples that they would be labeled as criminals after his resurrection (Luke 22:37), and again, we find Jesus preparing his followers beforehand with the news to prepare. Defensive weapons will be essential to all living in the last days before Christ's arrival. In the current state of world affairs, we see increasing encroachment upon the right to bear arms in the United States. Despite what many desire to believe, it is not unthinkable that arms could be outlawed altogether in a fashion similar to what we see in Europe. Plenty of firearms will remain in the wind, but the majority may no longer have ready access to them. Some other things to consider are that firearms make noise. So, in an urban environment, they are not always the best course of the first action for defense. Guns require ammunition, which is heavy. While crossing dangerous areas on foot, a minimal loadout is your best friend as it permits swift movement as you progress toward your primary or alternate safe locations. A capable defensive pistol with a few spare magazines should be sufficient for this task. Knives and stabbing weapons offer discretion and relative silence and are easily crafted from the urban landscape from various materials. But before delving into creating improvised tools for self-defense, let's talk about your body as a weapon.

Self-Defense is a classification of martial arts. While all martial arts can claim they are a form of self-defense, not all self-defense systems can claim they are martial arts. Martial or military arts have come down through primarily Middle Eastern and Asian influences. With those influences come cultural expressions and religious aspects that formulate each discipline's artistic expression. Because of this influence, you will not find any real Christian martial arts. Traditional martial arts pose a risk to the spiritual development of the serious Christian. I am a member of the U.S. Martial Arts Hall of Fame and, as a life-long martial artist with black belts in multiple styles, I can attest first-hand that the godly person has no business immersing themselves in traditional martial arts. Christian martial arts associations have popped up over the years, many of which implement Bible study in their teaching curriculum, but they fall short of practicing authentic Christian martial arts. Such organizations merely sanction traditional arts, including their theories, traditions, and occult practices, so long as they include religious modifiers in their programs. For a martial art to truly be a "Christian Martial Art," it must not reproduce any of the worship methods hidden within the original traditional system, and it should not reproduce anti-Christian worldviews, traditions, or ceremonies.

One danger in traditional arts, for example, comes from Taekwondo. Many Taekwondo practitioners learn Tae Guek Poomsae (kata/ forms).

The Tae Geuk patterns, according to the Kukkiwon Training Manual, mimic the eight divination signs as represented upon the Korean Flag. Upon examining the Tae Geuk, you will discover that it is a religion hidden within Taekwondo in honor of the Korean war god. Therefore, by moving through these worship patterns, traditionally, you summon the war god's energy and power (divination). The Bible provides dozens of examples of divination and sorcery, and in every instance, it is condemned. This type of teaching is pervasive in all Asian martial arts and many of those of Europe. Today, your local martial arts club is more concerned with keeping the doors open than imparting ancient spiritual knowledge, but there are still some that insist on keeping the old ways alive. So please be cautious of Christian martial arts groups that endorse traditional Asian arts as they have always been taught, touting ranks and lineage from the "source" of the art, for you are not getting a Christian art at all.

Christianity as a lifestyle is by and large marked with acts of non-violence and pacificism. The fact is, God does not want us to initiate violence, but he wants us to train ourselves to master our emotions. He wants us to prepare our hearts to respond humbly when we are tempted with feelings of anger, jealousy, and rage. I believe the study of self-defense instead of martial arts provides this kind of training. When you study the scriptures, you will find hundreds of examples of combative applications. These applications range from Cain murdering Abel with a rock (Gen. 4) and Jacob wrestling with Jesus (Gen. 32) to the Battle of Armageddon (Rev. 16). There are also many cases for Biblical self-defense, such as in the book of Nehemiah. As Nehemiah was rebuilding Jerusalem and tribal neighbors were seeking to carry out vigilante attacks on the Jews, he instructed his people: *"Don't be afraid of them. Put your minds on the Master, great and awesome, and then fight for your brothers, your sons, your daughters, your wives, and your homes."* (Nehemiah 4:14 MSG). In this manner, we'll examine self-defense so that we may fight for our brothers, sons, daughters, wives, and homes.

> *Greater love hath no man than this, that a man lay down his life for his friends.*
>
> ~John 15:13

Proficiency

You do not need to achieve a black belt level in self-defense to be effective. The average person does not have much if any, self-defense training. If you can reach a paltry 20% efficiency, you can overcome 80% of the threats you will ever face. Meaning, you only need to have a solid foundation of basic skills. Strikes, kicks, grappling, and weapon usage are what's needed. Because it's not likely you will be able to train with me personally, here are three programs you can access nation-wide or online to attain these skills.

1. Krav Maga, the Israeli self-defense system, is useful for the average person. It will teach you strikes, kicks, and defenses against common street attacks.

2. Gracie Combatives, the 36 lessons up to Blue Belt, will allow you to dominate almost anyone in the average street fight. Gracie Jiu-Jitsu is related to but is not technically considered competitive Brazilian Jiu-Jitsu. That said, any grappling training is better than none at all. Wrestling, Sambo, and Judo are all beneficial.

3. Libre Knife Fighting or Filipino Combatives. Filipino-based combatives start students out with sticks and knives. Once you gain a solid understanding of how to move your body concerning such weapons, you quickly realize that nearly everything is a weapon and can be manipulated in much the same way. Libre Knife Fighting offers a more direct and purposeful connection to self-defense and can be understood quickly. It's brutal and no-holds-barred, which is exactly what you need to know.

This training pursuit will also help you get into better physical condition as well. Fitness plays into survival as much as anything else, so train to be as functional and capable as you can be and be at peace with that.

Field-made Tools

As mentioned previously, it may be better to create your tools after you've passed through secured areas. Blades and stabbing weapons will be the most practical to build on the run, which stresses the importance of proper training in the defensive use of such armaments beyond general utility and outdoor survival needs.

Ink Pen Ventilator

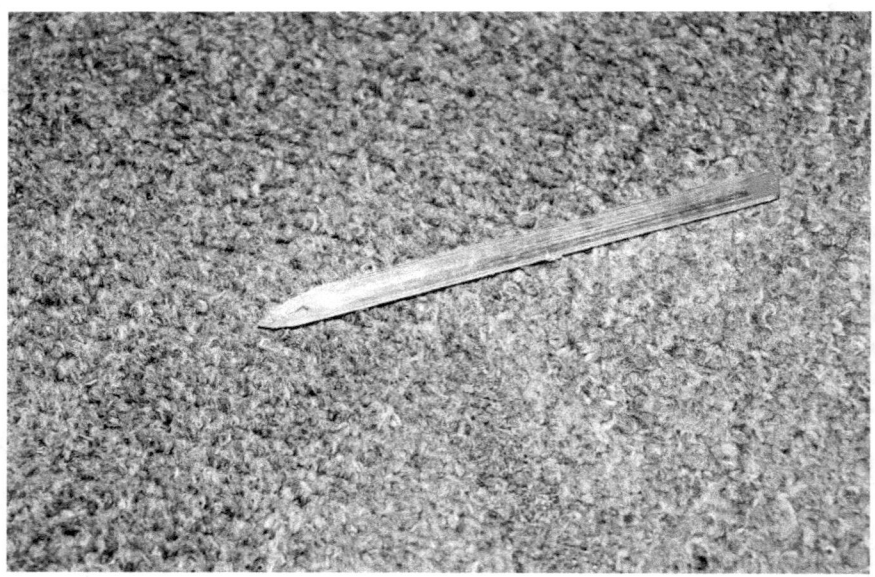

Bic brand crystal pens make fast ventilators. A ventilator is a tube with a sharp point, making it a useful defensive tool when used as a weapon. After all, no one likes holes poked in them. To make one, remove the cap, then the ink tube. Take the empty crystal tube and rub it briskly across some office-style carpet to melt it into an edge shape.

THE GOSPEL OF SURVIVAL

You can do this in about thirty seconds. Any tapered tube that is rigid enough to stab with will make a decent improvised defensive tool.

Reinforced Chop Sticks

Chopsticks, those same ones found at Asian restaurants, can be reinforced to make handy weapons. Dampen the sticks with water, then roll them through some baking soda; follow that with a coating of cheap super glue, and you've just created a plastic reinforced stick. The chemical reaction between baking soda and super glue does create some heat and fumes, so use caution and make this in a ventilated area. Scrape it against a rough surface such as asphalt to make an improvised stabbing weapon.

Nail Knife

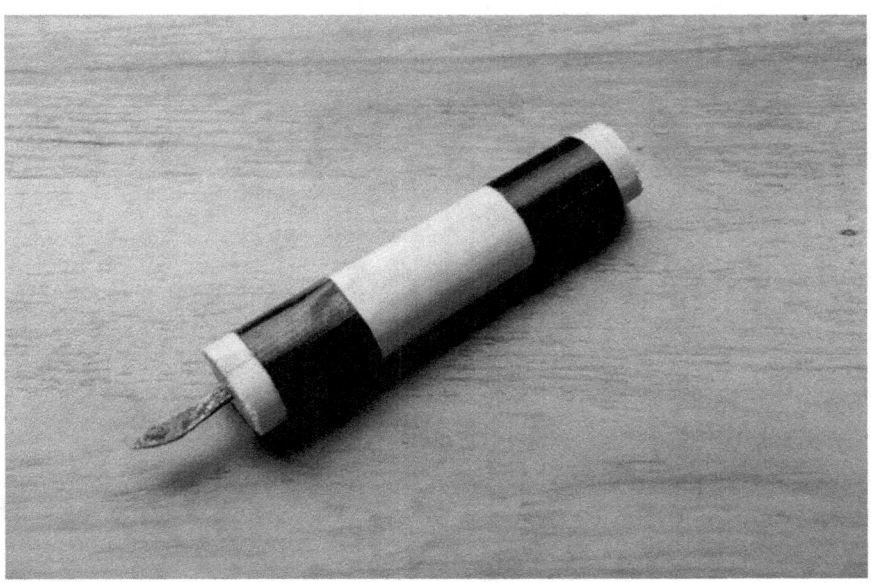

Pick up an aluminum roofing nail; the longer, the better. Steel can also be used, but it requires more effort. Pound the nail flat using two stones or a hammer and some anvil device. Sharpen the nail by rubbing it against a rough surface or sandpaper. Now collect a broom handle or something similar, cut or break it to about five inches in length, then split it down the center. You can split it by placing one end on a sharp edge and striking the back with a stone. Now, press the nail tightly between the two slabs of wood. It will not seat at first, so scrape out the nail's impression using your new nail blade. Once appropriately installed, secure the two slabs together with binding. You now have a handy cutting tool for hundreds of tasks.

Carabiner Karambit

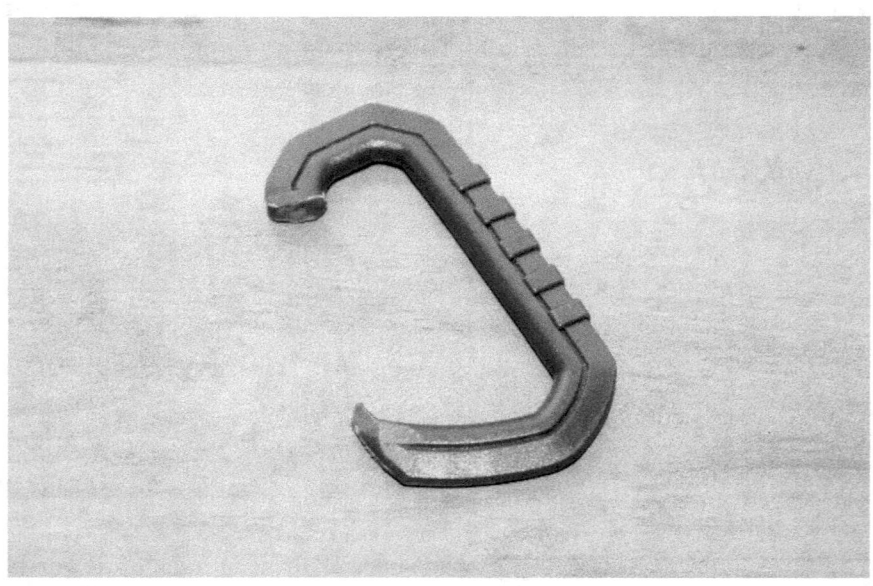

If you come across a plastic carabiner, break off the gate and rub the wide end's edge against something rough to create a sharp edge. You can leave the top so that it rides over the top of your finger or abrade it off for a clean edge. You have a last-ditch defensive tool.

Push-Dagger

THE GOSPEL OF SURVIVAL

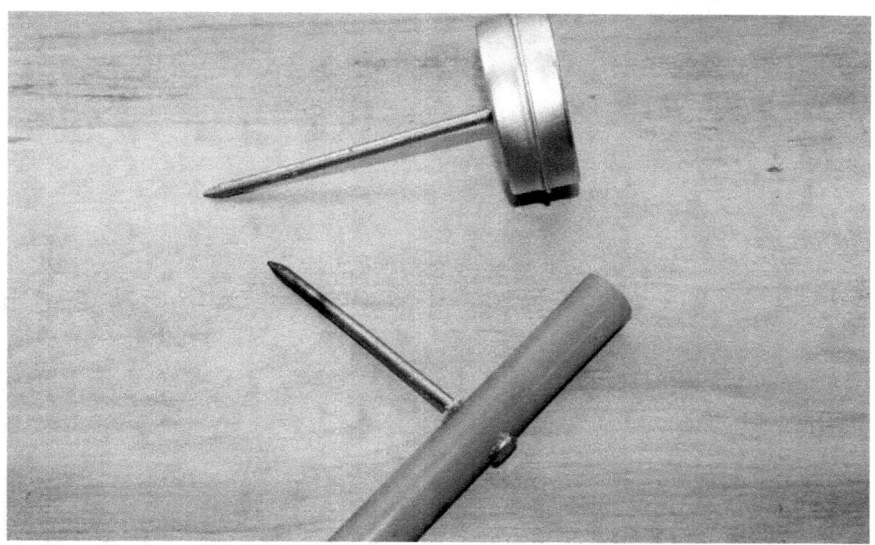

You can utilize Chapstick tins or hose and pipe pieces to construct push daggers. Drive a 3-inch nail through your hose or pipe piece and secure it with some binding such as duct tape, jute twine, super glue, or cloth wraps. If using a tin, open the tin and drive it through the bottom. Fill in the tin with material to keep the nail in place. The top of the tin will act as protection for your hand.

Tile & Toilet Knives

If you can find ceramic tile and a nail, you can knap out a knife blade. Apply pressure to the edge of the tile to shear off small fractures. Flip the tile over and repeat this process until an edge develops. You can use a bopper to break the tile into more manageable pieces or create shapes before or as you knap. It takes a lot of practice to make a quality edge, but you can create a crude edge in an afternoon. You can repeat this same process with a toilet tank or bowl made of Johnstone. Toilets break into very sharp pieces and also make excellent arrowheads. Haft (attach) it to a pipe with some bindings, and again, you have a defensive weapon.

Ceramic Tile Knife

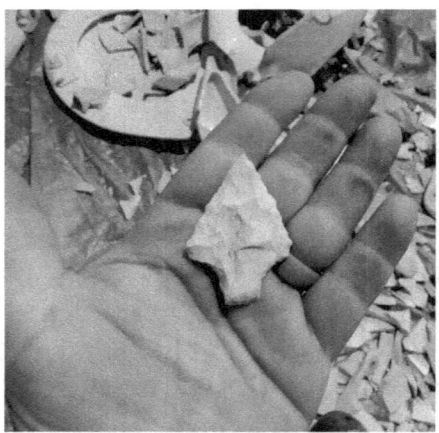
Toilet Tank arrowhead

THE GOSPEL OF SURVIVAL

Regardless of the type of tool you carry, use, or create, think of as many uses for that tool as possible and make it part of your narrative. For example, if you usually carry around a tool bag in your day job, no one would bat an eye if you had an electrician's knife, ice pick, or a sharpened screwdriver. Never overlook the most obvious as your life or the lives of those you care for may depend on it.

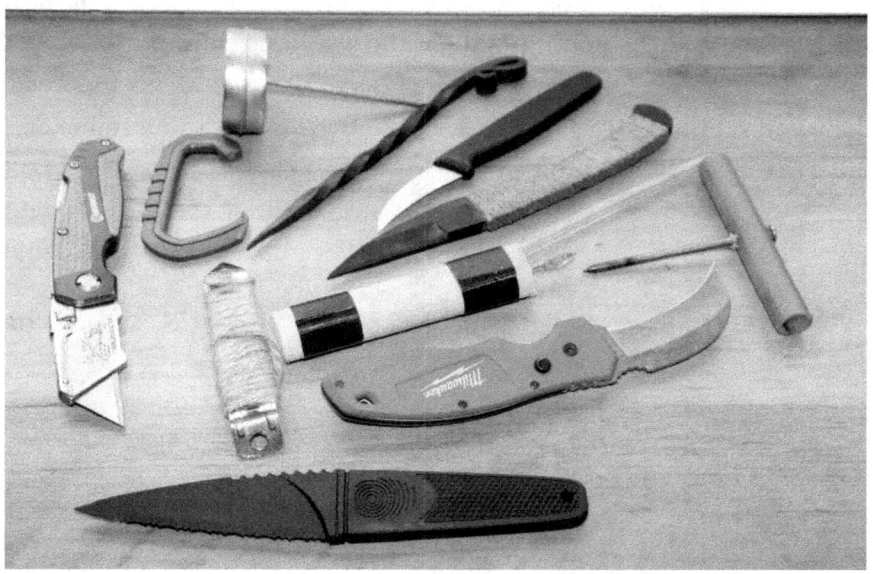

Now, armed with the fundamentals of a ditch kit, improvised weapons, and camouflage, let's put it all together by examining navigational methods through masses of people during civil unrest. Recently, civil unrest unfolded on the Capitol Building steps in Washington D.C. Protests were happening to overturn the 2020 election results. A protest or riot of any type is not the place to remain. All it takes is one person's poor choice to create a domino effect that will affect everyone. Your best bet is to move with the crowd until you can make your way out. You do not want to try to swim upstream against the crowd, so to speak, as that's the quickest way to end up being pushed to the ground and trampled upon or worse.

Law enforcement will employ riot control weapons such as tear gas, water, and pepper sprays. Avoid areas where these tactics are being used, as you will blend in with everyone else. Law enforcement officers will not be able to distinguish between those trying to leave the area and those causing the problem in the heat of the moment. Should you need a gas mask to cross through a location, grab a 2-liter bottle or juice jug, remove the cap, and cut one side of the jug off so that your chin sits near the cap end and the opposite side of the jug covers your face and eyes. Stuff some cotton under your chin to serve as a filter. This mask will help you get through a gassed area with relative ease without immediate danger to your eyes or lungs.

Your sole objective should be to get home to secure your family or get out of the area. You are not trying to be the hero, so stay focused. As difficult as it might be to resist the urge to intervene, doing so likely won't help anything and may cost you your life. Get yourself and your loved ones to safety and leave the rest to the police. As you traverse the streets, don't get pinned in. Getting pinned in by roadblocks, riot control, or the crowd can be detrimental to your progress and ongoing safety. Seek cover as needed, or as able, indoors. If a storefront is open, you may consider ducking in until the crowd passes. If, however, the rioting is several blocks or city-wide, you'll be better off staying on the move and blending in until you can break away to safety.

Therefore, let us not sleep, as others do, but let us watch and be sober.
~1 Thessalonians 5:6

We offer a comprehensive urban survival training course online and onsite at our school in Kentucky. Visit us at CampcraftOutdoors.com for additional information.

25

The Wheat and the Tare

> *"Go in through the narrow gate. The gate that leads to destruction is broad and the road wide, so many people enter through it. But the gate that leads to life is narrow and the road difficult, so few people find it."*
> ~Matthew 7:13-14

I pray that you are one of the few that are hiking this narrow path. It is essential that you be able to tell the difference between imposters along these paths toward eternity. Let's begin with the most important question, do you know Jesus Christ? Do you have a personal relationship with him from which connection you can discern his voice and obey his teaching? The truth is, many will say "yes" to this question, actually around 76% of Americans according to a religious survey[14]. The majority of people professing to be Christian have no actual relationship with Jesus Christ at all. They instead hold to a form of religion to which they bear some affiliation due to family upbringing or social connection. It's sad to say that many believe that agreement with the story of Jesus' death, burial, and resurrection, attending a church faithfully, paying a tithe, and getting preached at qualifies them to be a Disciple of Jesus Christ.

However, the Bible teaches that none of these things make one a Christian any more than standing in a barn would make you a tractor. So, let's move from one that's in agreement with the message of Christ to one that obeys the message of Christ. The first step on the narrow path is realizing your need to be saved from death and eternal punishment. When you talk to people in general and ask them where they believe their loved ones have passed on to after death, the vast majority will say "heaven" or "a better place." You may also think that when you die, regardless of your current life or situation that you too will one day go to heaven. However, Jesus Christ tells us that "no man shall enter the kingdom of God unless he is born again" (John 3:5).

We know that it is not possible to be born again through our mother's womb literally. Of course, Jesus was speaking of a spiritual rebirth wherein we would die to our current life, wants, circumstances, and desires to be reborn to a new life with Jesus Christ living in line with His will for our lives. This rebirth is done by first realizing that all men have committed sins against God; this means they have done things that He said never to do. The punishment for breaking His commandments is spiritual death and eternal separation from Him (God).

Romans 6:23, *"The penalty for sin is death..."*

But, because God loved His creation (man) so much, He sent His only Son, Jesus Christ, to suffer sin's death penalty for all humanity by dying upon the cross. Jesus came to earth; was born of a virgin; raised as a Jew; lived a sinless life, and was ultimately beaten beyond recognition. As an innocent man on earth and in heaven, he was crucified so that through his perfect act of obedience to God's commandments, all men might be saved from sins death penalty.

Romans 6:23 *"...but the Gift of God is eternal life through Jesus Christ, our savior."*

Although it's hard to understand how God placed all the sins of the world upon Jesus without extensive study beyond this text's scope, we can rest assured that all the sins that we have committed past, present and future have all been covered under the shed blood of Jesus. And now, God demands that all men come to repentance and belief in the name of Jesus Christ (Acts 17:30).

The Philippian Jailer that asked the Apostle Paul and Silas, "Sirs, what must I do to be saved?" received the following answer: "Believe on the Lord Jesus Christ, and you shall be saved..." (Acts 16:30-31)

And we see in Romans that *"whosoever shall call upon the name of the Lord shall be saved."* (Romans 10:13).

You, being *whosoever*, can also be saved; in the Gospel of Luke, the sinner prayed: "God be merciful to me a sinner" (18:13). We also see that those that confess Jesus before man shall also be confessed by Jesus before His Father in Heaven: "*Whosoever, therefore, shall confess [testify of] Me before men, him will I also confess before My Father which is in heaven"* (Matthew 10:32).

You too can confess now to receive Jesus as your Savior:

"Lord Jesus, I know I am a sinner and have broken your commandments. Jesus, I ask you to forgive me and save me now, thank you for dying on the cross for me, and thank you for rising from the dead to prepare a place for me in your Father's Kingdom. I now receive you as my Lord and Savior, baptize me with your holy spirit so that I can become the person you want me to be. Amen."

Now that you have confessed Jesus Christ as your Lord and Savior- be baptized. When you join Christ in baptism, you die to your sin, thereby breaking its power in your life. Baptism (immersion underwater) is how we identify with the death, burial, and resurrection of Christ as we see in Romans chapter 6:2-11: "Since we have died to sin, how can we continue to live in it? Or have you forgotten that when we were joined with Christ Jesus in baptism, we joined him in his death? For we died and were buried with Christ by baptism. And just as Christ was raised from the dead by the glorious power of the Father, now we also may live new lives.

Since we have been united with him in his death, we will also be raised to life as he was. We know that our old sinful selves were crucified with Christ so that sin might lose its power in our lives. We are no longer slaves to sin. For when we died with Christ, we were set free from the power of sin. And since we died with Christ, we know we will also live with him. We are sure of this because Christ was raised from the dead, and he will never die again. Death no longer has any power over him. When he died, he died once to break the power of sin. But now that he lives, he lives for the glory of God. So, you also should consider yourselves to be dead to the power of sin and alive to God through Christ Jesus."

To be baptized, you do not have to seek out a pastor or church, you as a believer, striving for obedience to the word of God, can indeed baptize yourself by faith. Get in your tub, swimming pool, or find a creek and Baptize yourself in the name of Jesus so that you may receive the gift of the Holy Spirit (Acts 2:38).

Learn to Love Jesus more than man
What exactly is love? According to Webster's, love is "a deep and tender feeling of affection for or attachment or devotion to a person or persons," thus we see that love is based on feelings and emotions we have toward something or someone.

What, however, is God's definition of love?

I John 5:3, *"For this is the love of God, that we keep his commandments: and his commandments are not grievous."*

John 14:21 *"He who has My commandments and keeps them, it is he who loves Me. And he who loves Me will be loved by My Father, and I will love him and manifest Myself to him."*

II John 1:6 *"And this is love that we walk after his commandments. This is the commandment, That, as ye have heard from the beginning, ye should walk in it."*

From these statements, we gather that God's definition of love is obedience to His will, as revealed in the commandments. And to remain in His love, we must:

John 15:10 *"...keep my commandments, and you will abide in my love; even as I have kept my Father's commandments, and abide in his love."*

We often hear of why we should not keep God's commandments more than keep them after becoming a Christian. Preachers say that the commandments are "under the old law" and are not for the believer today. Yet, these same preachers pluck old laws to suit their needs (tithing anyone?). We know full well that it is the blood of Jesus that saves by His grace (enablement), through faith (our acting on His enablement), but most fail to live the Christian life after being born again. How many times have we fallen back into sin, or have you seen others do the same—only to think or declare, well, *"I'm saved, and God will forgive me."*

It's true; God is very loving and forgiving. So much so, He sent His son to die for you and me. But that is the extent of His love and forgiveness according to:

John 15:13 *"Greater love has no one than this than to lay down one's life for his friends."*

There is nothing more significant one can do than die for another. You love your neighbor as yourself- even unto death, is this not what Jesus has done? Now some would contend that keeping the commandments of the Lord is works-based. If that be so, then being obedient to the Word of God is also a work, as is being obedient to the leading of the Holy Spirit.

Think of this for a moment. If loving God; having no idols; keeping His name holy; remembering His Sabbath; honoring your parents; not murdering; not committing adultery; not stealing; not giving false testimony, and not coveting are works; then going door to door to seek and save the lost are greater works. Feeding the hungry is also a more extraordinary work, as is giving to the poor.

"But!" you say, *"We're under grace and not law."* True, we are under grace until we are saved.

Ephesians 2:8 *"For it is by the grace of God you have been saved through faith, not of yourselves, it is a gift from God".*

Now that we have been saved, we are now subject to be judged by the law of Christ- for the law in itself could not save us. Regardless of how well one kept the law, they always missed the mark, and the Bible declares that if you fall in any area of the law, you are guilty of breaking it all. Now, by His grace or "enabling power" we can keep or "be obedient to" His commandments, for we have already been saved and made righteous through the blood of Jesus.

Now, what of those that teach against obedience to the commandments of God?

They do not have a love for God, for if they did according to Christ in John 14:15 they would keep His commandments. 1 John 3:9 *"No one who is born of God practices sin, because His seed abides in Him, and he cannot practice sin because he is born of God"*. *We know we must be holy, for without holiness no one will see God* (Hebrews 12:14).

Many will say at the judgment, *"'Lord, did we not prophesy in your name and in your name drive out demons and perform many miracles?' Then He will tell them plainly, 'I never knew you. Depart from me, you who practice lawlessness!'"* (Matt. 7:22)

Notice that those at the judgment do not cry out, saying they remained obedient to Jesus' message- they only claimed to have done works on his behalf- this is a dangerous trend we are now witnessing in the church worldwide. If you picked up a bottle of water that stated 98% pure, you would wonder what was in the other 2%, right? When you look at the back, you find that the additional 2% is made up of raw sewage. Would you drink the water? Would you even waste your money on it? Of course, not- why then do we think God would?

98% holiness- 98% obedience- 98% love is not enough! What then is the problem with people today? FEAR- people fear the Lord will not provide; they fear He does not hear their prayer; they fear they will not make it in this world. All because they do not know him personally! Yet, the scripture again plainly states in 1 John 4:18 *"There is no fear in love, but full-grown (complete) love turns fear out of doors and expels every trace of terror! For fear brings with it the thought of punishment, and [so] he who is afraid has not reached the full maturity of love."* (AMP)

We already know that love to God is obedience- so from this passage, we render, *"There is no reason to fear if you're obedient, for obedience kicks fear out the door. Fear (disobedience), brings with it the thought of punish-*

ment, and he who is afraid has not yet reached maturity in their obedience." (Rendering Mine)

Additionally, 1 Peter 4:8 states *"Above all things have intense and unfailing love for one another, for love covers a multitude of sins [forgives and disregards the offenses of others]."* (AMP)- In other words, love one another as you love yourself, for in this is love perfected and your sins will be covered.

So, let us press on to maturity by remaining obedient to the unchanging Law of Love and Liberty in Christ. We are free of human-made doctrine, teaching, and tradition- we are now open to obey the Lord without the restriction of worldly guilt or indifference. While this road of true love for God is rocky and dangerous with vipers at every stop- we must press on as one running the race- with purpose in every step, looking only at those things which are eternal.

Discerning the True from the False

One of the most important things Christians need to know is how to tell the difference between a genuine and false Christian. Ultimately, this is the difference between the wheat and the tare, which will become of greater importance as we grow closer to the last days.

2 Timothy 3:1 *"In the last days it is going to be very difficult to be a Christian"* (TLB)

This statement seems very odd because we think it was Paul and the saints of old who had a hard time. Paul faced significant opposition, receiving thirty-nine stripes on his back on five different occasions, three times he was beaten with rods, once he was stoned, and he spent years in prison. YET- he states our days (the last days) will be even more difficult! Why? He gives the reason:

2 Timothy 3:2-4 *"People will be lovers of themselves, lovers of money, boastful, proud, abusive, disobedient to their parents, ungrateful, unholy, without love, unforgiving, slanderous, without self-control, brutal, not lovers of the good, treacherous, rash, conceited, lovers of pleasure rather than lovers of God."* (NIV)

In examining that statement, you may still wonder what point he's trying to make, for how does this list differ from what he faced in his time? In the apostles' time, all society also held these same traits- for Peter told them on the day of Pentecost, *"Be saved from this crooked and perverse generation!"* (Acts 2:40). So, WHY is Paul singling-out our generation? Again, he gives the reason:

2 Timothy 3:5 from the Amplified Bible: *"For [although] they hold a form of piety (true religion), they deny and reject and are strangers to the power of it [their conduct belies the genuineness of their profession]. Avoid [all] such people [turn away from them]."*

The New King James Version of the Bible states, *"They have a form of godliness, but deny the power."* So, you can see what makes it challenging to be a Christian in our generation. Many who profess to be Christian will not have allowed the cross to slay their self-life or worldly pursuits. We have this notion that what we want matters! They will not have decided to forsake all their hopes and dreams to follow Jesus. They will sincerely believe He is their Savior, but they'll affiliate with Him for the mere fact of what He can do for them, rather than who He is.

It's like a woman marrying a man for his money. She may marry him for his love for her, but ultimately for the wrong reasons. Out of this motive, they'll seek Him for the sake of salvation and success in this life and believe fully and sincerely that He is their Savior, but they never give Him control of their own lives.

The problem comes when the lines are blurry. Let's look at a self-seeking person that confesses a born-again experience, talks the language of a true believer, makes friends with the godly, and is even excited about believers' gatherings; yet there is no nature change. In essence, this person is unwittingly an imposter- and the difficulty arises in the fact that his self-deception spreads like a disease. Others base their lives on the "norm" in the Christian culture, and this "norm" is out of sync with heaven, thus making it hard to be a true disciple. In Paul's time, your life was on the line every hour of every day. There was no question about it- if you have your allegiance to Jesus, you put your life on the line. Paul continues:

2 Timothy 3:10-13 *"But you, Timothy, certainly know what I teach, and how I live, and what my purpose in life is. You know my faith, my patience, my love, and my endurance. You know how much persecution and suffering I have endured. You know all about how I was persecuted in Antioch, Iconium, and Lystra—but the Lord rescued me from all of it. Yes, and everyone who wants to live a godly life in Christ Jesus will suffer persecution. But evil people and impostors will flourish. They will deceive others and will themselves be deceived."* (NLT)

Paul made it clear. It wasn't only what he taught, but what he lived and his purpose in life that proved Timothy could trust him. It wasn't his answered prayers, supernatural gifts producing miracles, or his excellent ability to preach the Word. No, it was his lifestyle. This lifestyle was and still is to be the determining factor. He continued saying, *"evil people and imposters"* will flourish. Now we all know to stay clear from an evil person; however, it's imposters, those who assume an outward identity that does not match their true nature, who are most dangerous. They are the ones that profess and have a form of Christianity, but there is no evidence of the life-changing power of grace. Notice Paul stated they would deceive not only others- but also themselves!

This battle is one that not only Paul warned us about, but so did other New Testament writers. Jude tells us:

Jude 3 *"Dear friends, I had been eagerly planning to write to you about the salvation we all share. But now I find that I must write about something else, urging you to defend the faith that God has entrusted once for all time to his holy people."* (NLT)

Notice the urgency in his voice. He wanted to discuss the wonderful things we share in salvation but had to write about something different. He had to encourage them to fight, battle, wage war for the faith. What is the fight about?

Jude 4 *"I say this because some ungodly people have wormed their way into your churches, saying that God's marvelous grace allows us to live immoral lives. The condemnation of such people was recorded long ago, for they have denied our only Master and Lord, Jesus Christ."*

The war is against the influences created by people who have perverted God's grace to excuse their ungodly lifestyles. These assaults are more deadly than all-out persecution of the church. They're more dangerous than laws against biblical principles such as abortion and schools' requirement to teach evolution. They're more potent than any cult or false religion- because they're eternally fatal!

You may be asking, "But how does this apply to us today? No one could remain in a church and openly deny Jesus is the Messiah and go unnoticed." Think about it- how do they renounce Christ? Titus 1:16 *"Such people claim to know God, but deny Him by the way they live"* (NLT)- In fact, they claim to know God, they confess Jesus as Lord, but their works communicate otherwise- they fail to keep His commandments. Remember, they not only deceive others, but themselves- all the while being convinced, they're real Christians.

James 2:17-19 *So also faith, if it does not have works (deeds and actions of obedience to back it up), by itself is destitute of power (inoperative, dead). But someone will say [to you then], You [say you] have faith, and I have [good] works. Now you show me your [alleged] faith apart from any [good] works [if you can], and I by [good] works [of obedience] will show you my faith. You believe that God is one; you do well. So do the demons believe and shudder [in terror and horror such as make a man's hair stand on end and contract the surface of his skin]!* (AMP)

James identifies a considerable gap today in our teaching. We pull out scriptures like *"Believe on the Lord Jesus Christ, and you will be saved"* (Acts 16:31). If just believing is enough, and confessing Jesus is the son of God is all that's required to be saved, James shows that even the demons will be saved- which we know isn't right! To drive it home more, James points out that the demons shudder. In other words, the demons fear God more than some who say they have faith but lack obedience!

THE EVIDENCE of our truly being saved by the grace of Jesus Christ is that we will have a lifestyle to prove it. This is why John the Apostle states,

"And we can be sure that we know him if we obey his commandments. If someone claims, "I know God," but doesn't obey God's commandments, that person is a liar and is not living in the truth. But those who obey God's Word truly show how completely they love him. That is how we know we are living in him. Those who say they live in God should live their lives as Jesus did." 1 John 2:3-6 (NLT) {emphasis mine}

Can this be any clearer? The proof we know Jesus Christ is that we keep his commandments. The one that says he knows Him but doesn't keep His commandments is deceived, and a liar estranged from the truth, even though he confesses with his mouth his knowledge of the Word of God. For this reason, John says, *"My little children, these things I write to you, so that you may not sin. And if anyone sins, we have an advocate with the Father, Jesus Christ the righteous"* (1 John 2:1-2)

Notice he doesn't say, "These things I write to you so that *when you sin*, you have an advocate." No, the goal is not to sin. We have the power through the grace (enabling force) of God, so we can set our sights on a life like Christ, for we are free from the control of disobedience. But if we do succumb to sin; we do have an Advocate.

Why then have we only heard one part of the gospel? It's because the majority of those preaching are deceived and don't truly know Him. If someone claims, "I know God," but doesn't obey God's commandments, that person is a liar and is not living in the truth.

1 John 2:1-2- be not deceived friends, remain obedient to He who saves- for disobedience leads to destruction.

Thus, the Gospel of Survival, in reality, is the Full Gospel of Jesus Christ applied to daily life. The good news is that God sent his son to die so that humanity may receive forgiveness of their sins, which separate us from our Creator (John 3:16). To learn and live by the leading of His Holy Spirit (John 14:26, Acts 2:38). This good news also shows us the way we can love our Creator (Mark 12:30, 1 John 5:3) and fellow man (Mark 12:31) and how we can endure (Mark 13:11) until the end and prepare for the establishment of the Kingdom on earth (Exodus 13:14-19, Isaiah 57:13, Matt. 4:23, 24:1-51).

When this good news is practically applied in the day-to-day life of the modern Christian, they will be prepping! Prepping for the King's arrival in the last days and sharing this good news that in the midst of worldly chaos, our hope has a name and He shall soon come to establish His throne and bring true justice to the broken-hearted. The last days are no time to be fearful, but are a time to be expectant and excited!

And proclaim as you go, saying, 'The kingdom of heaven is at hand'... What I tell you in the dark, say in the light, and what you hear whispered, proclaim on the housetops.

~ Matthew 10:7 & 27 (ESV)

26

Experimental Archaeology Applied

The biblical text comes to life when you put into practice all that it has to offer. In my own journey, my family and I just did what the Bible said, and doing this led me to the desire to learn more outdoor skills because building debris shelters from natural materials without getting wet takes some practice. So, I started seeking training in survival skills, preparedness, etc. only as a means of fulfilling what I plainly saw as Biblical teaching. This wasn't always popular among those I went to church with. We most often limit this type of thinking to Jesus and the Apostles. This limitation is one of the many reasons we miss out on understanding the context of biblical teaching and the skills spoken about in specific passages. Paul's exhortation to the Thessalonians sums up Biblical Experimental Archaeology in my perspective.

> "Test all things; hold fast to what is good."
> *1 Thessalonians 5:16-22*

I am a firm believer in doing things; by gaining hands-on experience coupled with historical and biblical evidence, it's nearly impossible to sway someone's opinion (James 1:22- be a doer of the word not easily deceived). When I see practical skills in the scripture, I try them. By doing these skills, I am grounded just a bit more in the time of the Bible. This process allows me to meditate on the hardships and struggles of the ancient people and grasp why God put a mention of a specific skill in there (by now, I hope you realize it was to train us for the end-times). Experiencing skills in this way makes me appreciate all that God has given us in modern times and aids me in memorizing more passages of scripture because they are now a part of me through experience.

Context clues matter for Biblical interpretation a great deal. One famous example is the phrase Jesus used *"...it is easier for a camel to go through the eye of a needle than for a rich man to enter the kingdom of God."* from Matthew 19:23–26. The "eye of a needle" is what locals called the Eastern Gate in Jerusalem, which was closed at dark each day. Late-night travelers arriving could not get their camel through the smaller gate (a man-sized door) unless it was stooped and had all its baggage removed. Context clues lead us to a picture that would show that a rich man would need to humble himself and rid himself of his baggage (riches) to enter the Kingdom. Fortunes then, as now, were a typical idol that people contend with continually. God shall supply all our needs, not necessarily our wants.

Let's look at a couple of examples of how we can glean survival skills from the biblical text, then apply them. We'll begin by examining Exodus 15: 22-26 (NLT):

"Then Moses led the people of Israel away from the Red Sea, and they moved out into the desert of Shur. They traveled in this desert for three days without finding any water. When they came to the oasis of Marah, the water was too bitter to drink. So they called the place Marah (which means "bitter"). Then the people complained and turned against Moses. "What are we going to drink?" they demanded. So Moses cried out to the Lord for help, and the Lord showed him a piece of wood. Moses threw it into the water, and this made the water good to drink. It was there at Marah that the Lord set before them the following decree as a standard to test their faithfulness to him. He said, "If you will listen carefully to the voice of the Lord your God and do what is right in his sight, obeying his

commands and keeping all His decrees, then I will not make you suffer any of the diseases I sent on the Egyptians; for I am the Lord who heals you."

I will share a glimpse into my survival skills development process and how I extrapolate information from the Bible to apply it in a class or teaching. So, what interests me here is that God told Moses to throw a specific piece of wood into the water, which made it safe to drink. God also said that listening carefully to his voice and doing right in His sight would prevent the diseases that were sent upon the Egyptians. I want to know what that wood is, and I also want to see if it will make water safe to drink for me today. I am also curious about what diseases the Egyptians suffered from because plagues are not mentioned here. So, we'll examine this too. I will not, however, look at the Theological concept of Typology, which also applies here as that is outside the scope of this specific study.

In Hebrew, "Vayorehu Hashem etz" means "God instructed Moses about the tree." Some Hebrew scholars such as Rabbi Simeon bar Yohai believe God took Moses to the last part of the Tree of Life in the Garden of Eden, which he threw into the waters. I disagree with this and feel a more practical example is warranted because God uses the practical to prepare His people to depend upon him through simple obedience. Recall at the beginning of our journey how God taught Adam to "make" clothing from animal skins. We know he did more than we accept at face value, so it only makes sense that as He "instructed Moses about the tree," he did far more than show him the location of a tree but revealed to him its properties.

All scholars agree that the etz mentioned in this passage refers to a bitter tree or shrub growing at the Oasis of Marah. The only tree prevalent in this region is the Acacia tree. Palm trees and cedars are always noted in the Bible, and they are nowhere near this vicinity even today, so we can rest assured that it was not a palm or cedar tree. Additionally, the Acacia tree is the only tree that is both a tree and a bush in that region due to two native species. The location of Marah is roughly 1000 yards from the Caves of Jethro, which should sound familiar to you as this is where Moses was raising his father-in-law Jethro's sheep. This oasis is noted in British explorer St. John Philby's book, The Lands of Midian. Dr. Colin Humphreys, a Cambridge University physicist, has also done extensive research in this region and notes that the wells in this region were known locally as the salt wells (al Maliha).

Acacia wood is used in herbal medicine and is in the Mimosa tree family. They share many characteristic uses, one of which is that they provide a bark that can be used medicinally. This bark, once processed, is also very stringy and can be used for cordage, and guess what else? Water filters. By carefully examining the text and the specific instructions given to Moses and then to the people, it appears that they constructed an inner-bark fiber water filter. This filter is why water was thrown through it. Historically, Bedouin tribes have created these same-style fibrous water filters for thousands of years. With this greatly abbreviated understanding, let me now jump you over to the application stage of making a tree-fiber water filter. Because actual acacia trees are not native to my area, I was forced to examine a cousin that is considered invasive to my region called Mimosa (*Albizia julibirissin*, aka Silk Tree, or Silky Acacia). Mimosa trees are those that look beautiful for a short time in your yards or in parks then wilt and turn yellow by mid-summer and grow long pods that transmit seeds everywhere.

JASON HUNT

Mimosa Flower by Julia Freeman-Woolpert

In Herbal Medicine, the inner bark is prepared as a decoction (boiled in water) and used to aid happiness, uplift the mood, and hold properties that help alleviate depression and anxiety. The Mimosa is known as the Happy Tree in Traditional Chinese Medicine. These properties elude to the benefits of using filter material made from the tree; the medicinal properties would relieve the Israelites fear and anxiety and make them happier for remaining obedient to God, whereas the Egyptians lived in constant fear of their gods.

For medicine or filters, it's the inner bark we are after. The best time to peel the bark is in spring; as the sap warms up and allows the bark to slip more readily, a bark tool, such as a chisel tip stick, will aid you in keeping longer sections of bark together for later processing.

You can see the stringiness of the bark
Photo by Ralph Giunta at rememberplants.com

When scraping the inner bark, you may use any sharp edge to create strings and fuzz, which will be molded into a bird's nest fashion. An increase in surface area is what is most important. The next image shows the green bark fibers I scraped using the back of my knife. I took this fist-sized amount off a small branch in just a minute or so, so you can imagine how much an entire tree could produce. It was also effortless to process, and doing so with stone tools could easily be accomplished.

Green bark fibers from a branch

Now that we have ready-to-use filter media, how would they most likely have used it? According to the Passover story, we know the families took all they could carry; this included their cooking vessels. It makes sense that each family would have taken their containers full of water, then thrown that water through the filter into another vessel. Conversely, they could have just as quickly taken the filter media and tossed it into the bottom of their vessel, which would have allowed sediment to separate from the cleaner water. The acacia fibers would have helped remove the water's bitterness, but from experience with these filters, that would have taken some time. Something else that could be done quickly by each family and would have made the water safe to drink; would have been to use a three-stage gravity filter. The materials would have been available around them- Acacia fibers, sand, and charcoal. Again, this process required water to be "thrown" in from the top and works for a long time.

The Sushruta Samhita ancient Sanskrit text on medicine and surgery (compiled between 1000–600 BC) specified various water purification methods, including boiling and heating under the sun. The text also recommends filtering water through sand and coarse gravel. Images in Egyptian tombs, dating from the 15th to 13th century BC, depict various water treatment devices. A three-stage filter is entirely within the realm of possibility. Having been Egyptian slaves for over 430 years, the Israelites would have most certainly been aware of their water purification practices and likely would have been the ones employed to do it.

I refer back to our scripture reference to highlight *"If you will listen carefully to the voice of the Lord"* Moses was responsible for carefully listening for specific instructions to lead an entire nation to survive apart from the known world. So which technique that I described based upon practices used will work best to clean water? Well, I had to test them all as 1 Thessalonians 5:16-22 notes; only then could I arrive at a definitive solution for my spiritual and skills improvement.

Coyote Well with Mimosa Fiber Filter

After trying a coyote well (a hole dug near a water source) and putting fibers into a vessel directly, I came up with the same result.

While the water's turbidity was resolved, the water remained cloudy and filtering only marginally improved the taste. In ancient times, this may have been great. But, to my modern palate, I know I can do better, and I strongly suspect they knew this too, which is why a three-stage filter makes the most sense to me.

Three Stage Filter in action

Using simple pieces of cloth, you can tie to a tripod; you can create three levels. In the first level, we used tree fibers, the second level was sand, and the final was finely crushed charcoal. Prime the filter with a few vessels of water until the water coming from the filter runs clear. It's then ready to use for drinking. I have run soda through these filters and have gotten clear water out. They work that well when adequately constructed.

So, here are the takeaways from this lesson. There is no definitive evidence of any water filter being created anywhere in the Bible. We have only conjecture and can only glean additional clues as to the methods they may have used, which are congruent to those drawn in pictographs or mentioned in other historical documents of the time. This is the experiential part of archeology. This skills journey solves no theological question, nor does it add any significant archaeological discovery due to the scant evidence. What this does is allow us, as biblical learners and doers, to press into the scriptures in a more personal way to experience learning through biblically-based research and skills application. These unique experiences allow us to relive in a small way the biblical narrative and demonstrate the various methods they likely used to survive. Digging into the Bible to find relevant examples of each of our five smooth stones (Safety, Fire, Water, Shelter, and Food) and putting the skills to practical use today is a profoundly enriching process for all involved that can be used to lead and equip others in the Christian life.

27

Tactical Ministry

Tactical Ministry is the concept of utilizing any ministry method to elicit a result, which would be the salvation of souls and workers' training for the end-times church. Paul most effectively used this ministry style, which he alluded to in his first letter to the Corinthians.

1 Corinthians 9:19-23 *"Even though I am a free man with no master, I have become a slave to all people to bring many to Christ. When I was with the Jews, I lived like a Jew to bring the Jews to Christ. When I was with those who follow the Jewish law, I, too, lived under that law. Even though I am not subject to the law, I did this to bring to Christ those under the law. When I am with the Gentiles who do not follow the Jewish law, I too live apart from that law so I can bring them to Christ. But I do not ignore the law of God; I obey the law of Christ. When I am with those who are weak, I share their weakness, for I want to bring the weak to Christ. Yes, I try to find common ground with everyone, doing everything I can to save some. I do everything to spread the Good News and share in its blessings."*

This example is our tactical ministry method that will reap a mighty harvest for the Kingdom of God when used throughout these end-times. To put this yet another way, perhaps you are one that grew up in the outdoors and has always taken pleasure in hunting, fishing, and just being outside. Your friends are into the same thing too, and that's pretty much your primary interest when you do not have to work. However, this interest, this calling on your life, is shelved on Sunday mornings because it's never revealed to us how we take the things we love and turn them into ministries for God. We're often under the impression that as long as we're showing up each week for an hour and paying our tithes at church, God accepts us, and that is our purpose.

The church, however, is comprised of individuals, not buildings and pews. The church is a living organism made up of those that call themselves Christians. To truly support the church's work, you must be actively involved in its labor. So, by continuing to shelve those things in your heart, you're limiting the impact the church can make on the world. Think of it this way, and if you're outside, then the church is also outside. If you're hunting, then the church is also hunting, you are the church, and you can use your gifts and abilities to draw others interested in the same things that you are closer to Jesus by merely doing what you love to do.

When you add new skills to your arsenal, those become outreach tools through which others can be drawn to Christ through you! This outreach is the core meaning of ministry. When Jesus began his earthly ministry, he first went to the fisherman; have you ever wondered why that was? It's because Jesus started his ministry as one desiring to catch men and draw them to himself; thus, he told them, "Follow me, and I will make you fishers of men" (Matt. 4:19). We, like Jesus, should exploit our jobs, hobbies, and interests as opportunities for ministry. If you are a hunter, invite others to go scout sign or clear a shooting lane so that you can share the word of God with them. If you enjoy canning and gardening, invite people to come and join you, impart skills to them, share the story of God and the importance of being prepared. Put your skills to action- using whatever ministry methods necessary to get the results God has commissioned us to obtain (Mark 16:15-16).

This book has been the preaching of this gospel of the Kingdom. I sincerely hope it has stirred something within you for good and that perhaps you might act upon it by sharing it with others. Please, teach the skills contained in this book to others. Start Clubs and Youth Groups in your churches and follow along in the skills curriculum chapters. We have made video training resources and onsite classes to equip you further when you are ready. Connect with us at Campcraft Outdoors.

References

1. etymonline.com: c.1600, "act of carrying off," from M.Fr. rapture, from M.L. raptura "seizure, rape, kidnapping," from L. raptus "a carrying off" (see rapt). Originally of women and cognate with rape.

2. Strongest Strong's Concordance, Greek word 1996, 1997

3. Strongest Strong's Concordance, Greek word

4. Ibid, Hebrew word 7451

5. Strongest Strong's Concordance, Hebrew word #4150

6. A History of Christianity by Kenneth Scott LaTourette, page 81 "Persistent Opposition and Persecution"

7. The Strongest Strong's Exhaustive Concordance, Hebrew entry "matteh", pg 1525

8. http://messianicgentiles.blogspot.com/2009/11/tzitzitprayer-shawltallit.html

9. Talmud, B. 122a; Sanhedrin 16a; comp. Yer. Yoma 41b

10. Encyclopedia Britannica, article: Origins of Agriculture, Harvesting and Processing, tribulum

11. https://www.who.int/water_sanitation_health/emergencies/qa/emergencies_qa17/en/

12. https://www.nbcnews.com/news/us-news/california-pastor-church-found-contempt-fined-over-covid-rules-n1250481

13. https://www.weforum.org/agenda/2020/06/now-is-the-time-for-a-great-reset/

14. Barry A. Kosmin and Ariela Keysar (2009). "AMERICAN RELIGIOUS IDENTIFICATION SURVEY (ARIS) 2008" (PDF). Hartford, Connecticut, USA: Trinity College. http://b27.cc.trincoll.edu/weblogs/AmericanReligionSurvey-ARIS/reports/ARIS_Report_2008.pdf. Retrieved 2011-09-06.

Training Resources

Survival Gear & Classes: www.campcraftoutdoors.com
This is my website. You will find the classes I offer as well as the variety of survival tools and outdoor gear we make, use, and sell.

Outdoor Core: www.outdoorcore.com
Here you will find a variety of skills-based courses in survival, preparedness, and outdoor skills from qualified instructors including my own Modern Survival class series.

Survival Skills: www.survivalskillofthemonth.com
Survival Skill of the Month is a monthly survival skill sheet delivered to you that will enable you to learn something new each month. You can receive this digitally or in your mailbox.

Edible & Medicinal Plants: www.wildedibleplantofthemonth.com
Wild Edible Plant of the Month is a monthly skill sheet delivered to you that will enable you to learn a new wild edible/ medicinal plant each month. You can receive this digitally or in your mailbox.

Books:
Building the Perfect Bug Out Bag by Creek Stewart
Bushcraft Boxed Set by Dave Canterbury with Jason Hunt
Driven by Eternity by John Bevere
Essential Wilderness Navigation by Craig Caudill
God, where are you? By John Bevere
Practical Self Reliance by John McCann
Preppers Long Term Survival Guide by Jim Cobb

Dr. Jason Hunt is the owner and founding Instructor of Campcraft Outdoors, a softgoods manufacturing and preparedness company located in Kentucky. His survival and outdoor knowledge are backed by thousands of man-hours in the field. Jason is a frequent contributor to Backwoods Survival Guide, Prepper's Survival Guide, and various other magazines. His degrees are in church ministry, practical theology, and outdoor ministry leadership. Jason is also a wilderness emergency medicine instructor and volunteer firefighter with multiple specialty rescue qualifications. He's the author of Reasons for the Seasons, Walking the Narrow Path, and co-author of the best-selling Bushcraft First Aid.

www.ingramcontent.com/pod-product-compliance
Lightning Source LLC
Chambersburg PA
CBHW071233290426
44108CB00013B/1394